COACH TRAINS
and TRAVEL

Southern Pacific 4-8-4 gets a 2-10-2 helper engine at San Luis Obispo with the northbound No. 95, the all-coach Starlight. The 2-10-2 will drop off on the other side of the Cuesta grade at Santa Margarita, leaving the 4400 class 4-8-4 to take it alone to San Francisco. This photo was taken in 1954 by Richard Steinheimer.

COACH TRAINS and TRAVEL

by

PATRICK C. DORIN

SUPERIOR PUBLISHING COMPANY, SEATTLE

Library of Congress Card Number 75-2683

Library of Congress Cataloging in Publication Data

Dorin, Patrick C.
Coach trains and travel.

Includes index.
1. Railroads—United States—Trains. I. Title.
TF23.D66 1975 385'.262'0973 75-2683
ISBN 0-87564-521-6

FIRST EDITION

Printed in The United States of America

Dedicated
To
Eugene Kerik Garfield
and
The Auto-Train Staff
for
The Development and Operation
of the
Nation's Newest Concept in Rail Coach Service

Coaches of the late 1820's resembled four wheeled buckboards or wagons on rails, but by 1831 the stage coach design was incorporated. The DeWitt Clinton was an early train, and its historic design fortunately has been preserved. The Clinton is shown here at the Chicago Railroad Fair of 1948 during the Wheels a Rolling show. Lake Michigan is in the background. (Bob Lorenz)

Foreword

The purpose of this book is to trace the development of coach and chair car travel from the DeWitt Clinton to the Metroliners and Turboliners of 1975. The time span covered is about 175 years, and during that time precious little has actually been written about the backbone of rail passenger service.

This book is actually the third in a series of books written by this author covering rail passenger service. This new book covers most of the types of coach services offered in the USA and Canada including the doodlebugs, RDC's, the world famous Challengers, all-coach streamliners, local runs, commuter trains, milk, mail and express trains, slumbercoaches, special tour trains, and finally the two newest organizations in the USA: Auto-Train and Amtrak. Canadian roads are represented by the Algoma Central and Ontario Northland, but the Canadian Pacific and Canadian National passenger services are covered in other volumes by this author. In fact, the next book to be written by this author will be entitled *The Canadian National Railway Story*.

Most railroad companies used the terms chair cars and coaches interchangeably. Such is the case in this book. However the term "chair car" usually indicates that each set of seats on each side of the aisle is divided into two reclining seats. Parlor cars with single seating on each side were generally not referred to as chair cars.

The railroad passenger coach has received little attention but yet some of the Nation's finest trains were "All Coach" trains. The coach was, and is, the most economical form of transportation and has served in the widest variety of train operations. No other car can boast such a service record.

North Branch, Minnesota   Patrick C. Dorin
October 1, 1974

Acknowledgments

Many people gave freely of their time and resources to this writer during the research for data, materials and photographs for this book. For their time, assistance and encouragement, the author wishes to gratefully acknowledge the following people:

Mr. Albert P. Salisbury of Superior Publishing Company for his encouragement and work with layout through to the final publication of the book.

My wife, Karen, for her time in checking materials and the manuscript for errors, Mr. Luther S. Miller of Railway Age Magazine for permission to use materials from Railway Age and Railway Age Gazette from 1890 to 1974: Gerald Delling for his kind assistance with photo selection and printing, and the following railroad photographers: Charles B. Gunn, Herbert H. Harwood, Jr., Robert Johnson, Robert R. Larson, Bob Lorenz, Jim Morin, Jergen Fuhr, Wayne C. Olsen, Al Paterson, Albert C. Phelps, H. W. Pontin of Rail Photo Service, Jim Scribbins, Stanley F. Styles, Paul H. Stringham, W. C. Whittaker, Dale Wilson, William Raia, Dick Steinheimer, Jack W. Swanberg, Elmer Treloar, George Moore, John H. Kuehl and Russ Porter for the photo on the dust jacket.

A special note of thanks must go to the following operating and public relations men of the following companies: Algoma Central — John R. Skinner, Amtrak — James A. Bryant, Auto-Liner Corporation — William W. Kratville, Auto-Train — Richard J. Church, Burlington Northern — Peter A. Briggs, Chesapeake & Ohio — M. B. Dolinger, Chicago & North Western — Thomas J. Judge, Duluth, Missabe & Iron Range Railway — Donald Shank and Frank A. King, Louisville & Nashville Railroad — Edison H. Thomas, Milwaukee Road — C. C. Dilley and Dennis Preuter, Norfolk and Western — William A. Martin, Ontario Northland — W. B. Antler and Mrs. Linda Montemurro, Missouri Pacific Lines — Harry Hammer, W. C. Schultz (T&P) and J. R. Beckman (C&EI), Penn Central — Robert S. McKernan, C. G. Muldoon and Ed Nowak, Pullman-Standard — John Kniola, Reading Company — Lois M. Morasco, Santa Fe — Bill Burk, Seaboard Coast Line — Don Martin, Southern Railway — A. S. Eggerton, Jr., Southern Pacific — Robert A. Sederholm, Union Pacific — E. C. Schafer.

Without the complete and unselfish cooperation of the above men and women and their staffs, this book would not have been possible. Should an acknowledgment have been left out inadvertently, this writer trusts it will be found in its appropriate place within the book.

Table of Contents

CHAPTER 1

The Development of Coach Travel

It is believed that railroading began in the United States in 1795. During that year a construction railroad was built to haul building materials on Beacon Hill in Boston. This first line was an all-freight line as were a number of other such lines before the construction of the Baltimore & Ohio around 1830. Passenger travel did not begin until that time, when the B&O laid track from Baltimore and began service with open wagons fitted with flanged wheels and a roof. The motive power was a horse. Service was opened on the line between Baltimore and Ellicott's Mills (13 miles) and in early 1831 the railroad was in the process of investigating steam to replace the horses. Most everyone is aware of the race between the Tom Thumb steam locomotive and the horse car between Relay and Baltimore, in which the horse won. But changes were coming, steam would become the prime mover for railroad motive power until the 1950's. Meanwhile the work horse of the passenger train, the coach, also began to undergo changes that are still taking place in 1975.

Coach car design and style has changed almost continuously since the late 1820's. From the early wagon cars and stage coach designs, the coaches evolved into cars that resembled flat top transfer cabooses of modern times. Sides and windows replaced the open sides. Bulk heads replaced the ends plus an open platform and steps for boarding the cars. The interiors were equipped with wood stoves for heat and wooden benches. During the winter one roasted near the stove and froze if he sat too far away. The stoves were also fire hazards. Comfort of the passengers was very low with very few of the cars being equipped with cushions of any kind. Yet this totally enclosed car was the backbone of coach travel by the 1840's.

At first exterior designs were plain, but as time went on that changed too. First the roof line began taking on graceful curves instead of being simply flat or with a slight pitch for the rain water to drain off. The sides were soon decorated with ornamental indentations and hand painted lines in graceful patterns. The size of the cars grew from 20 or so feet in length to over 60 feet by the time of the Civil War. Single axle wheels gave way to four wheeled trucks under each end, and a number of the heavier cars would ride on six wheeled trucks. The development of the four wheeled truck led to a greater comfort index in terms of riding qualities. Most of these developments had taken place before the 1860's and from that time on the car simply grew in size.

The open platform eventually gave way to a modified open platform. the steps remained the same with the railings,but doors were fitted at the top of the steps and a diaphragm fitted to the end framing. Passengers could now walk from one car to another without being exposed to the elements, and without the danger of falling between the cars. These semi-vestibules were in use by the 1880's and the full vestibule was in use by the 1890's. This innovation was one of the more significant advancements made by the railway car designers as it permitted full use of the entire train by all passengers. The open platform cars, however, were not retired from service immediately. Some of these cars were still in use in commuter service on the Burlington Route in 1948, and on the New Haven in the 1950's. A few open platform cars even received steel sheathing, but few new cars of this type were built after 1895. It is interesting to note that the Milwaukee Road constructed a steel open end combination baggage-caboose-coach for use in mixed train service in South Dakota. Open end cars were still in operation in 1975 on the Rio Grande's Silverton in the Narrow Gauge country of Colorado. One might say that the open end design has been with American Railroading for a whopping 145 years as of 1975.

By 1900 passenger cars were reaching the length of 80 feet, and some were rolling on the six wheeled trucks mentioned earlier. All equipment was of wood construction, but this was to change by 1910. Indeed the Pennsylvania Railroad was running the first all-steel train by 1908.

The next stage included built up sides and bulkheads with a roof, end platforms and four wheeled trucks during the 1840's. This car was the first coach for the Galena & Chicago Union Railroad, now the Chicago & North Western Railway, and was constructed in 1848. It represented quite an advancement over the earliest cars. (Chicago & North Western Railway)

Pennsylvania Railroad coach No. 3556 represents equipment built in the 1850's through the 1880's. This car represented an improvement with a curved roof, larger stoves, bigger seats, (some even had cushions) and more weight for greater safety and improved riding qualities. This particular coach is preserved at the Strasburg Railroad Museum in the Pennsylvania Dutch Country of the Keystone State. (Patrick C. Dorin)

The exterior of the coach had reached a peak in its design with the adoption of full vestibules and steel construction that would not change until 1934.

Interiors of the coaches were generally painted in light greys or browns. Seats were straight backs but by 1914 mohair plush began to replace the typical rattan seats of the earlier eras. Before the end of the 1920's, bucket seats were installed in cars that were operated on some of the Limited trains. The New York Central's Motor Queen was a typical example of a train that carried at least some cars with bucket seats. By the late 1920's some of the coaches were painted a little more cheerfully.

Reclining seats made their appearance in the late 1920's too. For the first time, the passenger's comfort was taken into consideration in a piece of equipment other than a Pullman sleeper or parlor car.

Most of the coaches — until the 1940's — were non air conditioned. They were not much fun to ride for adults, but as a child this author delighted in opening the window to listen to the exhaust of a Chicago & North Western 4-6-2 Pacific, the clickety-clack, the two longs, one short and one long of the whistle blowing for grade crossings as we rode the Ashland Mail. The Mail was the old day train between Chicago and Ashland, Wisconsin before the streamliner Flambeau 400 took over. Often to the discomfort of the passengers, the car would fill with smoke from that old Pacific. Travel by coach was a real adventure.

The Standard coach made most of its technological advances from about 1900 to 1929. During that time period, the railroads were simultaneously developing still another facet of coach travel — The "Motor Cars" or doodlebugs as they were often called. This development in turn eventually led to the streamlined motor cars and articulated streamliners. (Motor cars are covered in Chapter 2.)

This Milwaukee Road coach No. 3 rode on six wheeled trucks and represents the same time era as the Pennsylvania coach No. 3556. The car was photographed at the Milwaukee Road shops at Milwaukee before the Turn of the Century. (The Milwaukee Road)

The Union Pacific coach, riding on six wheeled trucks, was built in 1869 by the UP's shops at Omaha. Note the ornate painting, which was becoming quite common. Another interesting point during that era was that sleeping cars and coaches were built with the same exterior window configurations. It was quite common for many sleepers to be later rebuilt with coach seats. (Union Pacific Railroad)

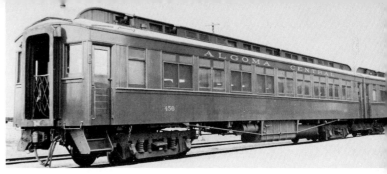

Union Pacific coach No. 521 brings us up to the 1890's and 1900's with simpler paint schemes, the dark olive or Pullman green for all or most coaches. The semi vestibules were already in service by that time and the open platform was becoming a thing of the past. However, this coach was still in service when photographed on April 12, 1909. (Union Pacific Railroad)

The 1900's dawned with the wood coach in full blossom with complete vestibules such as this Algoma Central coach No. 456. Four wheel trucks were standard on all but the heavier cars. End windows were also common and the seating capacity of the 456 was 72 passengers on "walk over" seats. (Stan F. Styles)

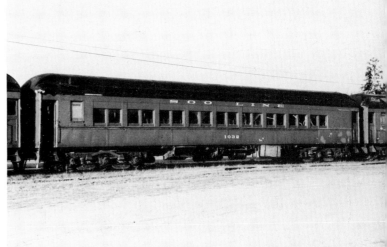

The vast majority of the seats on all coaches from about 1890 on were similar in style to these walk over straight back seats in this Algoma Central cafe coach. They were quite comfortable for short distances, but for long distance or overnight travelers they rated a 0 comfort index and were simply a means of getting from one place to another. (George Moore)

Among the last standard coaches constructed were the 1300 series for the Northern Pacific in 1935. Indeed even the roof line had changed from the previous curves. The new cars were even air- conditioned. (Pullman Standard)

As we move into the 1920's coaches were becoming longer and heavier. The Soo Line ordered many cars from Barney and Smith with six wheeled trucks, and for awhile the Soo even outdid the big roads like the Great Northern in passenger service. (Patrick C. Dorin)

Steel coaches were being built by 1910 and they represented the safest construction and finest riding qualities up to that time. Union Pacific coach 654 was built in 1910. (Union Pacific Railroad)

Seating was vastly changed too. Introduced in the late 1920's, reclining seats were installed on the NP cars built in 1935. The interior decor was also much more cheerful and the seat cushions were soft enough for one to be able to sleep with comfort. The coach was beginning to make some dynamic changes for the first time since 1910. (Pullman Standard)

THE ADVENT OF THE STREAMLINER

The 1930's mark a turning point in the coach and chair car history. Here we have the development of the streamlined coach, articulated streamliners and streamlined self propelled gas or diesel electric cars. It was a period when both standard and streamlined coaches were coming out of the car builders' shops almost hand in hand, or shall we say coupler in coupler. While Pullman was building light weight cars for the New Haven and Boston & Maine in 1935, it was also building standard coaches for the Northern Pacific and the Burlington.

It was during this decade that reclining seats really came into the luxury classification as well as the leg rest. The unsung hero of the passenger train — the lowly coach — was not so lowly anymore. In fact, it was becoming down right comfortable; and it is safe to say that from 1934 through 1975, the coach and/or chair car has continued to develop not only in terms of comfort and style, but also in exterior design.

The year 1934 brought the first streamliner when Union Pacific's M-10000 hit the rails. Otherwise known as the City of Salina, the articulated locomotive and two car train provided seats for 100 passengers and included a buffet in the rear car. During the same year, the Burlington's Pioneer Zephyr rocked a traditional railroad

Large lounge rooms were provided at the ends of these NP coaches for extra passenger comfort. This room was for the men who enjoyed talking and smoking after the early evening had slipped away. (Pullman Standard)

The Women's lounge room was equipped with softer seats and also with a small dressing table and mirrors. These NP coaches were approaching the standards of a Pullman Sleeping car. (Pullman Standard)

12

industry into realizing that there was more than one way to carry passengers. The Zephyr, also made up of a locomotive, mail & baggage car; baggage buffet grill and coach observation, provided seats for about 50 revenue passengers. These two trains are significant in the history of coaches and chair cars because of the conditions that brought about their creation.

In the late 1920's and the 1930's, the competitive automobile was beginning to make itself felt more and more in the railroad passenger business. The UP and CB&Q, being positively oriented, began to look around for ways and means to reverse this trend. The City of Salina and the Pioneer Zephyr started a trend that has continued until the present time, and most likely will continue. This does not mean that sometimes progress almost came to a stand still, but that it did continue despite an erratic flow forward. The development of the articulated streamliners was in full bloom by 1936 as several trains were on order by the Union Pacific, Burlington, Illinois Central, New Haven and the Boston & Maine — Maine Central. The details of some of these light weight pocket streamliners is outlined below.

The City of Salina was the first articulated coach streamliner, and indeed, the first streamlined train built by Pullman. It included three units one of which was a full coach and the other a buffet coach. (Union Pacific Railroad)

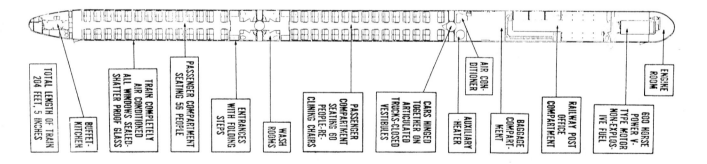

THE BOSTON & MAINE — MAINE CENTRAL'S FLYING YANKEE

One can say that the Pioneer Zephyr directly sired the Flying Yankee. The Yankee followed the Zephyr construction with almost a duplication of the original train. The only exception being more coach seats than the Zephyr provided. The Flying Yankee too has not received the historical attention it deserves because it followed too closely on the heels of the Pioneer. Apparently the Greek god of the west wind wanted to grab all of the publicity for itself. In fact both the City of Salina and the Pioneer received more attention than any other train developed during the mid to late 1930's, with the exception of the all-coach Florida trains. At any rate, it is hoped that the treatment of the Flying Yankee in this section of this book will give some credit to a train — where credit is due.

13

As 1934 drew to a close and 1935 blossomed into the new year, the Edward G. Budd Manufacturing Company completed a three car or section articulated high speed train of light weight, stainless steel construction with seats for 140 passengers. The new streamliner was built for the B&M and MEC, and can lay claim to being the first streamlined train in the east. (Not to be confused with the Wind Splitter built in 1900 on the Baltimore & Ohio Railroad. This train never entered revenue service, and operated experimentally only.)

The Flying Yankee entered New England on a Saturday, February 9, 1935 after making a press run for the railroad companies and the Budd Company to Mechanicsville, New York. The train was then placed for public inspection at Boston, and several other cities and towns on both the Boston and Maine and Maine Central. This public display lasted for several weeks before going into service running a grand total of 730 miles daily.

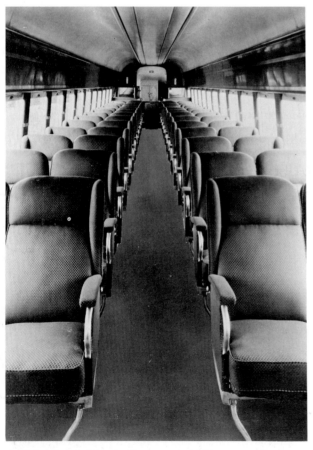

The interior of the buffet coach looking back through the coach to the buffet section. The four facing seats at the forward end of each coach accommodated removable tables. (Union Pacific Railroad)

The Flying Yankee streamliner replaced a steam train operation between Boston and Bangor via Portland. The steam train departed Boston at 9:40 AM and ran non-stop to Portland, Maine (115 miles) in two hours, five minutes. From that point the Maine Central scheduled the train for the 135 mile run to Bangor with 14 intermediate stops. The new Flying Yankee cut nearly two hours off the running schedule for the service, and in so doing permitted just one set of equipment to replace the former two sets with steam power. The new schedule between Boston and Portland called for an average speed of 55 miles per hour, and a slightly lessor speed between Portland and Bangor. Furthermore, the Flying Yankee made an additional evening trip back to Portland from Boston after its fast afternoon run from Bangor. In the morning, the Yankee departed Portland for Boston at 7:30 AM. What an operation! The train replaced not only two conventional trains, but was able to make an additional round trip between Boston and Portland on a daily basis. The new streamliner not only cut costs for the B&M-MEC, but gained new passengers not only for the Bangor run, but for a Portland run besides. The streamliner not only had the public taking notice, but the industry as a whole was intrigued by the pocket all-coach streamliner.

The train was smoothly contoured as was the Burlington's Zephyr. It is interesting to note that wind tunnel tests at the Massachusetts Institute of Technology indicated that at a speed of 95 miles per hour, the total resistance to motion was reduced to about 47% of that of a train with three coaches of conventional shape but of the same weight.

The train contained a baggage compartment, a buffet and four passenger coach seat sections plus a lounge observation room. The interior decorations consisted of a deep shade of blue green on the walls and ivory ceilings. The seats were upholstered in mulberry taupe with brown leather arm rests. Drapes of lemon gold and striped with green were placed at the windows. The floors were carpeted with meadow green coloring under the seats and sand color in the aisles. The observation lounge was slightly different with carpeting the color of cedar. The window drapes were lemon gold but striped with deep brown instead of green.

The window shades were of a neutral color facing inside and were silver on the outside to match the exterior of the train.

Lighting was indirect in all of the cars and was designed to produce a minimum intensity of eight foot candles at reading height.

The Union Pacific's City of Salina is shown here on a press run on the Boulder City line in Colorado. (William Kratville)

The City of Salina was displayed nation wide, and everywhere the crowds poured out to view the train inside and out. The "City" can lay claim to being the first all-coach streamliner. (William Kratville)

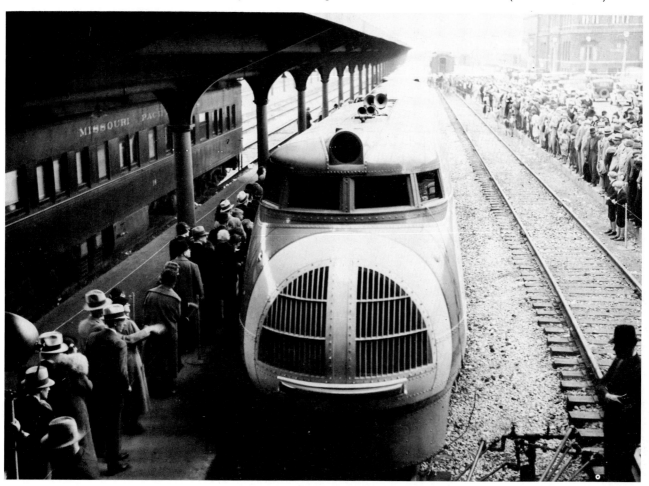

The Pioneer Zephyr went on display just at the City of Salina did before going into service. The Zephyr attracted crowds in the same fashion, and was part of a dawn to dusk run from Denver to Chicago. The Pioneer began a whole new fleet of streamliners that would eventually become World famous. (Burlington Northern)

The coach seats were built on light weight tubular aluminum framing. The height of the seat and the angle of the back were carefully chosen for passenger comfort. There was a clear space beneath the seats, 8½ inches high, for the stowing of hand baggage. Robe rails for holding jackets and overcoats were provided on the backs of the seats.

The buffet was designed to supply grill service, ice cream and hot and cold drinks. The buffet included a refrigerator, electric grills, coffee and hot water urns and storage space for dishes, utensils and food. Service was provided either at the counter or at one's seat. Individual trays which could be attached between the seats served as dining tables. Large sleeping car section tables

The rear of the Pioneer Zephyr on display at Philadelphia in 1934. (Harold K. Vollrath)

Originally the Zephyr consisted of three articulated units with 20 coach seats in the second car, and 40 seats plus a 12 passenger observation lounge with folding tables. In 1935, a 40 seat chair car was added to the train. This was later replaced in 1938 with a dinette chair car. When retired in 1960, the train retained its original three unit consist. (Burlington Northern)

could be set up at opposing seats at the end of each car. The buffet section was in the lead car or engine section.

The Flying Yankee ran on the schedule previously described until 1939. At that time, the train was removed from Yankee service during the summer months to operate between Boston and Bethlehem, N.H. as the Mountaineer. From 1947 on the Flying Yankee streamliner ran as the Cheshire between Boston and White River Junction until 1952. For the next four years she took on a Boston — Troy, New York assignment as the Minute Man. For a short period of time in 1956 and 1957, she again ran as the Cheshire. However the year 1957 brought a close to regular operation and she was retired from active service for long distance runs. She led an active and varied career, and on some rare times she even served as a special ski train. It is probably a matter of opinion if the Flying Yankee had a

more varied career than the Burlington's Pioneer Zephyr. The Pioneer did cover more of a geographic territory for some of her runs, but it is doubtful she ever ran as a ski train. One might say that the Flying Yankee went down in history as the forgotten streamliner. The Pioneer even won in retirement with a berth at the Museum of Science and Industry at Chicago. Perhaps we can call the Flying Yankee the silent hero. She was built for New England and she served her public well, as well as putting needed cash in the till for her owners. She was a superb little train and knowledge gained from her (and also the Pioneer) gave the Budd Company much needed information for them to play a major role in the development of some of the finest coaches and all coach streamliners that have ever been built. For this, the Flying Yankee also deserves the crown of distinction in the history book of American Railroading.

The service record of the Pioneer Zephyr was simply outstanding. She began service in 1934 between Kansas City and Lincoln. Four years later she ran as the Ozark State Zephyr between Kansas City and St. Louis. Four years later in 1942 she took on a Lincoln and McCook, Nebraska turn. In 1949 she ran on the Denver to Cheyenne route for the Colorado & Southern. A year later she went on the Galesburg-Quincy run, and in 1953 she became a Kansas City Zephyr connecting train from Brookfield to St. Joseph. Her last CB&Q assignment took her to St. Joe and Lincoln in 1957, and from 1960 on the Pioneer Zephyr has been assigned to the Museum of Science and Industry in Chicago. (Burlington Northern)

The **Burlington** invested heavily in articulated streamliners, and they often saw service system wide. For example, when the 9901 was replaced on the Twin Cities Zephyr route in 1936, she began service as the Sam Houston Zephyr between Ft. Worth and Houston on the Fort Worth and Denver Railroad. The Zephyr is shown here passing Irving, Texas carrying green flags indicating a following section. (Harold Kl. Vollrath)

The Denver Zephyr was the largest of the articulated trains to go into service on the CB&Q, a whopping 12 cars including the power units. The 1936 Denver Zephyr is shown here at Denver in July, 1943. (Harold K. Vollrath)

The Union Pacific did not take a back seat to the CB&Q with articulated streamliners. The UP invested heavily in either articulated trains and/or cars for its new "City" fleet that was growing in the late 1930's. (Harold K. Vollrath)

NEW HAVEN'S COMET

1935 brought another concept in coach train travel to American Railroading, and that concept was found in the New Haven Railroad's Comet. This particular train was an articulated three car, high speed streamliner with diesel power plants at both ends of the train. The Comet can lay claim to being the first American train with such an arrangement. The unusual train was designed and built by the Goodyear-Zeppelin Corporation of Akron, Ohio in collaboration with the New Haven. In addition, the Comet was unusual because it was built to provide a special high speed, frequent transportation between Boston and Providence. Even during the Depression, this territory consisted of a dense traffic pattern where rapid turn arounds were not practical with steam. It was for this reason that the double end design was selected and all of the space not used for power plants was arranged to accommodate coach passengers only for trips of less than 60 minutes.

The operation of the Comet involved five round trips per day between Boston and Providence. The New Haven began the new service in June, 1935. Initially the schedule called for making the nearly 44 mile run in 44 minutes in each direction. The only exception to this operation was the last west bound run from Boston (after 11 PM). This particular run was a local trip and its scheduled running was longer than the usual 44 minute timing. During the mid-1930's, the steam train schedules between Boston and Providence varied from 55 to 75 minutes. (Should the

reader desire further information concerning the Boston-Providence operations, see Chapter 1, *Commuter Railroads*, Superior Publishing Company, Seattle, Washington, 1970.)

The Comet consisted of three body sections articulated and carried on four trucks. The train was 207 feet long and was powered by two 400 horsepower Westinghouse Diesel engines, one at each end of the train. Being a totally new concept in 1935, the double end design presented a rather interesting aero dynamic problem because of the symmetrical design for double end operation. Research was conducted through a series of wind tunnel tests on models at the Daniel Guggenheim Airship Institute at Akron and at Columbia University where a running belt was used to simulate the relative velocities between car bottom, air and the track.

The Comet had a cruising speed of 90 miles per hour, with a maximum speed of 110 miles per hour. Acceleration from 0 to 55 miles per hour could be accomplished in 120 seconds. The Comet was even able to operate at a speed of 68 miles per hour with one of the diesel engines completely shut down.

Each of the end body units consisted of the engine room and coach seats for 48 passengers. The center car contained a 36 seat passenger room and a 28 seat smoking compartment. The total seating amounted to 160 passengers. The interior of the car was painted in three shades of tan on the walls with a pink-white on the ceilings. Elaborate decorations were not the order of the day for this smart little train because of the short distance operations.

The seats were of the "walk over" type with aluminum framing. The seat cushions and back cushions were upholstered with a rust colored mohair. The appearance of the seats dominated the coach interiors. Each window had its own draw drapes, which were somewhat lighter in color than the adjacent chair upholstery. The outside of the drapes were a rich ultramarine blue which matched the blue belt of the exterior at the window level.

The Comet was a popular mode of transportation between Boston and Providence for a good many years. She ran from 1935 to 1951, almost exclusively in the service for which she was designed. The results of the Comet laid the ground work for the double powered low slung trains of the mid-1950's and the Turbo Trains now running between Boston and New York City. It is interesting to note that innovations that grew from the Comet's basic concept returned twice after the Comet's retirement to ply the very same rails. One could say that the concept of the Comet was a failure because it was not repeated with the purchase of additional Comet trains. On the other hand, the double ended power concept was utilized again with the Talgo train — although it

could probably be pointed out that the Talgo was a short lived operation. However again in 1967, the Turbo's were built with double ended power units, and these of course are still running in 1975. One could probably argue either way on the success or the failure of the Comet. The Comet was popular with the traveling public. It provided five round trips daily on its route. This meant that its use was an extremely high percentage of the 24 hour day. With such a high utilization factor, the New Haven must have been pleased with the streamliner.

There is an interesting post script to the Comet train's concept and service. While the New Haven was in the process of developing the Comet, they were struggling with another problem that they never really did solve. That problem had to do with the passenger loads of certain local main line and branch line runs that were too heavy for a single gas-electric car. The problem produced an experimental two car streamlined steam train that contained a good deal of the features found on the Comet. That train became known as the Besler, which is covered in Chapter 2.

The Flying Yankee looked very much like the three car articulated trains built for the Burlington by the Budd Company. The Yankee is shown here at Boston in July 1940. (Harold K. Vollrath)

The Comet represented still another concept in articulated streamliners, and she operated on a very fast, short, turn around run that would have been impossible for steam. The Comet deserves credit for its contribution to double ended powered trains, and today's Turbo trains can trace their development back to the Comet. (New Haven Region — Penn Central)

The Illinois Central, not be outdone by neighbors Burlington and Union Pacific, purchased the Green Diamond and was one of the fastest trains on the Chicago-St. Louis route. The train is shown here on display at Peoria, Illinois in September, 1936. (Harold K. Vollrath)

ILLINOIS CENTRAL'S GREEN DIAMOND

The Illinois Central also joined the Depression era articulated streamliner club. The IC's train more closely resembled the Union Pacific streamliners than either the Zephyr, Flying Yankee or the Comet. Thus it added still another concept during the dawn of streamliners.

The Green Diamond was built in 1936 and consisted of a power car and four cars. The first car was a Rail Post Office Baggage car and consisted of three compartments. At the forward end was an eight foot storage area. Next came a 31 foot RPO section and finally a 23 foot baggage area. The total length of the car was 64 feet.

The second car was a 64 foot coach with two coach compartments. The forward end included washrooms for both men and women and a four seat table arrangement on both sides of the aisle. Next came three pairs of regular coach seats of both sides of the aisle for a total seating capacity of 20 passengers in what would be called the smoking compartment. The smoking area was divided from the rest of the coach by a low partition with grille work. The non-smoking compartment consisted of 36 seats and a luggage storage area.

The second coach included a four seat table arrangement on both sides of the aisle at the forward end. This was followed by 36 coach seats,

which in turn was followed by a 16 seat table section. The entry doors of the car were next at the rear of the car ahead of the washrooms. The entry doors were ahead of the articulated truck at the rear of both coaches.

The last car was a diner observation lounge car. The car's entry doors were at the head end of the car behind the articulated truck. Washrooms were located forward of the entry doors. To the rear of the entry vestibule was a 18½ foot kitchen, which was equipped with cooking ranges, refrigerators, sinks, coffee and hot water urns and food storage areas as well as a candy bar, cigarettes and cigar storage cabinet. There was table seating for eight in this car, plus coach passengers were also served in the sixteen seat table section in the car ahead. The final section of the last car consisted of 20 lounge seats that were sold as parlor car accommodations.

The Green Diamond went into service on the Chicago-St. Louis run in 1936 and continued running on that route for eleven years. In 1947 it was transferred to the Jackson-New Orleans run as the Miss Lou. The second assignment lasted but two years, and the entire train was scrapped in 1950. The Green Diamond will be remembered for generations as the train that heralded streamliners on the Illinois Central — the Main Line of Mid-America.

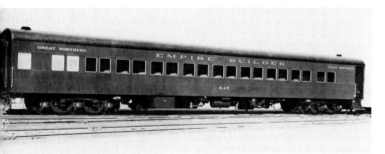

Among the first, but not the first, streamlined coaches that hit the rails were the Great Northern's Empire Builder coaches of 1937. Although some dispute if these were streamlined cars or not because of the use of bolts instead of welded car sides, the cars are squared off and carry the smoothly rounded roof and therefore qualify as a streamlined coach. Furthermore when the Great Northern operated these cars in the Gopher and the Badger, the trains were refered to as streamliners or as part of the streamliner fleet. The Milwaukee Road coaches of 1935 probably take the honors for the first true streamlined coach with the smooth roof line, and were operated in streamliner service. (Pullman Standard)

The interior of the Empire Builder coaches contained fully cushioned reclining seats, spacious men's and women's lounges and restrooms and ice water coolers. The company maintained the cars in excellent condition and some continued to operate until 1971. (Pullman Standard)

CONVENTIONAL MODERN EQUIPMENT

As the New Haven and other railroads were experimenting with various types of power plants, some trains were becoming more and more popular as time went on. Streamlined coaches began to roll out of the car shops in greater numbers for conventional trains. The Hiawathas were under construction in the Milwaukee Road shops. The individual cars, rather than articulated trains, meant that the capacity of the train could be increased or decreased according to traffic requirements. A number of articulated trains would still be built, but their number was to taper off. Trains, such as the Challenger, became very popular and the Union Pacific and the Chicago & North Western ordered an entire fleet of Challenger coaches for service between Chicago and the West Coast. The Great Northern ordered new coaches for the Empire Builder, and these particular cars have been the source of discussion among many people ever since their construction. Some have called them streamlined as they definitely have the streamliner concepts built in. However, the use of bolts instead of welded sides has caused the cars to be designated semi-streamlined by many people. The reader can take

his choice but should remember that Pullman was building the Empire Builder coaches at the exact same time the streamlined Challenger cars were rolling out of the erecting shops. The streamlined coach was here to stay by 1937, and furthermore it could be coupled with standard passenger equipment.

This combination of streamlined and standard passenger cars made for some very interesting passenger trains, and did so right up until the time of Amtrak. The streamlined coach was basically a step ahead of the standard coach. It generally had a lower seating capacity and lounge rooms located at one or both ends of the car. Some cars included powder rooms in addition to wash rooms for the ladies. They were built with reclining seats and they have offered literally hundreds of little niceties since 1937.

As we move into the 1940's, there were a number of developments that were taking place. Developments that, in many peoples' opinions, would set North American rail coach travel in a class far above any other area of the World.

There was a substantial amount of progress with coach service during the period immediately

The Pendulum coach was built with curved sides and when one looks at today's Turbo, the rounded contour brings back memories of these unique coaches that saw service on the Santa Fe, Burlington and Great Northern Railways. (Santa Fe)

The interior of the Pendulum car was smoothly contoured and contained baggage racks the entire length of the car that blended smoothly with the side walls. Car lighting was contained in the overhead baggage rack as well in the center of the ceiling. The windows in all three of the cars built were of the oval type, which were not the best for little children who wanted to look out the window. (Santa Fe Railway)

before the War. Also there was a substantial amount of research going on by both the railroads and the car builders. Because of financial conditions, very few of these innovative ideas hit the rails. One such car however was the Pendulum Coach built by Pacific Railway Equipment for the Santa Fe, Great Northern and Burlington in 1940.

The Pendulum Coach was constructed with curved sides, oval windows and a unique suspension system that was attached to the upper part of the car internally. The three cars were among the smoothest riding cars ever built, but the expense involved in maintaining the pendulum system was far too great. The three lines operated the cars in various types of service, and the general reaction by the traveling public was positive. Eventually the equipment was retired, and it could be classed as a successful venture but too expensive. The idea was not laid to rest forever though. In 1967 the new Turbo Trains went into operation with a similar system.

Throughout World War II not much went on except for the construction of a number of streamlined coaches. These were however, simply duplicates of cars built before the war. There were no new innovations until 1945.

As most everyone knows, 1945 brought the idea of the dome car. The Burlington rebuilt a streamlined coach with a dome, and Pullman-Standard teamed up with General Motors to construct the Train of Tomorrow. The history of dome cars and trains was covered in *The Domeliners*, Superior Publishing Company, 1973. The dome car certainly ranks as one of the greatest travel innovations ever devised by the transportation industry.

Immediately following the War, orders for streamlined coaches and other equipment poured into the car builders. Dozens upon dozens of new streamliners hit the rails from 1947 through the early 1950's. It was a golden time in railroad history, and very few people realized the impact that the automobile was to have on the train in a very short time. Nevertheless it was a fine time to travel by train.

Nearly all of the cars on order were conventional streamlined coaches. However a number of innovations began to take place in 1947 and 1948. For example up to this time, lounge accommodations were almost exclusively reserved for Pullman passengers. There had been exceptions to this rule, but by and large coach passengers did not have access to club and lounge car facilities. This changed with the purchase of coach lounge cars by the Northern Pacific in 1947; and by the MKT and Frisco for the Texas

Many railroads painted their streamlined equipment and lettered it for particular train service. Missouri Pacific coach No. 770 is a typical example of a coach painted for The Eagle. Note the road's initials in small letters at each upper corner. (Missouri Pacific Railroad)

The interiors of streamlined coaches were exceptionally bright and cheerful and included murals on the bulkheads, drapes, individual reading lamps in the baggage racks, full reclining seats with foot rests, low density blue lights for night operation, and spacious lounge rooms at the ends of the car. (Missouri Pacific Railroad)

Special in 1948. This was quite a change for the coach passenger.

With the thousands of streamlined car orders pouring into the car builders, the railroads were faced with delayed deliveries. Consequently many railroads used one or more of three different solutions to compensate for this problem. One was to secure tourist or 12 section, 1 drawing room sleepers from the Pullman Company and rebuild them into coaches. The outside window configurations were generally not changed and drawing rooms became smoking rooms. This equipment was most desirable because it was already air conditioned. The second method was to take old standard equipment and rebuild them with streamlined style picture windows, air conditioning, reclining seats and often with semi-streamlined roofs. The third method was the conversion of parlor cars to coach seating. In most cases the cars were repainted in the road's streamlined color schemes, and just as often as not, the rebuilt equipment's riding qualities exceeded that of the new streamlined, light weight equipment. With completely refurbished interiors the rebuilds were indistinguishable from the new equipment on the inside. These cars were a fascinating part of coach car history.

Transcontinental coaches were equipped with leg rest seats, and often with carpeting in addition to all of the things mentioned in the previous photo. (Santa Fe Railway)

Not all coaches were constructed as straight coaches. This Great Northern diner coach was originally built by ACF Industries for the Internationals. It later saw service on trains 3 and 4, the Dakotan. Amtrak operated the car on the eastern seaboard and it is shown here in Penn Central's Sunnyside yard, New York City on March 25th, 1972. (J. W. Swanberg)

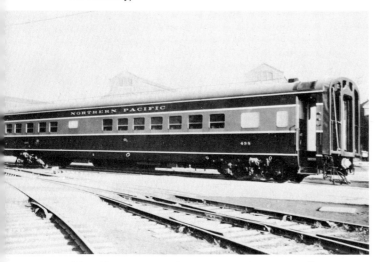

The Northern Pacific purchased coach buffet lounge cars for the new streamlined North Coast limited in 1947. It is another example of a combination type car. (Pullman Standard)

The coach section contained day-nite leg rest seats, with the leg rest folding down from the seat ahead. This arrangement did not interfere with the reclining operation of the seat, but it was not as good as the leg rest seats shown in the Santa Fe car previously in this section. (Pullman Standard)

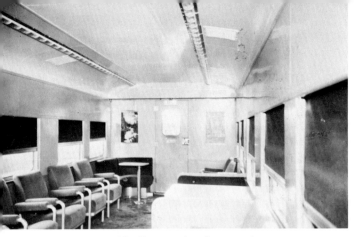

Lounge and buffet service for coach passengers was very rare until after World War II. After that time, the Northern Pacific, Union Pacific and other lines began to provide such equipment. The photo shows the lounge section of the NP coach buffet lounge car, which was the equal of many a First Class club lounge. (Pullman Standard)

The Northern Pacific coach buffet lounge cars were rebuilt to the World famous Traveller's Rest cars in 1955, and provided coach passengers on the North Coast Limited the finest of lounge car services. The interior of the car featured Old West decor with reproductions of the Lewis' and Clark's diaries, guns, maps and other items concerning the Lewis and Clark expedition. The interior of the car is literally a rolling museum. (Burlington Northern)

Another example of coach lounge car service was the Frisco — MKT's coach lounges on the Texas Special. (Pullman Standard)

Although many railroads rebuilt Pullman sleepers into air conditioned coaches after World War II, a few lines rebuilt standard coaches into high quality cars. One example is this fine rebuilt heavyweight coach of the L&N, 2577 pictured at Etowah, Tenn. on October 29, 1967. The car was operating on a National Railroad Historical Society Atlanta Chapter excursion via the Hiwasee Loop line. (Jim Scribbins)

The ultimate in coach car design was the dome coach, the first of which was built in 1945. Three car builders produced domes in various styles, the most prevalent however was the Budd built short domes. Burlington Northern dome coach 555 (ex-Northern Pacific 555) continues to operate for Amtrak and will soon have in excess of 20 years of continuous operation for dome coach passengers. (Patrick D. Dorin)

The interior of one of the same type of upgraded coaches; L&N 2575 on the same excursion. It would be difficult for even an experienced rail traveler to determine from the interior alone that this was not a light weight streamlined coach. (Jim Scribbins)

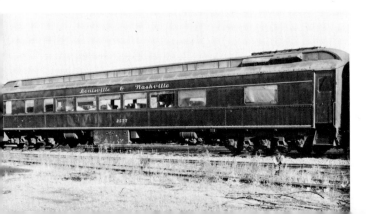

The Great Northern rebuilt a number of coaches from parlor cars. The 4th and 5th cars were such rebuilds and are part of the consist of the Great Northern pre-streamlined Gopher departing St. Paul for Duluth. (Great Northern Photo, Collection of Wayne C. Olsen)

Rebuilt coaches often were assigned to streamlined trains as is the case with train No. 106, the Missouri River Eagle departing Omaha for St. Louis on the MoPac in September, 1948. (Elmer Treloar)

The coaches in the consist of Monon train No. 6, the Thoroughbred, are rebuilt hospital cars and represent still another way in which railroads obtained high quality coach equipment without purchasing new cars. The train is departing Louisville decked out entirely in what was certainly one of the finest of liveries to grace any passenger equipment: the stunning red and grey. The date is July 10, 1952 and ten years from now, trains 5 and 6 will be longer but with additional head-end cars and fewer coaches. (See chapter 8) (Jim Scribbins)

Not all rebuilds from standard coaches or sleepers resulted in coaches. In 1950 the Illinois Central converted a full standard coach to this streamlined baggage coach. On the day this photo was taken, the 1850 was assigned to the headend of the "Governor's Special" between Chicago and Springfield. The 81 foot car rode on six wheeled trucks and was equipped with a 29 foot baggage compartment as well as accommodations for 36 coach passengers. The photo was taken in early 1971 at Homewood, Illinois. (Patrick C. Dorin)

Finally not all coach rebuilds resulted in full coaches. The Soo Line converted coach No. 2017 to a Dining Club Lounge car for service on the Laker in the early 1950's. The "Best Meals on Wheels" (by the Soo's own admission) were served in the car and it was a pleasure to ride the Laker just for the French Toast and the Lake Superior Lake Trout. The car is now located at the Lake Superior Transportation Museum at the Duluth Union Station. (Patrick C. Dorin)

The process of converting sleeping cars to coaches continued until the 1960's, when the Pennsylvania Railroad converted 50 Roomette sleepers to coaches. The exterior window configuration remained the same and cars operated system wide. (Patrick C. Dorin)

Very often during the rebuilding process, coaches like GM&O No. 243, received semistreamlined roofs. The car was assigned to the Chicago-Joliet suburban trains when this photo was taken in September, 1971. (Patrick C. Dorin)

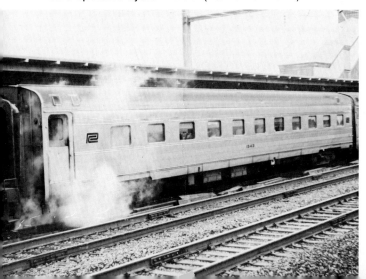

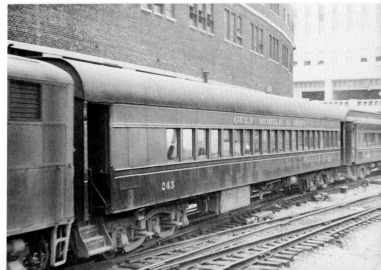

One of the orginal double deck coaches constructed for the C&NW in 1954 and 1956. No. 39 is shown here after its conversion from steam heating to electric operation for use with other push pull trains. (William A. Raia)

THE DOUBLE DECK COMMUTER COACHES

The Burlington was faced with operating and cost problems at the Chicago Union Station; and when Budd and Burlington got together on the problem — the double deck coach was the result. Initially the CB&Q ordered 30 such cars in 1950 from Budd. They have had several repeat orders ever since then.

Meanwhile these coaches with capacities in excess of 150 and as much as 169, began to look attractive to other railroads. In 1954 the Chicago & North Western purchased 16 cars from St. Louis Car. 1955 brought an order from the Southern Pacific for Pullman Standard for 10 double decks. Other builders such as ACF Industries and Canadian Vickers also got into the act and double deck coaches have been built almost continuously since 1950 through 1975.

The rarest of all Slumbercoaches was the Missouri Pacific's "Southland." With the exception of the New York Central, all Slumbercoaches were operated by Pullman. (Missouri Pacific Railroad)

The interior of nearly all of the double deck coaches was pretty much the same. Baggage racks extend over the center aisle, seats are of the flip over variety, stairways to the upper floor are adjacent to the car entrance ways, single seating is provided up top and coat hooks are provided in the wall at each seat. This is an interior of a C&NW coach constructed in 1971. (Pullman Standard)

Besides the Burlington, the North Western, and Southern Pacific; the Rock Island, Milwaukee Road, Illinois Central and the Canadian Pacific operate double deck passenger coaches in suburban service. They have rarely ventured out of suburban territory, but the Milwaukee Road did run double decks in special Wisconsin Dells, Wisconsin tour trains. Overall the double decks have been very successful in reducing costs and increasing ridership. The double deck or gallery cars, as they are sometimes known, have been a real star in the history of passenger coach development. But again the Budd Company was not content to be complacent in their commuter victory. Their next step was to go after the overnight trade in coach traffic — the Slumbercoach.

SLUMBERCOACHES

It was in 1953 that the Budd Company engineers came up with what they called a Siesta-Coach. The original design was an all single room configuration. Initial reaction to the design was rather dull. It reminded many railroaders of the tourist sleeper, which by 1953 had been phased out by nearly all U.S. railroads with the exception of the Soo Line and the Milwaukee Road. (Indeed Tourist sleepers on the Milwaukee Road were designated Touralux cars and space was sold on a coach fare plus space charge basis.) However, the Burlington took a very hard look at the

Here and there on some rail-roads coach tickets were good in sleeping cars. During the last years of Touralux Sleeping Cars on the Milwaukee Road, the Company honored coach tickets for travel. This photo shows a section in day service on a Touralux, the finest tourist cars ever operated in the USA. (The Milwaukee Road)

Siesta-coach. The new Denver Zephyrs were being constructed (including the newest design in leg rest seat coaches) and it was logical that this new concept in coach travel be included. Four cars were ordered, and they were designated Slumbercoach instead of Siesta-coach, and the name stuck — except for the New York Central. The end of 1956 saw the first Slumbercoaches operating between Chicago and Denver — Colorado Springs, Colorado. The CB&Q cars were also a modified design with 24 single duplex rooms and 8 double rooms for a total capacity of 40 passengers. The cars were an immediate success with a fare structure consisting of a coach ticket plus a space charge. It marked for the first time that passengers could travel in a private room on a coach class ticket.

As the Burlington Slumbercoaches went into service in 1956, the Milwaukee Road-Union Pacific leased two 21 Roomette sleepers from the Pullman Company (Pennsylvania Railroad's Bedford Inn and Coatesville) for competitive service between Chicago and Denver. The service did not last long, only from October, 1956 to April, 1957. To this writer's knowledge, this is the only time that sleeping cars have been actually designated "coach" although sleeping cars have been used in coach service.

The Burlington Slumbercoaches were in operation for more than a year before the next pair of cars went into service on the Baltimore & Ohio. In 1958, the B&O purchased two cars and like the CB&Q's, the cars were operated by

Pullman. At the time of purchase, the B&O debated about which Chicago-Washington train should carry the Dreamland and Slumberland. It was finally decided to operate the cars in the All-Coach Columbian because it was coach tickets that passengers were purchasing to ride the cars. Again ridership on Slumbercoaches was exceeding 80% on all runs.

1959 turned out to be a big year for Slumbercoach operations. The Northern Pacific ordered four for the North Coast Limited. The cars went into a combination Burlington-Northern Pacific pool where 4 NP and 2 CB&Q Slumbercoaches operated a Seattle - Chicago - Denver - Chicago - Seattle circuit. This operation would release a Slumbercoach off the North Coast Limited for the Denver Zephyr in Chicago. The car would make a round trip and upon its return to Chicago would be switched into the North Coast Limited consist. Arrival in Chicago on the DZ permitted enough time for the transfer, and the same held true with the afternoon arrival of the North Coast. Slumbercoaches did not layover 24 hours in Chicago as the rest of the North Coast's equipment did.

The B&O went back to the Budd Company for a repeat order in 1959 for three more Slumbercoaches for the National Limited. At the same time, the Missouri Pacific purchased one car and with the total of four cars the railroads provided a through Washington-Texas service. As of 1959, the B&O was the largest owner of Slumbercoaches, a grand total of 5.

The New York Central also purchased four Slumbercoaches in 1959 for operation on the New England States and the Twentieth Century Limited. Success of these four cars led the New York Central to rebuild 10 sleeping cars into 10 new Sleepercoaches (as the Slumbercoaches were designated on the NYC). The 22 Roomette sleepers were rebuilt to a 16 single room and 10 double room configuration for a passenger seating capacity of 36. This was four less than the standard Budd Company version. The rebuilding project was carried on by the Budd Company for the New York Central. As of 1961, the NYC was the largest operator of Slumbercoaches, a grand total of 14. In addition to the Century and the New England States, the cars ran in the consists of the Ohio State Limited, Cleveland Limited, and Wolverine. The New York Central operation was the most extensive in the United States.

As the passenger business declined, the Northern Pacific took advantage of discontinued Slumbercoach runs on the MoPac, B&O and NYC to pick up eight cars of the 24-8 configuration. The NP then became the second largest owner of Slumbercoaches with a grand total of 12, all of which went into a pool with the Burlington. The cars operated on the Denver Zephyr, North Coast Limited, Mainstreeter and the Blackhawk. After the BN merger, the new company owned 16 Slumbercoaches to set a new record for single company car ownership. Initially Amtrak purchased 11 of these cars, but now operates 30 cars of the 24-8, 16-10 and 16-4 configuration (1974). The latter are 16 duplex roomette, 4 double bedroom cars, which were built by Budd for the B&O in 1954.

The Pullman Standard Company also came up with a Slumbercoach design, but it never left the drawing boards. A car diagram with 19 single rooms and four double rooms was proposed in 1956, but that is all the farther it got. It contained the smallest capacity of any Slumbercoach designed.

It can be said that the Slumbercoach was and is a success. Repeat orders were most likely lost because of the automobile inroads that came with bigger leaps and bounds after the mid-1950's. It is interesting to note that Northern Pacific and New York Central invested heavily in Slumbercoaches, while Great Northern and Pennsylvania barely took notice of the equipment. The addition of Slumbercoaches on the North Coast Limited added an even greater variety of accommodations to be found on that train. What other train can one think of that offered domes, leg rest seats, Slumbercoach rooms, a complete line of sleeping car space plus that unique Traveler's Rest — that rolling museum of the Lewis & Clark Expedition. Some trains may have been fancier, charged extra fares, even sported a dome car but few have offered the wide variety of the North Coast Limited — and the Slumbercoach added just that much more.

The future is hard to predict for Slumbercoaches as we know them. It may be possible that they will run for quite some time depending upon passenger demands, and who knows, perhaps Amtrak will come up with still another design or configuration.

The Slumbercoach was only the beginning of a new series of coaches developed by the Budd Company. The long haul market was sought after next in 1954 by the ever popular Hi-Level Chair Cars.

HI-LEVEL CHAIR CARS

Sometime before 1954, the officials of the Santa Fe Railway and the Budd Company went to work to design a luxury car for the long haul market. The objective was to produce a car that was the ultimate in luxury and would be comfortable for a forty hour trip. The result was the hi-level chair car and the first two experimental cars rolled out of the Budd Company shops in 1954. The two were assigned to the El Capitan, a train that will be covered in Chapter 5.

The hi-level cars are 15½ feet in height. Passengers are eight feet above the rails and are treated to a view from a point a full four feet

The Hi-level cars were equipped with spacious leg rest reclining seats, carpeting, ice water, luggage racks, individual reading lights and decorated in Southwest Indian motifs. (Santa Fe Railway)

higher than in a standard level car. Because of the extra height and extra weight, the cars run smoother and with less noise and vibration than conventional equipment.

The Santa Fe owned and operated two types of hi-level coaches. One set contained step down stairs at one end so that the equipment could be operated with conventional cars. The other type is simply an all hi-level floor plan.

As we stated previously, the first two cars were built in 1954. The El Capitan was completely equipped with hi-level Chair cars, Dining and Lounge cars in 1956. The Company purchased additional hi-level cars of both types in late 1963 and early 1964. At that time, the older equipment was re-assigned to the San Francisco Chief with the new cars going on the El Capitan. A number of hi-level cars were also assigned to the Texas Chief.

With the advent of Amtrak, hi-level cars have operated on the Super Chief, Texas Chief and Sunset Limited. As of 1974, the hi-level cars have been studied for different operating possibilities but no new ones have been ordered for 10 years.

The Slumbercoach single and double rooms contained everything that could be found in a First Class roomette except that the bed is only 24 inches wide. This is a single Slumbercoach room on the Denver Zephyr. (Burlington Northern)

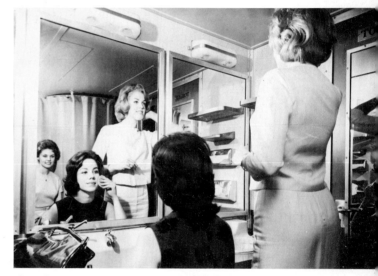

Spacious rest rooms are located on the lower levels of these chair cars. Both the men's and women's rest rooms were equipped with mirrors, electrical outlets, sinks and dressing tables for the ultimate in travel comfort. (Santa Fe Railway)

Roomy shelves on the lower level accommodate the baggage of passengers aboard the hi-level chair cars that operated on several Santa Fe trains. (Santa Fe Railway)

An artists concept of an early design low level train on the New Haven Railroad. (New Haven Region — Penn Central)

A low level train as compared to a standard height streamlined train. These designs were among many that never left the drawing boards. (New Haven Region — Penn Central)

COACHES WITH A LOW CENTER OF GRAVITY

From 1950 on, the automobile began to make even greater inroads on passenger train travel. The railroads began to cast about for new ideas that would increase speed, reduce operating costs and permit the railroads to reduce fares to attract passengers back to the rails. The investigation led ACF Industries, the Budd Company, Electro-Motive Division of General Motors and Pullman Standard to design and construct a number of experimental trains. Indeed, ACF Industries actually built a light weight Talgo train for Spain in 1949. The train was tested on American Railroads before exportation and was the forerunner of the trains to come in 1955. There were about six experiments known as the Talgo, Aerotrain, Train X, a modified Rail Diesel Car design, the Pennsylvania's Tubular train — the Keystone and the Pioneer III. Each of these designs had varying degrees of success. Of the trains, only the Keystone would survive until Amtrak. Train X would fade away and reappear again in modified form as Turbo in 1967. The Aerotrain and Talgo designs were almost totally unacceptable and as of 1975 there have been no new designs with these concepts. All in all, the designs brought back memories of the 1930's set of streamliners on the Burlington, Union Pacific and other lines. The articulated concept came back in full. In many ways, 1955 was a repeat of 1934. It lends evidence to the theory that history repeats itself only in different ways.

The original Talgo train was tested on the New Haven before it was shipped to the Spanish National Railways. The curved contour of the cars reminds one of the Pendulum coaches of 1941. (New Haven Region — Penn Central)

34

The **New Haven's Talgo** was named the John Quincy Adams and is shown here at New Haven under overhead wire. (Charles B. Gunn)

The Talgo

The Talgo actually was the first of the new light weight low center of gravity trains. The first one having been built in 1949 for the Spanish National Railways, who were rather pleased with its performance. According to the Spanish National, the Talgo concept provided a passenger seat for nearly 75% less weight per passenger than conventional Spanish designs. Further the trains were able to cut as much as 25% off the train schedules with very little increase in top speed. This was due to the light weight and low center of gravity which permitted higher speeds around curves. Naturally with this type of experience in Spain, ACF went ahead with an American design for the Rock Island, New Haven and Boston and Maine Railroads.

The original Spanish Talgo was built with a series of articulated two wheel units each riding piggyback on the unit ahead. The arrangement created a difficult situation when it was necessary to switch out a car for repairs and change the consist of the train. Although dolly wheels were used when the car was alone and out of service, they were not suitable for switching and so forth. Therefore, the American design consisted of a three unit car. The center unit was a four wheel car with the two end units riding piggyback toward the center unit. Each three unit car could then be switched in or out of the train with no difficulty. Furthermore, the cars could be operated in either direction at any speed instead of just the one way situation with the original Talgo. The first Talgo could not be

backed up with any degree of speed because the wheels of the units would be forced toward the outside of the curve. This created a tendency to derail. This situation was corrected with the newer American design in 1955.

The Talgo 3 unit cars were standardized to accommodate all interior accommodations such as coach, parlor, dining and lounge and sleeping car rooms. A Talgo coach (3 units) could accommodate 84 passengers on 42 inch seat centers and 96 people on 39 inch centers. In both cases, rotating reclining seats were (or could have been) used. With a sleeper configuration, the three unit car could accommodate 24 roomettes or 12 bedrooms or any combination of the two. The floor height of the Talgo varied from 26 to 28 inches depending upon load conditions. ACF built three Talgo trains and were delivered to the New Haven, Boston and Maine and Rock Island in 1956.

The New Haven train was named the John Quincy Adams and began actual service during the Spring of 1957. The original consist included five cars of three units each, with each car seating 96 passengers. The train operated between New York and Boston and was powered by

The interior of the John Quincy Adams was plain compared to full size streamline coaches, yet it was attractive. (Charles B. Gunn)

35

The Rock Island's Jet Rocket Talgo train was built with more class than the New Haven's or Boston & Maine's. Powered by a General Motors diesel, the train is shown here at 90 miles per hour just north of Peoria, Illinois on August 18, 1957. (Paul Stringham)

The only car to merit repeat orders was Pioneer III, however that was for commuter coaches such as Pennsylvania 153. Long distance cars never did materialize with that particular venture. The commuter cars are in service out of Philadelphia. (Budd Company)

Fairbanks-Morse "Speed Merchant" passenger locomotives designed for the Talgo. One of the New Haven coaches was rebuilt to a grill car in 1958. The train was taken out of Boston-New York service before 1960 and wrapped up a very short career, the shortest of all the Talgos.

The Boston & Maine's train was made up of 5 coaches, and was initially intended for Boston-Portland service. The train, like the New Haven's was unsuccessful and was transferred to commuter service on the Boston-Reading and Boston-Dover runs. She continued service in that capacity until the mid-1960's, and had followed almost the same pattern as the most luxurious Talgo of them all, the Rock Island's Jet Rocket.

The Rock Island's Jet Rocket went into service on the Chicago-Peoria run in February, 1956. She replaced the conventional Peoria Rocket and consisted of a baggage coach, a combination dining room, bar lounge and parlor car and two coaches. The train went into service after a display period in Chicago and Peoria, Illinois and at Gary, Indiana. It was at Gary that this author first viewed the Jet Rocket. It was not in service

The Keystone is the only low-level train that was not put in moth balls after she went into service. Furthermore, she was the only light weight low level train that passengers did not make efforts to avoid riding. (H H. Harwood, Jr.)

The Keystone was powered by GG-1's and generally served in the New York-Washington run. She could be coupled to standard equipment, such as the New Haven box express car behind the 4872. The train is southbound departing Baltimore in April, 1966. (H. H. Harwood, Jr.)

This photo will give the reader an idea of just how low the Keystone cars were in comparison to the high level platforms at 30th St. Station in Philadelphia. Yet passengers could board the Keystone at such high level stations. The Keystone was almost a case of where one could have their cake and eat it too. (H. H. Harwood, Jr.)

The Budd Company's RDC innovation was the Roger Williams constructed for the New Haven Railroad. However the concept was too expensive as compared to standard RDC's which could perform the same type of service. The fact that the Roger William's equipment is still operating under Amtrak attests to the Budd Company's fine workmanship on passenger cars. (Charles B. Gunn)

for long, when the passengers began to complain about the rough riding qualities. It was this problem that plagued all of the Talgos. Rock Island responded to customer demands, the conventional streamlined Peoria Rocket went back into service. The Jet Rocket was then transferred to commuter service between Chicago and Joliet in 1957. The Rock Island then ordered another coach for the train to provide additional seating capacity, and was the only order for a single Talgo coach ever placed. The train ran as the Banker's Special until about 1961, when it was placed in storage near the Rock Island's testing laboratory on the south side of Chicago.

The Talgo cannot really be considered a success. They were appropriately decorated in the

interior, and they were pleasant to look at. However, the riding quality — even on good to excellent track — was poor. Further the noise level seemed to be telegraphed through the entire train. These two points did more to kill the idea off than anything else. It could be said that the B&M and the Rock Island did get at least part of their investment back with commuter train service. It was a valiant effort, but Talgo just didn't have what the American Rail Traveler wanted. The Talgo goes down in history as simply a wink in the development of coaches and chair cars.

Budd Company's Low Level Innovations

As ACF was building low slung trains for the New Haven and other lines, the Budd Company was also involved with three types of new trains. The Budd Company, however, took more of a conventional approach to the designs. Although it could be considered a matter of opinion, it seems that the Budd Company designs were more successful than either the Talgo, Train X or the Aerotrain. In all three Budd trains, there were either repeat orders for the type car, or the train itself continued in operation into the 1970's.

Strangely enough the most successful of the three was Pioneer III. Pioneer III was a light weight low level coach with an 11 foot, 9 inch overall height. The test car weighed in at 83,000 pounds comparing with the 115,000 to 130,000 weights of conventional streamlined equipment. Meanwhile, the coupler height remained standard and could be used with other passenger cars. In fact, during tests on various railroads,

The interior of the Roger Williams featured individual reading spot lights, full baggage racks, reclining seats and cheerful colors. (Charles B. Gunn)

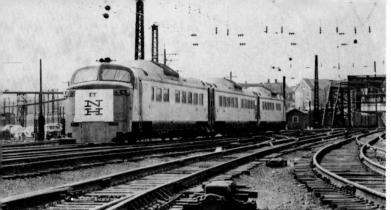

The chief advantage of the Roger Williams over the low level articulated trains was that it could be broken down in consist for different traffic levels. Here a three car train zips along at New Haven. (Charles B. Gunn)

The Roger Williams was one of only three RDC sets that contained a dining section. (Charles B. Gunn)

Pioneer III was pulled by Budd's Rail Diesel Car demonstrator.

The interior of the test car contained 88 bucket type seats on 35½ inch centers. Budd also designed four other interiors for Pioneer III: A deluxe coach for 52 passengers, dining car, club lounge car and a 16 duplex roomette, 3 single bedroom and 1 double bedroom sleeper. A unique aspect of the sleeper was the fact that the roomettes faced each other and could be opened ensuite if desired. This innovation, with the lower duplexes only, would be well worth its installation in roomettes today.

Pioneer III was ordered by only two railroads, the Pennsylvania and the Reading. These two lines purchased a fleet of standard height (not low level) electrified Silverliners with seating from 124 to 127 passengers for use in Philadelphia suburban service. (See Chapter 4, *Commuter Railroads*, Superior Publishing Co., 1970)

The year 1956 also produced another train that was similar in many ways to the Pioneer III. Known as the Tubular train (and named the Keystone by the Pennsylvania Railroad), the train consisted of a power-kitchen car and seven chair cars. The train was 11 feet, 9 inches high with a standard coupler height. Vestibules, as with Pioneer III, were standard height with the ramp and step downs for the lower floor levels in the main passenger compartments. Each chair

The Roger William's coaches were somewhat different from standard RDC's in exterior style, size and weight. However they could be operated with standard RDC's with no problem whatsoever. (J. W. Swanberg)

car carried 68 passengers with a 14 passenger lounge at the vestibule end of the car. Although there was a kitchen in the power-kitchen car, there was no food service. The first two coaches of the train once contained 16 seat dinettes, but these were eventually replaced with a standard 14 seat lounge. The only refreshment service was a small liquor bar in one of the lounges.

For most of the Keystone's career, she ran coupled to a standard height train between Washington, D.C. and New York City. She ran either on the head-end or the rear end of the train, always coupled to the power kitchen car. The seven Keystone coaches were powerless without that car. The Keystone ran continuously, and at the time of this writing (Summer, 1974) the train is being considered for other types of runs by Amtrak. Up to now, it has been almost exclusively operated between Washington and New York. The fact that this light weight low level train was not retired early in its career demonstrates its success as an operating unit. However, there were no repeat orders for the tubular construction (with no center beam or sill), and in this respect was different from Pioneer III which had a center sill. Keystone interiors featured plastics for ease of maintenance. It is interesting to note that Keystone was built at the exact same time the Budd Company was constructing the Hi-level El Capitan. Of the two, only the Hi-level chair cars earned repeat orders.

Budd was very busy in 1956 with new coach and train designs. The RDC provided the idea for the third innovative train, known as the Roger Williams. In this case, a six car train was constructed with streamlined cabs on each end of the consist. The end cars were and are known as coach cabs and the four interior cars were simply built with blind ends. However all six cars contained the same components as standard RDC

38

cars. The seating capacities were lower than standard RDC's because reclining seats were installed. The cab coaches seated 60 while the four center cars seated 76. Two years later one of the cars was modified to contain 40 dining room seats and 28 coach seats. The train was designed to operate at 110 miles per hour and for both standard operation and the third rail electric power going into Grand Central Terminal in New York City. The train could be broken down in shorter or longer consists if required, and could be operated with standard RDC's. As a long distance train, however, the Roger Williams did not prove itself well in that service. Many railroad men questioned the concept of six RDC cars in one train, which means there is a substantial amount of power. Each RDC is rated at about 600 horsepower at 300 HP per engine with two per car. This meant that the six car train contained 12 Detroit Diesel engines. It turned out that the RDC concept demonstrated considerable cost improvement over locomotive drawn short trains. But as the train becomes longer, the improvement diminishes and becomes equal at about 4 or 5 cars. Thus, the six car Roger Williams did not last long in Boston-New York service and was transferred to commuter service in the Boston area. It is interesting to note just how many of these 1956 experimental trains ended up in commuter service. This Rail Diesel Car concept did not merit any repeat orders, and the Roger Williams became one more statistic of the 1956 passenger train experiments.

While the Budd Company and ACF Industries were designing their light weight trains, GM was busy too. GM was selling passenger locomotives to the railroad industry in the form of the "E" units as well as road switcher types equipped with steam generators. Electro-Motive Division was very interested in continuing such sales, and indeed it must be noted that they are still selling passenger locomotives in 1974 in the form of the SDP-40F's to Amtrak. However, their 1956 venture in building complete trains was as short lived as the other light weight low level experiments.

Electro-Motive set up three objectives in the construction of the Aerotrain. First, the entire train including the locomotive should weigh as close as possible to 600,000 pounds gross weight. Second, all costs would have to be reduced with coaches costing only 50% of a conventional car. Finally, the style and concept must awaken public interest.

A new locomotive was designed (the same type ordered by the Rock Island for its Talgo train) and each car was designed to seat 40 passengers. The train was made up of 10 cars with a capacity of 400 passengers and a maximum speed of 102 miles per hour. Coaches were 40 feet long and 9½ feet wide and rode on four wheels. Each car was independent and not articulated with any other car. The doors and steps of the vestibule were at the front of each coach and could serve either high or low level platforms. The rear of each car contained a lavatory on the right side. Across

The Aerotrain operated as the City of Las Vegas on the Union Pacific. (Union Pacific Railroad)

The interior of the Aerotrain coaches resembled buses more than it did a train. (Union Pacific Railroad)

the aisle, space was provided for a galley or snack bar for serving light meals or refreshments. In the two trains constructed, four cars were equipped with different types of service to try the reception of each. (The Union Pacific installed a full food service while the train was in Los Angeles-Las Vegas service.) As stated previously, each car contained 40 seats of the reclining type with foot rests. The seats were filled with rubber and were equipped with changeable nylon covers, washable headrests, and ashtrays in the arm rests. Seat spacing was 35 inches apart. Package racks extended the full length of each car above the seats. The interiors were attractive and

durable and required a minimum of painting and maintenance.

The Aerotrain could have been called the train with the throw away body. Each coach was built with an undercarriage that was expected to last many years with a minimum of maintenance. GM believed that when the car required an overhaul, the old body could simply be replaced by a new one for less money per passenger than was spent for repairing and refurbishing conventional type cars.

After construction, the trains went into service. One ran as a special section of the El Capitan for a demonstration run between Chicago and Los Angeles. Then one train ran between Chicago and Cleveland as the Great Lakes Aerotrain on the New York Central, while the other ran as the Pennsy Aerotrain between New York and Pittsburgh. One of the trains ran for a short while as the City of Las Vegas on the Union Pacific. Such operation was unsatisfactory on all three railroads and the two trains were placed in storage. In late 1958, the Rock Island purchased both sets and placed them in commuter service between Chicago, Blue Island and Joliet. The Aerotrains continued in such service, with their wide bus body coaches until the 1960's. Aside from their Rock Island commuter service, the Aerotrains go down in history as failures in intercity passenger service. The Problem: the same as the Talgo, simply too light for a decent ride and too noisy. However, one must give credit to General Motors for at least trying to come up with a suitable train.

New York Central's Train X was powered by a Baldwin passenger diesel especially designed for the Xplorer. (Pullman-Standard)

Pullman-Standard's Train X

The history of Train X actually goes back to 1951 when through a joint arrangement between Chesapeake and Ohio and Pullman-Standard completed construction of a prototype coach. During that time, Pullman constructed a research car that could be coupled to a standard diesel locomotive and also to the Train X coach. This car was tested on the C&O in Michigan and at one time hit a top speed of 105 miles per hour. In fact, the C&O even planned a low slung coal fired gas turbine locomotive for a complete train. However, the plans for a C&O train were laid to rest. For a short while, the whole idea seemed to lay dormant except at Pullman-Standard's headquarters where work went on to modify and improve the designs. The results came to fruition in 1956, which was a big year for passenger car innovations.

Pullman built two trains, one for the New York Central and the other for the New Haven. The two trains were essentially alike in mechanical details but had some differences in interior and exterior treatments. The trains weighed about one third the weight of a conventional train of similar capacity.

Train X was designed for either single or double end operation. Each train carried 392 passengers and consisted of four two-unit single axle cars and one single unit double axle center car. (A total of nine units altogether.) The center car was provided so that cars ahead would have their wheels forward with each trailing end suspended on the car behind. Cars to the rear of the central car trailed their axles to the rear and were suspended by the car ahead. The entire

The interior of the New York Central's Train X coach. (Pullman-Standard)

car could stand alone and be switched from either end.

Each of the two unit cars were permanently coupled and integrally articulated. It consisted of one 51 foot, 3 inch 40 passenger unit with a vestibule and side door and one 48 foot 48 passenger unit. Automatically operated dolly wheels, interlocked with the coupling mechanism were provided on the non-suspension end of the latter unit to allow switching and coupling. The 40 passenger 48 foot two axle central car had lockers at one end of the car for food storage, refrigeration and preparation. There was also an area for housing two food carts for serving light lunches on board the train.

Entrance doors were provided at the center of each two unit car. Although these doors were lower than found on conventional equipment, the trains could operate with existing loading and unloading station facilities.

The head-end of the New Haven's Train X. (Pullman-Standard)

The New Haven named their Train X the Daniel Webster. This photo clearly shows the center car (with four cars on each side) as the Webster rolls through New Haven. (Charles B. Gunn.)

The interiors were decorated in such a way that no adjacent cars were similar. Floors were covered with lightweight vinyl tile. Lightweight reversible reclining seats were provided with an elastic backed, easily maintained vinyl upholstery. Tinted heat absorbing glass in the windows eliminated glare and eliminated the need for window shades and draperies.

Pullman completed the New York Central's train in 1956. It went into service between Cincinnati and Cleveland as the Ohio X-plorer. Unsuccessful, the train was withdrawn from service in 1958. The New Haven's train was named the Daniel Webster and it too was completed in 1956. The New Haven converted the central Buffet Coach to a 31 seat Grill-Coach. The Webster went into Boston-New York City service in 1957 and lasted only until 1958. The low slung light weight trains were already being placed on the bench as they were losing the game.

The mid-1950's low slung train story lasted less than three years not counting the Rock Island's operations in suburban service. It amounted to something of a disaster, and not much was written concerning the failure of the trains to measure up to expectations. What is really interesting about this is that at exactly the same time the low slung trains were being built, the Santa Fe "Hi-level" coaches were proving themselves in experimental operation from 1954 on. The Santa Fe cars were successful, and this was borne out by repeat orders by that railroad. In fact, even in 1975 the hi-level design has not been designated as obsolete and has implications for other service. The hi-level cars were smooth and quiet, while the low slung speedsters were noisy and rough. Needless to say, the railroads were disappointed in the performance. As the curtain fell on the low slung streamliner story, still another long distance coach was in the wings of the railway stage ready to make its debut in 1958.

THE CHICAGO & NORTH WESTERN BI-LEVEL 400's

As the low slung streamliners were placed into operation on the various railroads, the C&NW management took a long hard look at the speedsters. Consideration was given to possibly purchasing two such trains for either the Twin Cities 400 or Chicago-Green Bay service. However actual service was not turning out so well and the North Western began to look elsewhere for new designs. Then one day the dawn began to glow that the successful double deck commuter coaches had implications for long distance travel. Moreover, if the long distance trains were eventually discontinued, the cars could easily be converted for suburban service. The C&NW and Pullman-Standard got together and discussed the situation, and the result was the "Bi-level 400's."

These bi-level coaches seat 96 passengers with double seats on the main level and in single seats on the upper deck. Leg room is substantial. The cars were painted in the C&NW's Iowa corn colors of green and yellow, while the interiors were decorated in tans, browns and other soft complementary colors. Initially, the bi-level 400's ran between Chicago and Ishpeming on the Peninsula 400, and the Flambeau 400 from Chicago to Green Bay and the Green Bay 400 from Green Bay to Chicago. The trains went into operation in October, 1958. The following Spring, the Flambeau was equipped with bi-level equipment from Chicago to Ashland and return. The Green Bay 400 was re-equipped with conventional 400 equipment. The Flambeau 400, by the way, was the last long distance passenger train on the C&NW. The bi-level coaches were pleasant to ride in, and the C&NW was the only railroad to apply the double deck concept to long distance travel. The railroad purchased bi-level coaches, a combination coach-parlor car, a lounge coach known as the Country Club Lounge and a complete parlor car. Later in 1970 the C&NW converted the coach parlor to a coach snack lounge. The latter served hot sandwiches and other light meals. The Country Club was also converted for such service. Both of these cars operated between Chicago and Green Bay on trains 153, 209, 214 and 216. They provided table seating and in general were much more pleasant than the usual food bar coach. The bi-level coaches operated on several C&NW trains right up until Amtrak. They were successful operations, and because they secured heating, air conditioning, lighting and other required power from a Cummings auxiliary diesel motor on the locomotive, they were lighter and easier to maintain. In fact, the underside of the bi-level 400 coaches are strangely bare.

After Amtrak, the cars were stored for a short time. However, with increased passenger business Amtrak is operating the cars on the Illinois Zephyr and other trains. As of early 1974 the equipment was leased and retained the C&NW's green and yellow. Locomotives were also leased for the bi-level services. By late 1974 and early 1975, Amtrak colors began to replace the 400 green and yellow.

The bi-level 400 coaches were the last new development of coach equipment of the 1950's. Although it could have been predicted with the slide in patronage figures, the C&NW cars turned out to be the last new concept for nearly a decade. The Turbos and Metroliners would not arrive on the scene until 1967. Auto-Train's luxury chair cars were still another four years into the future. Therefore, the bi-level 400 coaches are not only significant in terms of a new concept — and a successful one at that — but also because they were the last innovation of the 1950's. Furthermore, the cars operated during a time span that covered a particularly bleak period in United States railroad passenger travel. The fact that the cars were not put in storage a few months after construction is a feather in the caps of Pullman-Standard and the Chicago & North Western Railway. The concept is sound, and we just may see more of this type of equipment in the future.

THE LATEST DEVELOPMENTS

From 1958 everything seemed to go wrong for the railraod industry. The bottom dropped out of the passenger market and train after train was discontinued. Disputes with the United States Post Office developed, Rail Post Office cars were dropped from trains which in turn reduced revenues still further. A side effect was the increased costs for mailing for the American Public. The 1960's had all the appearances of having the only all weather transportation system go down the drain. A good deal of the blame can be laid at the automobile, which was gulping gasoline faster and faster. We were headed for a crisis, few people saw what was coming; and very few listened to the warnings that this could not go on.

A few far sighted congressmen saw the hand writing on the wall, and the stage was set for the development of a high speed ground transportation system. A number of systems were investigated, and initially the rail system was all but ignored. It turned out that mono rails, air suspended vehicles and other innovations were simply too expensive and presented too many technical problems. Obviously the Buck Rogers style of transportation was not going to work. Attention was then turned to vertical take off aircraft, but the skies were already overcrowded and experience with helicopter traffic in Viet Nam demonstrated the impractability of such a venture. A mid-air collision over Manhattan would be a real disaster, and the military experienced many helicopter collisions. The Viet Nam experience revealed that the type of traffic patterns that would be required for high passenger capacity vertical take off aircraft would be too complex and dangerous. Meanwhile, the studies and investigations were not doing much to solve the increasing problems. Finally, once again the railroad system was called upon to bail America out.

A new series of studies was cranked out by the Department of Transportation and the result was the Turbo and the Metroliner. The Dome-Turbo and the Metroliner rolled out of the erecting shops of Pullman and Budd respectively in 1967. The Turbo was a joint project by Pullman-Standard and United Aircraft and was described in detail in *The Domeliners*. After tests, public displays, press runs and a fantastic array of operating bugs, the Metroliners and Turbos went into operation between Washington and New York City, and New York and Boston respectively in 1969.

The Bi-Level long distance coach made its debut in 1958. These C&NW "400" fleet cars could be compared to conventional equipment as a 747 airliner can be compared to a 707. The bi-level cars carried nearly twice as many passengers as a conventional chair car. The photo was taken at Ashland, Wisconsin. Patrick C. Dorin)

The Metroliner coaches are operated in pairs with the cab control apparatus at the outer end of each pair. Special diaphragms were designed to link various pairs of cars. There are two types of coaches, a 76 seat and a 60 seat snack bar car. The trains were designed specifically for the New York-Washington run, but now also operate over the former New Haven Railroad to New Haven, Conn. At one time, it was planned to run Metroliner service as far west as Harrisburg. The Metroliners are also built with a parlor car configuration.

Metroliners are capable of operating as fast as 160 miles per hour. Present plans include the complete rebuilding of the former Pennsylvania Railroad main line to handle 160 mile an hour operation. The Metroliner equipment is among the most advanced electrically operated train in the world.

1973 brought still another development to the Metroliner design. Amtrak placed an order with the Budd Company for an additional number of non-electrified Metroliner coaches for operation between Washington and New York to Boston behind electric locomotives and standard diesel power beyond New Haven. Initial plans called for the cars to be capable of 120 mile an hour cruising speeds on the Northeast Corridor Route. This equipment was to be delivered in 1974 through 1976.

1973 was also responsible for two more developments in American coach travel. During that year Amtrak laid plans for a standardized car that could be converted from coach designs to either a lounge or parlor car. Final plans were not yet announced by the Summer of 1974, but it is probable that they will be under construction by the time this book is in print by late 1975.

The Turboliners also hit the rails in 1973. Amtrak secured through a lease arrangement two five car train sets from ANF-Frangeco of Crespin, France. Each train is powered by two 1,140 horsepower aircraft type gas turbine engines, one at each end of the train and capable of operating in unison. The five car train consists of a power coach at each end, a grill bar car and two coaches for a total capacity of 296 passengers. The trains have a rated top speed of 125 miles per hour and a range of about 1,000 miles between refueling.

This sums up the development of coaches from 1967 through 1974 for Amtrak (which is covered in Chapter 9), but it was not the only activity going on in coach car development.

Auto-Train, which is covered in greater detail in chapter 10, has been working continuously from 1971 through 1974 in coach car comfort. They purchased ex-Santa Fe dome lounge cars for a new style coach for their Florida service. The cars are painted in bright and cheerful colors and the leg rest seats are among the finest to be found on any train. They are rebuilding different styles of dome cars for chair car service for new routes, and as of June, 1974 have the last word in coach car style and comfort.

WHAT ABOUT THE FUTURE?

It is always difficult to project what will happen in the future, and that is not the purpose of this section. However, the energy crisis is not going to go away. We are not going to be able to depend on foreign sources for crude oil, and we have to depend on our good ol' American "know how" and coal for our resources for the next few decades. Consequently, gasoline prices are probably going to continue to climb and as they climb, rail travel will become more and more important. The coach or chair car has always been the work horse or back bone of the U.S. travel market. There are going to be changes in America, and it is obvious the train is here to stay. With that kind of a background, one can feel sure that there will be new rail coach car developments as time goes on — and the American Public will continue to travel by train for work, pleasure, vacations or for whatever reason people may have for traveling on the only *All-Weather* transportation system.

CHAPTER 2
Doodlebugs, Motor Cars and RDC's

While the standard coach was developing toward its final external form in the early 1900's, the internal combustion engine was making its presence known. The first applications of this engine in the railroad field were installed in what would now be called very primitive looking buses on railroad wheels. There were two basic types of these motorized rail buses, enclosed cars and open side tourist cars. The latter was equipped with canvas covers that could be unrolled from the roof to protect passengers from the elements. In many ways these cars were similar to the interurban cars of the early era or four wheel variety. The only difference being the power used, and one might say it was a futile attempt on the part of some steam roads to compete with the electric interurban lines. The rail bus reached its apex in development in 1951 with the 50 passenger rail buses by Mack-General Electric. These streamlined city buses, mounted on street car PCC trucks, were operated by the New Haven on various short runs such as the Mansfield-Fall River, Mass. line, a distance of 17 miles. The history of the rail bus covered a time span of almost half a century.

However the development of the rail bus is not remembered for the final splash as a streamlined bus on rails, but rather for the development of the doodlebug. After the initial developments, the gas cars grew into full size cars both in terms of height and length. It was during the roaring 20's that the gas-electrics flowered into their apex of standard development. Streamlined designs did not show up until the 1930's and the Rail Diesel Car did not make its debut until after World War II.

As we stated previously, the summit of gas-electric development came in the 1920's and early 1930's. There were a number of basic reasons for this. With the evolution of the self propelled car, the motor or prime mover became more sophisticated and as it did so, the size

of the car could grow. Eventually the cars were of standard height and length and looked very much like the standard passenger cars of the day. In fact, they were even painted Pullman, Coach or Olive green as the regular passenger equipment. However there was another more compelling reason for the rapid development of the gas-electric.

In the early 1920's the automobile was beginning to make itself known. Local traffic began to erode and the railroads needed a more economical train to provide service. The gas-electric filled that need, and in time thousands were zipping across the USA on all type of runs. Most of these were local in nature, but they were assigned to branch lines, main lines, secondary lines and commuter service. They were built in a variety of styles with only one thing in common, and that was the gasoline engine in a small compartment located behind the engineer. From there on back the doodlebugs were built as full baggage cars, baggage and mail, combination baggage-coach, combination baggage, mail and coach, combination mail-coach and coach. Horsepower ranged from 150 to 660. They could be operated separately or carry as many as two or three passenger cars. Sometimes they even toted freight equipment in mixed train service. It depended upon the railroad company, but the uses and operations of such equipment was simply unlimited.

Most of the cars operated on branch lines and connected with main line trains. However it was not uncommon for these cars to run relatively long distances on the main line providing local train service. The Omaha Road operated one such motor train between Minneapolis and Ashland, Wisconsin, a distance of 200 miles, and included a lounge section in the second coach. The train even had a name, the Namakagon, which was most unusual for a gas-electric. The gas-electric coach was an unsung hero to say the least.

Canadian Pacific motor car No. 41 is a typical example of the self propelled cars early in this century. Note the canvas curtains tied around each pole for each seat, plus an additional curtain to go around the back of the car. The motor man did have the benefit of a windshield. Although many of the early cars ran on four wheels, CP No. 41 ran on six wheels. (Collection of George A. Moore — Canadian Pacific Photo)

CP No. 50 represents an improvement in both exterior and interior design. Fully enclosed and riding on two four wheel trucks, the car was far more comfortable and faster than its predecessors. (Canadian Pacific Photo — Collection of George A. Moore)

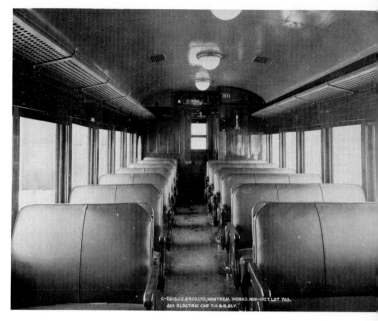

From 1915 to the mid-1920's, the gas-electric grew from the size of CPR No. 50 to full size such as illustrated here with Toronto, Hamilton and Buffalo Railway car No. 301. This car was typical of what many gas-electric cars looked like. No. 301 was constructed by Canadian Car and Foundry at Montreal in November, 1927. (Canadian Pacific Photo — Collection of George A. Moore)

The interior of TH&B No. 301 represented many advancements over the style of CPR No. 50. In this case, there are overhead baggage racks, larger windows, washroom and drinking fountain facilities and deep cushion seats. This particular car was also equipped with a 3-2 seating arrangement, whereas many gas-electrics were simply the usual 2-2 seating. Interior colors were usually tans, browns or grays. (Canadian Pacific Photo-Collection of George A. Moore)

The interior of CP No. 50 was comfortable for the short distance running for which it was built. The seats were constructed of rattan, and this type of seating was typical of many coaches built from the 1890's thru the 1920's. In fact, Illinois Central electric coaches were still equipped with such seating in 1974. The interior was divided into two sections, one with standard seating, and the other with bench seating facing the windows. The car was not unlike many interurban cars of the period. (Canadian Pacific Photo — Collection of George A. Moore)

Union Pacific M-29 is a more obvious rebuild. Originally a McKeen car with a pointed nose, the entire car has been extensively changed with a semi-streamlined appearance. The Union Pacific operated a number of such cars all over the system. M-29 was photographed at Oconto, Nebraska, which is 52 miles from Kearney, in March, 1955. At the time, she was assigned to trains 518 and 519 between Kearney and Stapleton, a distance of 102 miles. She connected with the Gold Coast, numbers 23 and 24 in both directions for through service to and from Omaha and Chicago. (Harold K. Vollrath)

Minneapolis & St. Louis GE-2 represents another variation in the styles of gas-electrics constructed. Whereas TH&B No. 301 contained coach and baggage sections, GE-2 also includes a Rail Post Office section. Furthermore, how many motor cars were named? This one was the "New Ulm" and was photographed at the Cedar Lake Shops, Minneapolis on May 26, 1948. (Jim Scribbins)

Many gas-electrics were built with enough power to pull trailers. Such as the case here with an Erie Railroad No. 3014 pulling one trailer on the high bridge near Moodna, New York. This particular car appears to be a rebuild with a semi-streamlined pilot, safety stripes, and an off center headlight. Imagine how that appeared coming down the track. The additional grill work and radiator equipment on the roof indicates that extensive work with the prime mover has been undertaken. (Bob Lorenz)

One of the few gas-electric runs to merit a name was the Omaha Road's "Namakagon." The Power-Mail-Baggage car was powerful enough to pull two trailers, which included a combine and a coach lounge car. This gas-electric run was most unusual with a name and lounge facilities. It ran through the beautiful "Indian Head" country (so named because the geographic shape of Northwest Wisconsin is a silhouette of an Indian Chief) and provided the only through service between Ashland, Wisconsin and the Twin Cities. This photo was taken at the Ashland depot in 1940. (A. Robert Johnson)

The two car flash steam Besler train of the New Haven Railroad. The flash steam power plant was also tried in several other self propelled cars. (Penn Central)

THE NEW HAVEN'S BESLER TRAIN

About a year after the Comet went into service, the New Haven placed a streamlined two car steam train in operation between Bridgeport and Hartford, Conn. This particular train was the result of an experiment conducted because the New Haven was searching for suitable coach facilities for certain types of runs. The patronage on these runs was in excess of the capacity for the gas-electric cars, and if a trailer was added a gas-electric would not have been able to maintain the required time schedule. The Bridgeport-Hartford run was operated with a steam locomotive, baggage car and two coaches. The New Haven needed a self contained unit with a small baggage space and a seating capacity of about 150 passengers. This would have been readily available with a diesel electric power plant. However, the Depression was taking its toll financially on the New Haven and that was too expensive for the use they could get out of the car. It was a different situation with the Comet, which was making five round trips daily. In this particular case, passenger capacity requirements were similar, but the operating conditions were totally different.

This problem was a particularly vexing one for the New Haven, and then in 1934 the Besler high pressure steam power plant was brought to the attention of the New Haven management. This power plant introduced another new concept in coach travel by rail. In this case, the Besler engine could provide the required amount of power with less weight and expense than was required at that time for the diesel electric power plant. In addition, the self contained Besler would be able to show substantial economy in operating expense over the steam engine and

terminal expenses would also be reduced. With these economies, the New Haven decided to go ahead and build an experimental two car train.

To accomplish the construction project, the New Haven took two old steel coaches (about twenty years old) and totally remodeled the cars into a modern appearing streamlined train. The interior was totally changed. In the new design both washrooms were located at the same end of the car. Mirrors were placed on the bulkheads and the flooring was completely redone with a composition rubber in a mottled gray design. The old seats were replaced with walk over seats especially designed for the cars. The seats were constructed with chromium plated tubular frames and the cushions were upholstered in a blue figured plush. Modern aluminum baggage racks replaced the old bronze racks.

The power car was compartmentalized as follows: an 8 foot section for the Besler boiler plant and auxiliary equipment, a 12 foot section for baggage and the rest of the car to coach seating. The trailer was a complete coach. Interior paint schemes were originally dark grey and light cream with red trim. The exterior was a royal blue up to the letter board with the latter being finished in aluminum. The two areas were separated by a stripe of pimpernel scarlet the full width of the belt rail. The roof was a darker shade of blue.

The Besler train was operated between Waterbury, Bridgeport and Hartford in the following manner: The train departed Waterbury for Bridgeport at 6:00 AM and continued on to Hartford arriving there at 9:05 AM. On the return trip it departed Hartford at 9:20 AM (Note the quick turn around capability of this train.) arriving at Waterbury at 1:30 PM. The total round trip mileage was 189.6 miles. After a twenty minute layover in Waterbury, the train departed for Bridgeport at 1:50 PM; making the 32 mile run in 50 minutes. The train returned to Waterbury during the afternoon; and then made still another round trip to Bridgeport in the evening. The total mileage for the daily schedule was 317.3 miles, and the train operated from 6:00 AM until 10:20 PM at night. Further the service was rather severe in that there were a large number of stops and stiff grades. The New Haven did not expect the unit to equal the performance of the Comet, but the Besler train did perform very satisfactory considering the horsepower weight ratio. It is interesting to note that the Besler train ran approximately 0.6 miles per gallon of fuel oil, while the Comet ran 1.6 miles per gallon of fuel oil including the use of oil for train heating. There is one point to consider however in making this comparison. The Comet was a non-stop train operation, while the Besler made a substantial number of stops and track conditions were totally different. Not only was the Boston-Providence trackage in better shape, but the Besler had to contend with grade and curve conditions much more severe than those under which the Comet operated. It would have been interesting to see how the Comet would have faired on the Besler's run. We can only speculate on this comparison of steam versus the diesel.

It might be of interest to ecologists and fuel experts that the Besler steam power plants were operated in Germany in the mid-1930's. As for fuel, can you believe this? They ran on coal or coke. Who knows? The Besler steam power plant may have an interesting application in today's railroading yet.

The Besler train was not entirely successful over the long run. It was withdrawn from service in 1943, and the New Haven did not involve itself with further applications of this type of power. Other railroads have used flash steam power plants, but economics, the diesel and perhaps a lack of continued research due to the War contributed to the demise of the concept. Despite the failure of this power plant, one must admit that the application of the Besler concept to coach travel was certainly an unusual page in the history of American Railroading. Will the energy crisis force us to look at the Besler concept again? Only time will tell.

THE CHICAGO & EASTERN ILLINOIS' EGYPTIAN ZIPPER

Now how's that for a name of a passenger train? Yet it was an appropriate name for a pair of passenger trains. The service was operated in what is sometimes called "Little Egypt" in Southern Illinois. A number of towns in that area are named after Egyptian towns and cities, such as Cairo.

The C&EI was faced with an operating problem on a run between Danville and Cypress, Illinois, a distance of 242 miles. The solution to the problem produced two streamlined air conditioned rail motor cars designed and built by American Car and Foundry. However instead of being either diesel electrically or gas-electrically operated, the two rail cars were driven by a gasoline motor with a mechanical transmission. The cars could carry 61 passengers and 5,000 pounds of mail in a 16 foot mail compartment. The cars were of streamlined design with a well rounded front with three large windows fitted with shatterproof glass. The exterior of the two cars was very attractive with its color scheme of silver, scarlet red, indigo blue and gold bronze with stripes of black. In addition to the individual seats (in pairs as in nearly all coaches), the chair car section contained a water cooler having separate compartments for ice and water. Most coaches were not equipped for ice water service. One must admit that these were unusual cars for such service, and they certainly added a rare chapter in the history of motor cars.

The original RDC-1 was built with both regular windows and variations of two other types of windows. This car literally toured the entire United States, and no self contained car before or since the RDC has had as much appeal not only to the railroad accounting departments, but to the coach passengers as well. The car in many ways was like a human being in that it could operate in a variety of environments. No single animal on earth has the range of habitat that the RDC has established for itself. RDC-1 was photographed on the Western Pacific at Oroville Junction, California in January, 1950. (Harold K. Vollrath)

Although the original consist of these Southern trains was but two cars, it was not unusual for them to pull two coaches. The Vulcan is shown here at Birmingham, Alabama in June, 1941 with the regular coach built for the train plus a dark green standard coach carrying the markers. (Harold K. Vollrath)

THE SOUTHERN RAILWAY'S
TWO CAR DIESEL ELECTRIC TRAINS

Faced with an operating and an economics problem, the Southern purchased six two car trains for service on a number of local runs in the states of Alabama, Mississippi and Tennessee and Georgia. Of the various types of self contained trains built, this fleet ranked among the closest to conventional steam train size and operation. The power cars included a 750 horsepower Fairbanks-Morse opposed piston diesel engine with Westinghouse electrical equipment, a Rail Post Office section and a baggage compartment. A 600 pound Vapor-Clarkson steam generator and a 600 gallon water tank were located at the rear end of the baggage room. The steam generator was used for heating the train and also to supply steam for the air conditioning during warm summer weather. Sounds like a conventional train, doesn't it?

There were two RDC-3's built with somewhat different than the standard exterior of six picture windows on each side. One was operated by the Duluth, Winnipeg & Pacific Railway with but four windows, while the Great Northern's operated with five on each side. The GN car was purchased for a rather tough assignment. No. 2350's day started early at 1:00 AM with a run from Billings to Great Falls arriving there at 6:15 AM for the 235 mile run. Train No. 43 ran on a daily except Monday basis. She laid over but 1 hour and 15 minutes before she continued on as train No. 235 to Butte, a distance of 171 miles. Her arrival time was 12:10 PM. Forty minutes later she departed for Great Falls as train No. 236 arriving there at 5:30 PM. 235 and 236 operated daily except Sunday. The car was serviced and departed Great Falls at 7:00 PM as train No. 42 arriving at Billings at 12:15 AM. 45 minutes later the cycle started all over again. Few RDC's in the country had such a tough assignment. 2350 is shown here at Butte in May, 1957. (Harold K. Vollrath)

52

The coaches built for the trains were 72 foot cars with two compartments, one with 32 seats and the other with 44 seats. Two washrooms were installed in each compartment. The seats were the walkover reversible type upholstered with plush, and had wooden arm rests. The interior of the coaches were painted in various shades of green.

The six two car sets replaced 6 steam locomotives and 16 passenger cars (six mail and baggage cars and 10 coaches). All of the trains went into local service as follows: One train between Oakdale, Tenn., Chattanooga and Tuscumbia, Alabama; three trains between Chattanooga, Birmingham, Ala., Meridian, Miss., and Mobile, Alabama; and two trains between Atlanta, Georgia and Brunswick and Jesup. In addition the trains were named, which was highly unusual for local train services. The Goldenrod ran between Birmingham and Mobile. The Joe Wheeler between Oakdale and Tuscumbia, with the Cracker and Vulcan holding down the Atlanta-Brunswick and Meridian-Chattanooga runs respectively.

The Southern Railway diesel electric trains, could in some ways, be considered the bridge between the gap of self contained cars and conventional trains. After 1939 there were not too many more self contained cars constructed. The Missouri Pacific's Eagle connection in Nebraska was built in 1942, which was a success; and the Rio Grande's Prospector which was a failure. Built in late 1941, the self contained Prospector was replaced by a conventional train by the summer of 1942. The next real advancement in self propelled cars would be the Rail Diesel Car, which will be covered next in this chapter.

RAIL DIESEL CARS

The RDC immediately became a hit in the rail transportation World — and I do mean a *World Hit*. They have been sold in both the eastern and western hemispheres, and on both standard and broad gauge trucks. The initials RDC stand for the generic name for the self-propelled stainless steel cars designed and constructed by the Budd Company. There were four models designated by RDC-1, 2, 3 and 4 and could be operated in either direction as single units, or in any required multiple all controlled from a single location. The coach seating capacities of the three types varies as follows: RDC-1, 90 passengers; RDC-2, 71 passengers and a 17 foot baggage-express compartment; RDC-3, 49 passengers and compartments for baggage-express and mail. The RDC-4 carried baggage-express and mail only. There was also a fifth type of RDC. Basically this unit was a partially powered trailer with an RDC-1 body without cab controls. The designation was RDC-9, although the Canadian National calls them RDC-5's. Only the Boston & Maine and the Canadian National operate this style of car.

Although the Budd Company sold most of the RDC's as off the shelf with walk over or flip over seats, they did make certain modifications. For example, the Baltimore & Ohio purchased two RDC-2's with cafe sections in 1956. This equipment along with two RDC-1's (two sets of three car trains) made up the consist for trains 21 and 22, the Speedliners, between Philadelphia and Pittsburgh. This application of RDC's by the B&O was one of just a few instances where RDC's were modified for a higher comfort index.

One of the more unusual all-coach streamliners was the Baltimore & Ohio's Daylight Speedliner. Equipped with RDC's was not so unusual, but the fact that the train carried an RDC-2, which was a modified cafe coach put the train in a class all by itself. Train No. 22 is shown here at Connellsville, Pennsylvania in November, 1956. (H. H. Harwood, Jr.)

Two of the more unusual RDC-2's were Western Pacific's 375 and 376. These cars carried both reclining and standard straight back seating. In this case the WP removed 22 of the commuter style seats from the forward section and replaced them with 18 reclining seats. Most RDC's contained but one washroom, but the WP added a women's washroom on the left side of the forward coach section, known as "coach section A." The single seat at the rear of coach section "B" was transformed into a conductor's office space. In addition the car received number boards above the vestibules and the name "Zephyrette" was splashed on the sides next to the baggage doors. It was a sharp RDC to say the least. (Bob Larson)

Also in 1956, Budd sold modified RDC-3's to the Duluth, Winnipeg and Pacific Railway and to the Great Northern. The standard 49 seats were reduced by 16 for the DW&P, and by 8 for the GN. The purpose of the modifications were larger baggage-express sections. In 1957 Budd sold two RDC-4's to the Minneapolis & St. Louis Railway with coach seats in the former mail section. These were the only RDC-4's to carry passengers, and were indeed unusual cars.

The RDC's were and are quietly efficient. They have in a very non-sensational way logged some spectacular achievements. For example, the Western Pacific's RDC-2's operating on trains 1 and 2 between Salt Lake City and Oakland saved the WP over $650,000 the first year in operation. The Budd Company reported in the early 1950's that it was not uncommon for an RDC to repay its purchase price in a single year, but the normal rate of return on investment was about 25%.

The purpose of the RDC was three fold: To save money; attract traffic and to preserve, improve and increase service. The RDC did indeed just those three things. The New Haven restored passenger service between Worcester, Mass. and New London, Conn. with one RDC Monday through Friday and two on week-ends. The result: 80,000 passengers during that year.

The Canadian Pacific often found itself short of seating space as RDC's were placed in service on previously faltering runs. The CPR reported to the Budd Company on one occasion that even airline patrons were riding the silver speedsters.

RDC's chalked up an availability record of over 95%, and their operation is still superb for such lines as the Boston & Maine, Penn Central, the Canadian lines and Amtrak. They can operate in all types of climate from 50 below in Canada to 130 degrees of desert heat in Saudi Arabia.

The RDC's were operated in both long distance service, and short distance local runs and commuter operations. The sky was the limit. The last RDC's were built for the Reading in 1962. At that time 12 cars were built for a variety of services for that railroad. As of 1974, Amtrak is rebuilding RDC's for various runs, such as the Black Hawk between Chicago and Dubuque, Iowa via the Illinois Central Gulf Railroad. In this case the former Western Pacific RDC-2's have been making the run which also offers snack and beverage service. There is one thing that no one can deny, and that is the RDC has certainly made its mark on the World in a very positive way in its first 25 years of history from 1949 to 1974.

CHAPTER 3
Coach and Chair Car Operations

The usual pattern for coach car operations in train service was to follow the head-end cars and separated from parlor or Pullman sleeping cars by a dining car or a lounge car. A typical line up of an overnight train was as follows:

Box Express Car
Baggage Car(s)
Mail and Baggage Car
Coach (For local passengers or "shorts")
Coach(es) For Through passengers
Dining Car
Lounge Car
Sleeping Car(s)

Coach passengers boarded the train and found a vacant seat. The conductor later came to punch the ticket, and would take it if the passenger were riding only within the conductor's assignment. However, if he was going beyond the train crew change point, the conductor would return the ticket to the passenger. When the next conductor came aboard, the entire procedure would be repeated. On night trips, this could be very burdensome to passengers desiring sleep.

Daylight trains were often made up in the same type of consist, with the exception of parlor cars instead of sleeping cars. Again coach passengers were required to have their tickets punched by each conductor along the route.

The position of the coaches within the consist of the train did not always hold to the typical operations mentioned above. For example, if a train carried set out coaches, these were often carried on the end of the train for switching efficiency. Often the Soo Line's Chicago-Duluth train carried special coaches for scouts on the rear of the train for set out in Southern Wisconsin. The Chicago & North Western's Duluth-Superior Limited carried a Madison set out coach on the rear end of that train. In still other instances, the sleeping cars were carried behind the head-end cars and ahead of a diner and/or lounge car. The Challenger, prior to April, 1956, followed such a procedure.

Sometimes the sleeping cars and coaches seemed to be simply mixed up. For ease of switching operations at Green Bay, the C&NW dispatched the northbound combined Ashland Limited and the Iron and Copper Country Express from Chicago as follows:

Head-end cars (For Ishpeming)
Head-end cars (For Ashland)
Pullman Car (For Ashland)
Coach(es) (For Ashland)
Cafe Lounge (For Ashland or Green Bay)
Coach(es) (For Ishpeming)
Pullman Car (For Ishpeming)

The Cafe Lounge car ran less and less by the late 1950's.

It was not uncommon in later years to observe passenger trains running with one engine, one coach and a head-end car running last. In fact, the C&O "Pere Marquettes" often ran with this consist prior to December 31, 1969 when the company lost the mail contract between Detroit and Grand Rapids.

While sleeping and parlor car passengers had access to a porter for various types of service and/or problem solving, coach passengers generally had to rely on the conductor or trainman. Very few trains carried coach or chair car porters. However, the Southern Pacific Daylights, the Great Northern's Western Star, the Union Pacific's "Cities" and many other trains carried coach porters. Often one porter was assigned to two coaches, and he assisted passengers with their luggage, had baby formulas warmed in the dining car and numerous other services for the convenience of the passengers. On trains with coach porter service, passengers were not required to have tickets punched at each division point.

On mail and express trains and mixed trains, the coaches were carried in different sections of the train. Mixed trains carried their coach and baggage car(s) or combination coach-baggage car either on the head-end behind the locomotive or on the rear of the train. Mail trains on the other hand could have their rider coach anywhere from the second car in the train to the rear end. Often if the coach(es), usually not more than two, were carried in the middle of the train, the railroad operated a baggage car with a rear-end brake-

Coaches and sleeping cars were generally separated from each other by dining and lounge cars. Such is the case with the Atlantic Coast Line's Miamian, a coach-Pullman New York-Florida streamliner. Seven and eight cars deep are a lounge car and a dining car with six sleepers bringing up the rear of the 14 car train. Note the excellent track for which the ACL was famous. (Seaboard Coast Line)

man's compartment on the rear of the train. This practice was followed on the Milwaukee Road and the Great Northern. Other railroads, such as the Pennsylvania ran a caboose on the tail end. The New York Central ran a special rider coach for the crew that looked like a coach at both ends but with no windows for the middle section of the car. These types of operations were standard operating procedures for long mail trains. On short trains, a coach was nearly always carried on the end with the possible exception of a set out baggage car behind the coach.

Basically, one could say that coaches were operated in just about any position in the train that could be thought of. Often it appeared that the coaches were mixed in with parlor cars and/or sleeping cars randomly. However, there was always a reason for the consist. Usually it had to do with the change in consist as the train traveled over its route. Train combinations at junction points, set out and pick up sleepers, coaches, dining cars and head-end equipment could completely change the consist or make up of the train as it moved from its initial terminal to the final terminal on its run. It can be said that any make up was and is prototypical.

Each journey begins with the conductor giving the engineer the high ball. In this case, we see Amtrak No. 8, the Empire Builder, ready to depart LaCrosse, Wisconsin on the final leg of its transcontinental journey over the Burlington Northern and Milwaukee Road from Seattle to Chicago. (Patrick C. Dorin)

Day trains too separated parlor cars from coaches with a dining car. The Kansas City Zephyr coaches are separated from the dome parlor by a single diner on the five car train. Such separation was not always the case and it depended upon the individual train operation. (Burlington Northern)

The Sun is beginning to burn away a morning fog at St. Paul, Minnesota as a second section of the North Western Limited negotiates curves and switches at the St. Paul Union Depot in 1945. It was not uncommon for railroads to operate an All-Pullman and an All-Coach section, when traffic levels dictated expanded operations. Such is the case here with 2nd 405, which is being pulled backwards from St. Paul to the Great Northern Station in Minneapolis. This photo was taken by the late H. W. Pontin, who founded Rail Photo Service. He was an outstanding man and a fine railroader for the Boston & Albany and a tremendous photographer. (Rail Photo Service)

Although most mixed trains carried a combine on the rear of the train, long trains such as Union Pacific 117 and 118 between Denver and Kansas City carried the passenger equipment on the head-end. Such a technique would be beneficial for expanding passenger service in the USA today, especially through the use of certain mail piggyback trains such as the Overland Mail and the Pacific Zip and other nameless mail trains on the Penn Central. (Harold K. Vollrath)

The usual arrangement for coaches and Pullman in a train would be revised if switching requirements dictated a different make up. Such is the case with the C&NW's Duluth-Superior Limited which carried a set out baggage car with mail for Janesville, Wisconsin and a set out coach for Madison. Both cars were carried on the rear of the train for easy set out by train crews. (Chicago & North Western Railway)

Often there was not enough business to merit a thru train between certain points, for example, Chicago-Portland on the CB&Q, GN and SP&S route. In that case, the railroads involved would run a connecting train which could be either a local or a thru limited train. The Spokane, Portland & Seattle ran such a train for the Empire Builder, which is shown here departing Portland on August 14, 1949 with four through cars plus a dining car and a lounge car that will stay on SP&S rails. The photo was taken before the North Coast Limited and Empire Builder connections were combined, and after the SP&S sole E-7, No. 750, was repainted from the Empire Builder or Great Northern color scheme. Note that the Pendulum coach was operated in Empire Builder service on the GN. (W.C. Whittaker.

The significant point about rail coach travel, be it commuter or long distance, is that it is the only all weather service. When the snow begins to fly, airports are closed and the highways become totally unsafe for travel. Only the train can bring travellers safely through any kind of weather. Here an Erie Lackawanna push pull train barrels through a snow storm in New Jersey. (Pullman-Standard)

Co-ordinated transportation is the key word here as the Rock Island's Quad Cities Rocket arrives at Joliet, Illinois. Passengers will make a cross the platform transfer to a suburban train which will depart after the Rocket, and make all stops to Chicago. The Rocket will run non-stop from Joliet to down town Chicago. The double deck suburban train stands ready in the left side of the photo. (Patrick C. Dorin)

It is the job of the Conductor and trainmen to answer questions, assist passengers with luggage and to supervise and assist passengers on and off trains. This gentleman has just detrained from the Rocket and will board the suburban train, shown in the previous photo, for an intermediate stop. Coach porters provide the same type of services and are available for all passengers at all times, whereas the conductor often has other paper work and duties to perform. (Patrick C. Dorin)

Prior to Amtrak, many passenger trains dwindled to very dismal consists of one or two cars. Most of these trains were taken off on April 30, 1971. One such train was C&NW No. 1, the former Kate Shelly 400, which is shown here departing Chicago on August 4, 1969. (John H. Kuehl)

Every once in awhile, coaches were used as cabooses. Such is the case with this New Haven Railroad Work Extra. (J. W. Swanberg)

Regardless of size, passenger trains sometimes had to be switched. It is the morning of June 21, 1955 and Duluth, Missabe & Iron Range Railway No. 5 is about to be shoved to the depot from the Endion round house. The train was en route to Ely, Minnesota. (Waynce C. Olsen)

As with most all interline train operations, each railroad owned a portion of the equipment to equalize wheelage charges. The fourth and fifth cars of the Southerner in this photo were owned by the Pennsylvania Railroad, over which line the All-Coach streamliner traveled between Washington and New York City. The PRR cars were constructed with a stainless steel exterior as the other equipment, but they were built with the standard Pennsylvania Railroad design which made them somewhat different from the rest of the train. It was but one more aspect of coach and chair car operations. (Southern Railway)

The Southerner was among several seven car All-Coach streamliners designed and built in the late 1930's and early 1940's. In 1941, the Southerner was the fastest reserved coach train and is shown here near Birmingham on its run between New York and New Orleans. (Southern Railway)

In order to guide passengers in the right direction for the right train, the railroads generally used signs displaying the train name and destinations at the depots. The All-Coach El Capitan awaits departure from the Los Angeles Union Station with such a sign adjacent to the motive power. It is interesting to note that the Santa Fe shunned articulated equipment, while its chief competitors — the Union Pacific and the Burlington — went in "big" for such trains. The five car El Capitan was the beginning of a career for a train that would eventually be the luxurious hi-level train, which is covered in Chapter 5. (Santa Fe Railway)

The Tennessean was originally designed to be an All-Coach train with the addition of heavy weight sleeping cars behind a squared off observation car. Virtually a twin of the Southerner, the seven car train picked up three sleepers south of Washington, D.C. Here the Tennessean breaks the morning quiet as it passes the Lick Creek Christian church in eastern Tennessee on a Sunday morning. (Southern Railway)

For a good many years prior to streamlining and the resumption of the Oriental Limited, the Empire Builder ran as a Pullman section and an *All-Coach* section. This May 23, 1945 photo by A. Robert Johnson shows the all coach Empire Builder departing St. Paul en route to Seattle with 12 cars including three head-end cars, one dining car and eight coaches.

One of the lessor known all coach streamliners was the Missouri Pacific's Valley Eagle, which was inaugurated between Houston and Brownsville, Texas on October 31, 1948. During the prime of the train's career, she offered deluxe chair car service as well as a grill coach for meals and refreshments. (Missouri Pacific Lines)

One of the best ways to offer a variety and greater frequency of service with fewer trains was a pool service. Not many railroads were involved in such modern thinking, but the Great Northern, Northern Pacific and Union Pacific were involved in such an operation between Seattle and Portland. The Great Northern's contribution was all coach streamliners 459 and 460. This photo shows 459 en route from Portland to Seattle with two "F" units, one baggage car and five coaches. Although the GN streamliners did not offer dining car service (Northern Pacific and Union Pacific did), they did offer sandwiches and refreshments by train sales service. (J. W. Swanberg)

One of the most versatile locomotives ever to be assigned to passenger service is the Electro Motive Division GP-9. Prior to dieselization, the Soo Line maintained two 4-6-2 Pacific type steamers at Sault Ste. Marie, Michigan for trains 7 and 8. One was kept as a standby in the event of failure upon the one arriving with No. 8 in the morning from Minneapolis. Furthermore neither engine did any other kind of work for the railroad. The GP-9 on the other hand could be assigned switching duties, transfer runs to Soo, Ontario to the Canadian Pacific and Algoma Central or a local freight eastbound to Gladstone. Provided, of course, the Soo had another steam generator equipped geep at the Soo terminal. There would be little dead time with the 550 upon her arrival at Soo, Michigan with train No. 8. Also for some reason, both Soo Line and Norfolk & Western Railway geeps looked mighty good on the head end of passenger trains. I don't know what it was — maybe it was the Tuscan Red color scheme. (A. Robert Johnson)

Perhaps the shortest all-coach streamliner with a name was the Sacramento Daylight. This Southern Pacific pocket streamliner connected with the San Joaquin Daylight at Lathrop, California and offered coach service between Los Angeles and the state capitol. (Collection of Patrick C. Dorin)

One of the more unusual coach operations is the power coach on Burlington Northern Chicago-Aurora commuter service. This equipment operates on the head end of trains going west, and on the rear end en route to Chicago. BN "E-8A" No. 9935 is powering train No. 219 out of the Chicago Union Station en route to Aurora. The time is September, 1971 and this Chicago day is very hot and muggy. (Patrick C. Dorin)

This photo shows Northern Pacific pool train No. 408 arriving at Portland with three "F" units and 12 cars at 3:15 PM in the afternoon, ON TIME. The train departed Seattle at 11:15 AM, and provided a convenient service for passengers off the Great Northern's Morning International from Vancouver. It also provided extra time for people en route to Portland from Washington points off the Empire Builder. Tickets were honored on all UP-GN-NP passenger trains between Seattle and Portland. (The Great Northern, Northern Pacific and Soo Line also had a similar arrangement between the Twin Cities and Duluth-Superior.) Although NP No. 408 carried through sleepers from Seattle to California points (Even NP cars painted in the Southern Pacific's Cascade color scheme of two tone grey.), she did not carry through coaches. Passengers had to change trains at Portland until Amtrak's Starlight went into service between Seattle and California. (J. W. Swanberg)

There were very few streamlined coach observation cars built, and only three dome versions. Such equipment nearly always operated on the rear end of trains, but such was not always the case. This photo is of a thin slice of time when the dome coach observation cars operated on the Chicago-Grand Rapids, Michigan Pere Marquettes. Displaced from the "Chessie" the cars were relettered "Chesapeake and Ohio" and eventually sold to the Rio Grande. See Chapter 19 of *The Domeliners.* (Rail Photo Service)

Nobody could know in the 1930's (during the Great Depression) that the Portland Rose would end up running as a long distance "scoot" with a humble two car consist. Train No. 18, which once ran a Chicago-Portland run via the C&NW, finished its days as a Kansas City-Denver-Portland train. The Portland Rose is shown here on May 1, 1971 (Amtrak Day) on its last run and last stop at Laramie, Wyoming. (A. C. Phelps)

CHAPTER 4
The Challenger

Although the Challenger was not an all-coach train throughout most of its career, the train is especially significant in coach travel history because of the introduction of economical luxury coach travel. It was during the year 1935 that the Union Pacific, faced with the Great Depression, decided to take a number of important steps concerning their passenger service.

One of the first steps taken was the removal of the coaches and tourist sleepers from the Los Angeles Limited. This equipment was then operated for a short time as a second section. However, in August, 1935 the coach-tourist train was given an identity of its own and christened the "Challenger."

The success of the new train was almost immediate and it lasted. It was not by any means a short term gain for the Union Pacific. Because of this popularity the Union Pacific made the decision to modernize the train.

During the winter and late spring of 1936, the Union Pacific shop forces were busy remodeling a number of cars for the Challenger. The company authorized the expenditure of $600,000 to remodel 47 coaches, 16 Pullman tourist sleepers, and five dining cars. This equipment went into service on May 15th, 1936, and at the same time the Challenger began operating through to Chicago over the Chicago & North Western Railway. At that time, the train departed Los Angeles at 8:00 PM and arrived in Chicago at 8:45 AM on the fourth day covering the 2,298 miles in 58 hours, 45 minutes. The west bound train departed Chicago at 9:30 PM and arrived in Los Angeles at 8:30 AM, 61 hours later.

The Challenger is noted because of a number of new innovations:

1. Special Women's and Children's coaches with large dressing rooms and smoking lounges.
2. A registered nurse-stewardess whose service was available to all passengers without charge.
3. Porter service throughout the train.
4. Elimination of tipping for "red caps" handling the hand baggage of coach passengers.
5. The complete elimination of the "penny-in-the-slot-machine" for drinking cups, and the installation of cups without charge.
6. Free pillow service to all coach passengers.
7. A lighting system that allowed the dimming of lights throughout the train during sleeping hours. In the 1936 remodeled coaches, aisle lights were equipped with "milk" globes to give indirect lighting. These were supplemented by side light fixtures located in the baggage rack supports and containing a white and blue lamp. The blue light was used during sleeping hours because it was found to be conducive to rest and sleep.
8. The punching of all tickets by conductors in the same manner as on Pullman cars so that passengers would not be annoyed by frequent ticket punching en route.
9. The calling of stations was eliminated during the sleeping hours. Passengers due to leave the train were awakened individually by the trainman so that other passengers were not disturbed.
10. The dining cars were operated as lounge and recreation cars during non-meal hours. (In May, 1937, the UP added a lounge car to the consist of the train.)
11. Air-conditioning equipment in every car.
12. Reclining and adjustable seats in all coaches.
13. Low cost meals with breakfast at 25¢, lunch for 30¢ and dinner for 35¢.

All thirteen of these points were incorporated in the new Challenger as it went into service. The train was extremely popular, and before the new equipment went into service, 78,322 people visited the train where its remodeled equipment

The San Francisco Challenger ran west on this February 14, 1941 day in two sections. 2nd No. 87 is shown here charging down the main with cab in front No. 4164 in the pouring down rain. The consist was typical of that time with 1 express car, 1 baggage car, 3 chair cars (First two are C&NW coaches, while the third is of SP ownership. All are streamlined and olive green.), 1 dining car, 1 lounge car and 3 tourist sleepers. (A. C. Phelps)

The Los Angeles Challenger, train No. 717 with engine 7856 and 16 cars prepares to depart Salt Lake City on September 30, 1940. Note that the engineer and conductor are comparing watches and going over the train orders. (A. C. Phelps)

was exhibited at nine towns from Omaha to Los Angeles during the time period March 22 to April 1.

By the Spring of 1936, the Challenger was running with one head-end car, two to three coaches for women and children, three or more coaches for both men and women, two or more tourist sleepers and one coffee shop diner. Seven sets of trains were required to maintain the schedule of this train that was "Challenging" the old ways of running passenger trains, the Depression and even the automobile and the bus.

The equipment, from the 1936 re-modeling program, was not changed as far as the exterior appearance was concerned. However, the name of the train was inscribed in large letters on the middle of each car below the windows. The interior decoration employed five distinctive color schemes, silver, blue, beige, brown, taupe and natural wood. Each of these was accompanied with the appropriate tapestries, curtain and floor coverings of a simple but restful design.

Thus in less than one year the Challenger was re-equipped. The train carried on with its challenge, and traffic continued to grow throughout 1936. In early 1937, the train's schedule was speeded up and as we mentioned before, a lounge car was added in April. The original consist had also been expanded by 1937 too. In addition to the through Chicago-Los Angeles coaches and tourist sleepers, a Minneapolis-Los Angeles tourist car was carried plus a Los Angeles-Denver car. The latter was transferred to and from the Challenger at Salt Lake City and handled between Denver and Salt Lake on the Pony Express. This was a new fast train which provided "Challenger"

service on its coaches and tourist sleepers. A Challenger tourist sleeper was also carried between Chicago and Portland.

The Union Pacific made plans to add a Portland Challenger in 1937, but instead elected only to carry a through coach and a Women's and Children's car from Chicago to Green River where they were transferred to the Portland Rose. Although the Pacific Northwest was never graced by a Challenger, the Union Pacific did provide Portland passengers with Challenger service to and from Chicago. The original plan was to run the Portland Challenger with the San Francisco Challenger, and the Los Angeles Challenger would run as an independent train. The San Francisco Challenger was added in late 1937 as planned, but a separate Portland Challenger never did hit the rails.

The Challengers, even before streamlining in late 1937, attracted passengers in large numbers. The Challenger was by the middle of 1937 the best paying train on the Union Pacific. The Union Pacific believed that it was the innovations listed earlier in this chapter that brought passengers in such record numbers. Often the train ran in two sections or more.

The Women's and Children's coaches made it very attractive for mothers traveling with children to go "Challenger." One car was reserved for women only, while the other was reserved for mothers traveling with their offspring. Nobody was permitted to enter these cars other than the passengers assigned to those cars. Uniformed trainmen in the course of duty were permitted in the cars, but had to request permission of the stewardess before entering.

The San Francisco Challenger often ran in two or more sections as is shown with Southern Pacific 2nd No. 87 heading for the Oakland Pier with green flags flying indicating a third section following. Often one section would carry all coaches with the other carrying the tourist cars and possibly one 12 section, 1 drawing room First Class sleeper. The third section would carry anything that was left that the first two sections couldn't carry. It was February, 1946 when this photo was taken, and passenger traffic was still heavy with military personnel coming home from the Pacific front. (W. C. Whittaker)

Promptly at 10:00 PM all bright lights were turned out and remained out for the rest of the night. Only the blue lights were used after 10:00 PM and passengers desiring to remain awake after that time could use the large commodious lounge rooms for men and women at the ends of the cars where chairs were available.

These innovations which proved so popular were the result of months of study by the Union Pacific. Further, in order to keep the train service at a high level every officer at all concerned with its operation including the executive vice president made frequent trips on the Challenger. They mingled with the passengers and listened to comments and suggestions. On one such trip, the vice president heard a women comment on the incongruity of having cuspidors in the women's lounges. The train was approaching Cheyenne, and the vice president immediately dispatched a telegram to the superintendent at Cheyenne. Upon arrival there, ash trays were substituted for the cuspidors. The management

The San Francisco Challenger, powered by a big Chicago & North Western Hudson No. 4009, barrels through Forest Preserve west of Chicago at 90 miles per hour. The C&NW always assigned the big Hudsons to the Challengers, and were painted dark olive green with yellow stripes to match the Challenger color scheme. (Cornwall-Martin Collection from Rail Photo Service)

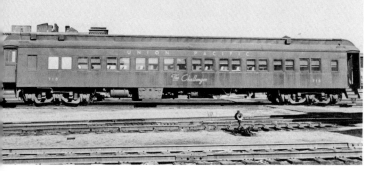

The Union Pacific assigned a variety of coaches to the Challenger. All were painted olive green with gold leaf lettering and the words "The Challenger" in red. The next few photos will illustrate the variety of cars and types of onboard service of the Challenger. (Union Pacific)

The interior of coach No. 710 was done up in a Scotish decor for Challenger service. (Union Pacific Railroad)

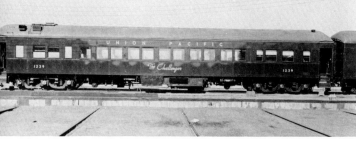

Coach No. 1239 is different from the 710 with its Harriman design. (Union Pacific Railroad)

The interior styling of the 1239 was more streamlined and stylish, and all head rests carried linens with the words "The Challenger" emblazoned on for all to see. The Challenger was one of the finest trains of the late 1930's, and was one of few that catered to economy minded travelers. (Union Pacific Railroad)

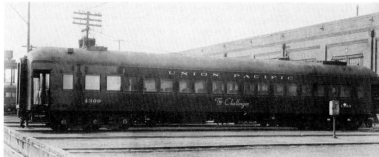

The interior of Coach No. 4300, as well as most all coaches, always contained reclining seats to provide the ultimate in seat service for coach passengers. (Union Pacific Railroad)

With the rapid increase in business for the Challenger, other styles of coaches were pressed into service. Often only the words "The Challenger" were quickly painted on with the Roman lettering left on instead of being replaced with Gothic lettering. (Union Pacific Railroad)

Interior of Challenger coach No. 522. (Union Pacific Railroad)

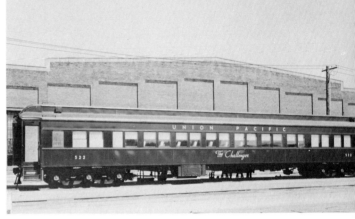

Exterior of Challenger coach No. 522. (Union Pacific Railroad)

of the UP felt that it was not consistent to provide the service and then allow it to shift for itself. The train was continually evaluated until World War II did not leave time for such activities.

The Stewardess-Nurse service was another innovation of distinction on the Challenger. In August, 1935, the company selected seven graduate nurses from Los Angeles, Salt Lake City and Omaha hospitals. As the Challenger service was extended, the UP also employed such nurses on the Pony Express and other trains. As of the summer of 1937, the staff had grown from seven to thirty nine.

Definite qualifications for stewardesses were established. Each one had to present an attractive

personality and appearance and show adaptability in understanding the situations confronting her. Each nurse was required to be registered and a member of the American Nurses' Association. A substantial amount of experience following graduation was required with recommendations from schools of nursing, superintendents of nursing and of hospitals where previously employed. The physical requirements included: age from 25 to 28; height from 5 feet, 3 inches to 5 feet, 7 inches with a corresponding weight from 125 to 145 pounds; and a physical condition which conformed to requirements established for railroad employees in general and which was determined by physical examination.

Attractive two-piece uniforms of French blue serge were worn, with a heavy cape of darker blue in the winter months. In the air conditioned train, there was little problem in keeping the uniforms fresh and clean. The length of the trip determined the rest period at terminal points, which varied from 12 to 36 hours at the turn around point, with a corresponding rest period of 36 to 60 hours between trips at the home terminal.

One coach on each Challenger was reserved entirely for women, and the passengers had the extra benefit of a stewardess-nurse. (Union Pacific Railroad)

Both the Chicago & North Western and Union Pacific operated Women's or Women's and Children's coaches. The C&NW purchased their fleet of such equipment (6160 to 6166) in 1937 and painted them slightly different. The cars were olive green but with yellow stripes and lettering plus the words "The Challenger" in red. (Chicago & North Western Railway)

The C&NW also purchased regular streamlined coaches (Series 6132 to 6147) for service on the Challenger in 1937. North Western "Challenger" paint schemes matched the Hudsons that were assigned to power the economy trains between Chicago and Omaha. (Chicago & North Western Railway)

At any time during the trip, the stewardess was subject to call, but her regulation rest period was from 10:00 PM to 6:00 AM. Comfortable sleeping quarters were provided in either a sleeping car or in an annex of a lounge room in a women's and children's coach. The Union Pacific assumed the living expenses incurred away from the home terminal.

One of the important duties of the stewardess was to assist mothers in the care of their children. Often there were more than 50 children under the age of 5 with which these nurses were quite busy with bottles to be sterilized, food formulas to prepare and vegetable and cereal feedings to be served. Each nurse learned to know the different types of formulas prescribed by the pediatricians from every section of the country. She did this work in the pantry of the kitchen in the dining car. Although at first reluctant to permit nurses into the dining car kitchen, the chefs soon freely conversed about the problems of child nutrition.

Stewardesses also worked with elderly people, the sick and the accidents that can occur from time to time.

The stewardesses were in the charge of a chief stewardess with headquarters in Omaha. The

The interior of the Women's and Children's coaches were as attractive as the coaches built for the "City" streamliners, and they continued the Scottish motif. (Union Pacific Railroad)

stewardess, at the end of each trip, delivered a written report of her journey, in person, at the office of the executive vice president and supplemented it with verbal details as required.

Dining car meals were inexpensively priced, and the result was that nearly 100% of the passengers ate in the diner. At first it was difficult to get the passengers in the diner because of previous bad experiences with dining car high prices. The UP standardized the meals, and with the high volume, was able to make a profit with the Challenger dining car service. By the beginning of 1937, it was necessary for the UP to operate two dining cars on the train in order to serve the meals required by the passengers. When the UP streamlined the Challenger in 1937, a double unit kitchen car and dining room car went into service. An extra charge was made for meal service outside the dining car, but this charge was waived for crippled or infirm passengers, who were served at their seats by the stewardesses.

The Union Pacific advertised the Challenger extensively nationwide, and all UP and Chicago

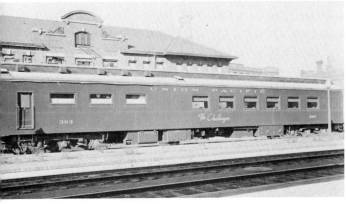

The Union Pacific and the Chicago & North Western both rebuilt standard dining and lounge cars for operation on the Challengers. (Union Pacific Railroad)

The Union Pacific purchased 30 more Challenger coaches in 1942 from Pullman-Standard, who had constructed nearly all of the streamlined cars operated by the C&NW, UP and SP on the Challengers. (Pullman-Standard)

Lounge car service for coach passengers was very rare in the 1930's, but the UP's Challenger carried lounge cars for coach passengers. Again the Scottish theme prevailed, and the cars provided nearly the same type of service as could be found on the Los Angeles Limited or one of the new "City" streamliners. Furthermore, the beverages were far less expensive, as were the meals in the diner, and this fact attracted passengers to the Challengers. (Union Pacific)

& North Western ticket offices advertised the Challenger prominently. In fact, it was believed that in Los Angeles nearly half of the visitors to the UP office building inquired for the "Challenger" office.

One of the problems of railroad service was the often rude treatment by railroad employees. The UP staff coming in contact with Challenger passengers was expected to be not merely polite, but actually friendly and helpful. As a result of this type of treatment, the UP learned that the

The Pullman tourist sleepers also carried "The Challenger" in red lettering on the side of each car. After the Challenger was discontinued, the cars were assigned to other trains. The 3012 is shown here in Santa Fe train No. 2 at Oakland, California. (W. C. Whittaker)

passenger was not a captious, peevish individual who cannot be pleased, but that he responded to courteous treatment and modern sales and service ideas quite as readily and as pleasantly as a customer in any other line of business. The result of this was a profit making train — and during the Depression at that. When the Union Pacific made arrangements to put on the San Francisco Challenger with the Southern Pacific Company, streamlined equipment was ordered by the Chicago & North Western, Union Pacific and Southern Pacific Railroads from the Pullman-Standard Company for delivery in late 1937.

The new streamlined cars added to the Challenger's popularity. Of the new fleet, the Chicago & North Western purchased 23 coaches, the Union Pacific acquired 45 cars while the Southern Pacific purchased 10 cars, four of which were made up of two articulated body units.

The 23 North Western cars included 16 chair cars seating 48 passengers and contained a men's

In 1938 streamlined double unit Dormitory-Kitchen and Dining Room cars were purchased by the Union Pacific. In both the standard and streamlined dining cars, the Scottish motif was carried throughout. (Union Pacific Railroad)

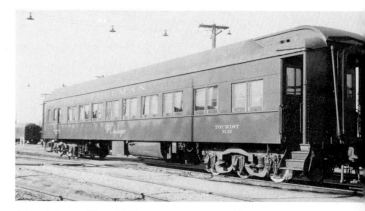

Tourist car No. 3132 was also a 14 section sleeper assigned to "The Challenger" with the name splashed across the center of the car below the window line. The car was photographed at East Los Angeles yard on February 14, 1946. Its career as a Challenger sleeper was all but over. The Challenger was one of a few select trains that were permitted to have the train name painted on the sides of Pullman cars. (Collection of W. C. Whittaker)

room at the forward vestibule and a ladies' lounge at the opposite dummy end. The other seven cars contained 56 seats, a ladies lounge and a nurse-stewardess room at the forward dummy end. There was a general toilet and a baggage locker at the opposite vestibule end.

Electric light was furnished by an axle-driven generator and storage batteries. Individually controlled reading lights included a blue light for night use. These were located over each seat and built into the parcel racks. There were also center lamps for general lighting.

The chair car seats were of the double rotating-type with three position reclining backs and rubber cushions. Lounge chairs in the men's room were of metal, upholstered in leather. Lounge and dressing chairs in the ladies' room were of similar construction and upholstered in fabric. The 23 chair cars were finished in four paint schemes with fabrics, floor coverings, etc. to match. Of the 23 cars, eight cars carried a tan and brown color scheme; eight cars, green; three cars, Chartreuse and blue; and four cars, rose and grey.

The 45 Union Pacific cars included 28 chair cars seating 48 passengers and having a men's and women's lounge rooms at each end of the car; 12 cars seating 56 passengers and containing a nurse-stewardess room in addition to a women's

Night time use permitted privacy through the upper and lower berth curtains. Although not quite as fancy as the First Class sleepers, Tourist cars were comfortable to ride in and provided economy travel for passengers desiring a sleeper. (Union Pacific Railroad)

Daytime use of a Tourist sleeper on the UP's Challenger. (Union Pacific Railroad)

lounge; and five two-unit articulated kitchen-dormitory-dining cars. The front half of the forward body unit of the articulated cars was used exclusively to accommodate the dining car crew, while the rear half made up the kitchen facilities. The total length of the two unit car was 144 feet.

The chair car seats were of the double rotating type with reclining backs, equipped with rubber cushions. Lounge chairs in the men's section were of walnut, and the upholstery was in leather. The lounge and dressing chairs in the ladies' room were constructed of aluminum and upholstered in fabric. Dining car chairs were of light walnut with rubber cushions. The tables were of inlaid patterns with blister proof Formica.

The interior architectural and decorative treatment utilized various color schemes to avoid monotony and add to the attractiveness of this economy train. Forty chair cars were finished in seven different paint color schemes with fabrics, floor coverings, etc. to match the distribution of colors including tan and brown, green, brown and yellow, light rose and dark red, orange, Chartreuse and blue, and rose and grey.

The five dining cars were finished in three paint schemes including two in grey and wine, two in brown and yellow and one in apricot and yellow. The dormitory-kitchen units were completed in apricot and wine with furnishings to match.

The Southern Pacific cars included six coaches for men and women and seating 48 passengers, and two two-unit articulated coaches. Each of these cars was made up of one body unit for women only and one body unit for men only. Each unit was 66 feet long and seated 50 passengers.

First No. 717, the Los Angeles Challenger, rolls through Ogden, Utah on July 6, 1941 with the Tourist car section. Trains 717 and 818 also handled "Challenger" service thru cars to and from Portland. The Portland cars operated in the Portland Rose between Green River and Portland. This arrangement lasted until June 1, 1946. Effective June 2, 1946, the UP-C&NW established the "Pacific-Challenger Service" operating eastbound on No. 16 Portland to Green River, and No. 22 Green River to Chicago. Westbound Challenger Service operated on No. 21 Chicago to Green River and No. 15 beyond to the Pacific Northwest. This service was discontinued on February 15, 1947. The Los Angeles Challenger was dropped during the Spring of 1947, while the San Francisco Challenger did not come off until the Fall of 1947. (A. C. Phelps)

Second No. 818 with engine No. 824 departs Salt Lake City on July 6, 1941 with 12 cars. (A. C. Phelps)

Southern Pacific train No. 87, the San Francisco Challenger, departs Ogden with 16 cars on a very clear and bright July 6, 1941 day. (A. C. Phelps)

Southern Pacific's train No. 24, the San Francisco Challenger heads eastward at Wells, Nevada on February 22, 1947 with Union Pacific 5510 for the helper engine, and Southern Pacific 4424 for the road engine. The length of this great train was 16 cars. The UP engine on the point was borrowed on account of a power shortage on the SP. (A. C. Phelps)

The general interior color schemes provided for the treatment of all cars in four basic sets of colors; and with these four sets of colors, two sets of interior furnishings were used. The sets of colors were: First, blue with ceilings of light cream, walls of light blue and base of dark blue; and second, green with ceilings of deep ivory, walls of light green and base of dark green. These two sets of wall colors came under the classification of cool colors and with them the upholstery fabric colors and floors followed the same warm tones.

The exterior color scheme of the entire train was olive green with gold lettering and the words "The Challenger" written in bright red lettering on the side of each car or articulated unit.

Because of the approach in marketing the train, Union Pacific crews were anxious to work the train. The approach in marketing brought people to the train that otherwise would not have traveled by rail, and consequently the clientele was a much friendlier group. The Challenger did not carry the snob appeal of the Century, Broadway or other extra fare all-Pullman trains.

The popularity of the Challengers was such that two and three section operation was not unusual. The Union Pacific, Chicago & North Western and Southern Pacific had to make arrangements for extra equipment to be available for Challenger service to accommodate all of the traffic. All coaches and extra dining and lounge cars carried the olive green color scheme with a few exceptions on the Union Pacific. A number of Challenger cars were painted in the two tone grey color scheme applied to such trains as the San Francisco Overland.

The Challenger served the Country well through World War II, and with the ending of the war, regular two section operation continued. New

Southern Pacific's San Francisco Challenger, train No. 23, pauses at Wells, Nevada for water in 7 below zero weather and clear. The total consist of the train is 15 cars. The UP coach to the rear of the baggage car was for the exclusive use of women and children. (A. C. Phelps)

In 1954, the Union Pacific and Chicago & North Western revived the Challenger between Chicago and Los Angeles. After seven years of inactivity, the Challenger once again hit the rails on a one night basis from Chicago to LA. This time, however, the train was not olive green but Union Pacific yellow. She carried at least 2 First Class sleeping cars instead of Tourist cars, although she did carry a 14 section streamlined sleeper during the Summer of 1954 and 1955. Numbered 107 and 108, the train replaced the Los Angeles Limited, and carried the double unit diner built for Challenger service in 1938. In addition, the train carried Omaha-Los Angeles coaches and sleeper, plus a full club lounge car for both coach and Pullman passengers. The 1954 Challenger was the finest ever, and more was yet to come. The Challenger is shown here in Rainbow Canyon. (Union Pacific Railroad)

cars had been purchased in 1942, and these continued to serve along with equipment dating back to 1935. The end of the war brought plans for the daily operation of the City of San Francisco and City of Los Angeles. With this daily operation, the Challengers were discontinued after 12 years of operation.

From 1947 through to 1954, the Challenger was all but forgotten. Challenger coaches were farmed out to other trains, such as the Ashland Limited and some of the 400's on the Chicago & North Western. The Union Pacific repainted a number of their cars for Streamliner service as did the Southern Pacific. The dark olive green Challenger cars were all repainted by the late 1950's. However as patronage declined in the 1950's, the Union Pacific once again decided to make a positive change in passenger train operations. The result was the Challenger Streamliner, which joined the "Cities" streamliner fleet between Chicago and the West Coast.

The Challenger Streamliner went into operation on a "one night en route" from Chicago to Los Angeles, 39½ hours from Chicago. Returning, the train departed Los Angeles in the afternoon and arrived in Chicago early in the morning the second day. The east bound running time was 39 hours, 45 minutes. The City of Los Angeles departed Los Angeles 2½ hours behind the Challenger, and arrived in Chicago 2 hours, 45 minutes behind the revised economy train. The Challenger was equipped with leg rest coaches, dining car, lounge car and a 10 roomette, 6 double bedroom sleeper and either a 14 section sleeping car or a 6 section, 6 roomette 4 double bedroom car depending upon the season. In 1955, the train was equipped with a dome coach and a dome lounge car. Later that year, the dome lounge went to the City of St. Louis and was replaced by a club lounge car. Also in October, 1955, the Challenger was removed from the Chicago & North Western between Chicago and Omaha and operated via the Milwaukee Road between the same two points.

When the new Challenger Streamliner went into operation, the Union Pacific gave passengers a silver dollar to spend in the dining car. Prices were lowered to 65¢ for breakfast and to $1.00 for dinner. Luncheons were served for 85¢. The new coach-Pullman streamliner was a hit.

From October, 1955 through April, 1956, the Challenger was combined with the Milwaukee Road's Mid-west Hiawatha between Chicago and Omaha. This changed the schedule for later running times on the eastbound run arriving at Chicago at 4:30 P.M. after a 40 hour, 30 minute journey.

This operation remained in effect until April, 1956 when the Challenger was combined with the

City of Los Angeles. From that time on the Challenger ran as a separate train only during the summer season. From 1960 on, the train ran as a second section to the City of Los Angeles which was not unlike the original Challenger running as a second section to the Los Angeles Limited in 1935. The big difference with the new seasonal operation (including the winter holidays) was that the Challenger was now an all-coach train. As with all Union Pacific passenger trains, the Challenger once again became part of history on May 1, 1971. Amtrak elected not to include the Challenger as part of the new services. The only passenger train now running on any part of the Challenger's route is the San Francisco Zephry, and that only from Cheyenne, Wyoming to Oakland, California over the Union Pacific and Southern Pacific's Overland Route. It has been suggested that Amtrak rename the Zephyr, the San Francisco Challenger because the train certainly is a *Challenger*. A Challenger not only to the automobile, bus and air competition; but a *Challenge* to the energy crisis as well. The Challenger will long be remembered by rail fans, historians and transportation geographers for the part she played in rail economy coach service.

In 1955 the Challenger became a Domeliner and carried a dome observation lounge car and one dome coach. The Challenger had reached a new height in equipment. However, the dome observation lounge was soon transferred to the City of St. Louis, and in October, 1955 the Challenger went to the Milwaukee Road between Chicago and Omaha. At the same time, the train was combined with the Midwest Hiawatha. The following April, the Challenger's schedule was changed and she ran as a second section to the City of Los Angeles. At that time, she became an all-coach train for the first time in her history. She continued to run either combined with the City or separately during the heavy travel seasons from 1956 to 1971 when her career was brought to a close by Amtrak. (Union Pacific Railroad)

CHAPTER 5

Some Superb All-Coach Trains

For decades in North America the most celebrated trains were the All-Pullman or All-Sleeping cars of the extra fare and extra care variety. Such trains as the Broadway Limited, Twentieth Century, Super Chief, Overland Limited, Panama Limited and the Lark have been ridden and written about by countless book authors, newspaper men and the subject of on train movies by Hollywood. To travel on the Broadway or the Super Chief meant upper social class or in other words, "snob appeal." The All-Pullman train caught the spot light in American Railroading.

However, as some railroads operated All-Pullman trains, many roads operated deluxe coach trains that were advertised as "All-Coach" trains. These trains offered economy travel, often with full first class dining car service and club lounge cars. The trains often carried a full complement of "Coach Porters" and were scheduled as "fast trains." The purpose was to entice people from buses and the private automobile. Many were successful for a time, and then faded away because of the Depression. Many lasted until Amtrak and a fair number became Coach and Pullman trains because of their popularity. As of 1974, Amtrak does not advertise or spot light any trains as being All-Coach streamliners. In a sense the All-Coach train has disappeared in much the same way as the All-Pullman train. There are all-coach trains to be sure in Amtrak's time table, but can the reader find the extra fare El Capitan, the City of New Orleans, the Challenger or the Pacemaker complete with dining, lounge and porter service in the 1974 time tables? The rest of this chapter is devoted to the Superb All-Coach trains, when and where they operated and the type of equipment they carried.

THE BLUE COMETS

Among the first, in fact the first, *DeLuxe* coach trains operated in the USA were the Central of New Jersey "Blue Comets." On February 21, 1929 the Blue Comets went into service between New York City and Atlantic City replacing a coach and parlor train service. The Blue Comets were a double daily service and the entire train was painted a beautiful Packard blue, Jersey cream and royal blue. The interior was also decorated in blue tones including the porters' uniforms; table service and linens.

The distance of 136 miles between terminals was covered in three hours. The train times were so arranged that New Yorkers could spend time at work in the morning and leave the city at 11:00 AM, have lunch on board the train and be able to spend most of the afternoon in Atlantic City. Or if they desired, they could catch the afternoon Blue Comet at 3:30 PM and arrive in Atlantic City in time for evening dinner. From the seashore resort passengers could depart on the morning Blue Comet at 9:15 AM or in the late afternoon at 4:35 PM. The afternoon passengers could enjoy dinner on board the train which arrived at New York at 7:35 PM.

The Blue Comets made but one scheduled stop between the two terminals at Hammonton, N. J. Other stops were made at Elizabethport, Red Bank, Lakewood and Lakehurst only to receive and discharge passengers to or from Hammonton and beyond. Non-stop connecting trains ran between Newark and Elizabethport for the Blue Comet passengers.

All coach seats on the Blue Comets were numbered. Special tickets, printed on blue paper stock, carried a number and a letter to designate the coach in which the seat was assigned. The method used here was designed from methods of seat and row numbers in theatres. With this type of system, passengers had no difficulty finding the coach with their reserved seat(s). No seats were sold in either the observation or smoking cars, and all passengers had full use of all the facilities on the train without extra or first class fare charges. This in itself was a radical departure from the traditional operation of permitting only sleeping or parlor passengers to use the lounge or observation cars.

Two Pacific type (4-6-2) steam locomotives were assigned to the Blue Comets. These engines were equipped with automatic train control and painted Packard and Royal Blue to match the train.

Thirteen standard cars consisting of two combination baggage smoking cars, two observation cars, six coaches, one dining car and two baggage cars were completely rebuilt for the new service. Each car carried the name of the train in gold letters on the letter board. The name of the railroad did not appear on any of the cars. The exterior blue scheme was even applied to the trucks and underframes.

The interiors of the smokers, coaches and observation cars were finished in circassan walnut with cream colored headlining and baggage racks. The window shades were made of blue Spanish pantasote material. Each car was furnished with drinking cup and towel vending machines for both men and women.

The smoking car contained 48 bucket type seats, each with center arm rests which could be lowered if desired. All seats were covered with a blue leather. Bulk head seats were non-rotating. Match strikers were attached to the bottom of each window post and on the back of each pair of seats was a cup type ash tray of royal blue. A table, which could be used for playing cards or writing letters, could be placed between the two pairs of facing seats next to the bulkheads. Each

smoking car was furnished with 22 nickel plated cuspidors. The floor of the smoker and all other cars was covered with a diamond pattern of blue and white tiling.

The coaches contained 64 bucket type triple cushioned seats upholstered in rich Persian-blue figured mohair material with wide golden tinted strips. A nickel plated coat hanger and umbrella holder was attached to the rear of each seat. The coach floors were covered with a thick carpet laid on Ozite. The carpet was Persian blue into which was worked an all over design in gold.

The observation cars were equipped with 48 silver blue reed arm chairs, upholstered in Persian-blue Avalon plush with a golden tinted flower design. The floor was covered with a deep blue carpet with a golden tinted meteor design. The observation platform accommodated six colapsible chairs. A nickel plated card holder was attached to the bulkhead wall on each side of the corridor. On one side was a card that read "Smoking Car Forward," and in the other was a card which under the caption "Train Crew Today," gave the name and years of service of the engineer and the conductor.

A 36 seat dining car was also completely refinished and re-equipped for use on the Blue Comet. The floor was nearly identical to the observation car. Above each window was a panel of frosted glass in each of which was a hand etched design representing a comet with stars and clouds. Blue bulbs were used in the deck lights, which gave a delicate blue lighting effect through the white shades. The tables were set with Czecho-

The Blue Comet pauses for the photographer at Asbury Park, New Jersey during the year 1938. The big Pacific type steam locomotive is equipped with "Automatic Train Control" and really sped the Comet over the rails during those Depression years. The Blue Comet was the forerunner for superb all-coach train service in the USA. (Harold K. Vollrath)

Slovakian table linen in a light tone of ultramarine blue. The color scheme was completed by the use of rich dark blue china and glassware. Each table was provided with a light which consisted of a silver base and a circular parchment shade on which were painted gold stars and comets. The dining car served a 75 cent blue platter luncheon and a $1.25 dinner in addition to a-la-carte service. The dining car made one round trip on the Blue Comet, from New York in the morning and to the Big City in the evening. The other Blue Comet ran without a dining car.

The Blue Comets were a fantastic step for the railroad industry as a whole. They started a new mode of travel for the coach passenger, who heretofore did not enjoy a First Class service. The Blue Comet started off with a bang, but the Depression killed the service and the equipment was eventually repainted Coach Green. Although the new train did not have a long history, nobody could know in the early 1930's the deluxe all-coach train service that would eventually criss-cross the United States.

THE MOTOR QUEEN

The next deluxe all-coach train to hit the rails was the Big Four's Motor Queen between Cinncinnati and Detroit. The Big Four, part of the New York Central System, virtually copied the Blue Comet. The train was painted blue with a cream stripe and gold lettering. The exception in this case was that the Big Four lettered the cars "New York Central Lines" instead of the train name. The name of the train brought up the rear of the train with the words "Motor Queen" splashed across the railing of the observation car.

The train consisted of a club smoking car, two coaches, a dining lounge car and an observation car. As with the Blue Comet, the Motor Queen's equipment was all rebuilt. The dining lounge car was somewhat of an exception to the usual type of car. This particular car seated 24 in the dining room, 10 in a lounge and 8 in a card section. The observation car was equipped with soft easy chairs and painted in soft light blue colors.

The Motor Queen was also powered by a Pacific type steam engine which made the trip in 6 hours, 45 minutes. The distance between Detroit and Cinncinnati is 270.3 miles and the 6¾ hours was hot running in 1929. The 1953 schedule of the Queen City was seven hours, and that was with diesel power.

Despite the fast schedule, the Motor Queen did not attract enough passengers, and the nation's second deluxe all-coach train went the way of all flesh during the Depression. The Queen City, was in a way, an out growth of the day schedule of the Motor Queen. However, it carried a sleeper for parlor car service and did not have the personality or the finesse of the All-Coach Motor Queen.

THE READING COMPANY'S CRUSADER

1937 brought a high speed streamlined All-Coach train to the metropolitan east coast, which may not seem like much at first; but this new train was unusual in many respects. First of all, it was powered by a streamlined steam engine. Second, it was not articulated and aside from the Hiawatha, was one of very few non-articulated streamlined trains. Third, it was run in hot competition with a high speed Pennsylvania Railroad between Philadelphia and New York.

The Budd Company built the unusual streamliner for the Reading Company, which went into service in December, 1937. The Crusader was made up of four chair cars and one tavern dining car. The two end cars were observation cars which eliminated the need to turn the entire train around at end terminals. The end cars contained 56 coach seats and 14 lounge chairs, while the other two coaches contained 56 revenue seats and 12 lounge chairs. The dining car accommodated 24

The Big Four soon followed the Central of New Jersey's example and put together the Motor Queen, the entire consist of which is shown here. Ironically, the Motor Queen served the very state (Michigan whose main industry would sound the death knell for the railroad passenger train. (Ed Nowak— Penn Central)

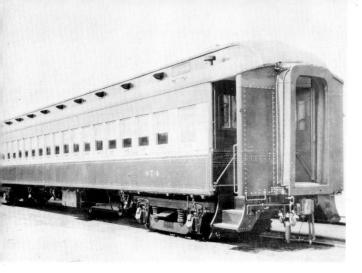

All coaches for the Motor Queen were completely rebuilt by the Big Four and were lettered "New York Central Lines" and sub lettered C.C.C.&St.L. At the time the Motor Queen was finest coach service on the New York Central System. (Ed Nowak—Penn Central)

The observation car was equipped with easy chairs and carpeting. Such lounge car service was not open to coach passengers on other trains of the period. (Ed Nowak—Penn Central)

people in the dining room and 27 in the cocktail lounge.

Although the end cars were identical in layout and structure, they differed widely in color treatment. For example, in car No. 1, the walls were olive brown and the ceiling was flesh colored where as car No. 5 had light aquamarine walls with a lemon cream ceiling. A utility table with open shelves was placed at the rounded end of the lounge sections of the two end or observation coach cars. A good deal of the exposed wood work was Sapeli mahogany. All of the seats were of the rotating type with individual reclining backs and sliding cushions. The seat cushions were molded sponge rubber and the backs were of spring construction. These types of seats were used in all four of the coaches of the train.

Car No. 2 had clay colored walls and a drab buff ceiling. The seat coverings were a green plush. Car No. 4 had light olive green side walls with a sand gray ceiling. The seat coverings in this car were a brown frieze. The flooring in all of the coaches was originally Linotile laid in geometric designs.

The middle car of the five car speedster contained a dining room, cocktail lounge or tavern and a kitchen. The tavern was fitted with sofas, chairs and tables for 27 passengers. This section was separated from the dining room by a low partition surrounded by glass panels that extended as high as the upper window rail. The color scheme of the car was olive brown, flesh and Indian red. The dining room chairs were of wood frame construction finished in gray oak and covered with Lackawanna tan leather with red piping. Cushions and backs were sponge rubber filled.

The tavern had 11 individual tubular steel chromeplated chairs upholstered and covered with the same materials as used in the dining room chairs. There were also four built in corner settees in the tavern. They were cushioned with sponge rubber and covered with red leather. The floor covering in this car was a Chase "Seamloc" carpet with a raisin colored background and a henna pattern.

The kitchen occupied 22½ feet at the end of the car. All equipment used in the kitchen was made of stainless steel, with the exception of a coal burning range. Other kitchen equipment consisted of a refrigerator, water boiler, broiler, two coal bins, steam table, coffee urn, a service shelf, a low kitchen refrigerator, a fruit chill box, a liquor refrigerator and locker and areas for the storage of dishes and supplies.

The Crusader was in many ways a long distance commuter train. She traveled from Philadelphia to New York in the morning and from New York in the evening. For awhile, the train made an additional round trip from New York (Jersey City) to Philadelphia and return between the morning and evening runs. However, this extra round trip was operated only Monday through Friday and it is interesting to note that the Crusader equipment did not run on Saturday even though the train did. On Saturdays, equipment from the Wall Street ran in place of the streamliner. By the 1960's the extra round trip had been discontinued and still later the five car train was sold to the Canadian National. The train is still in operation in Canada as of 1974.

The Crusader on the Reading-Central of New Jersey Route still operates Monday through

The five car all-coach streamliner was powered by a high speed streamlined Pacific capable of moving the train in excess of 100 miles per hour. (Harold K. Vollrath)

Friday between Philadelphia and the New York area, as well as the companion train, the Wall Street. This is the last long distance service on the Reading and the Central of New Jersey and we may be seeing the curtain drawn on these two railroads. It will depend upon the planning of the merger of the bankrupt railroads into a possible new system. However, if the Reading should disappear as a separate railroad; it will be remembered for its contribution to the deluxe All-Coach passenger trains, "The Crusader."

SEABOARD AIR LINE'S SILVER METEOR

February 2, 1939 ranks as a red number date in the railroad industry for on that day the Silver Meteor began service between New York and Florida. What is significant about the Silver Meteor is that it is the first of the seven car All-Coach high speed streamliners. Several of these trains were built in 1939 and 1940, and all of them proved so popular that eventually Pullmans were added to the consist and they lost the distinction of being All-Coach trains.

The Silver Meteor was constructed by the Budd Company and consisted of a Baggage chair car, 60 seat chair car, Tavern-coach car, 48 seat dining car, two 60 seat chair cars and a Chair

Observation Lounge car. The original consist carried a total of 280 reclining seats.

Between New York City and Washington, D. C. the train was handled by Pennsylvania Railroad electric locomotives. From Washington to Florida, the Seaboard assigned a 2,000 horsepower diesel locomotive built by Electro Motive Corporation.

The original schedule for the single train set called for a round trip every three days alternating between New York and Miami, and New York and St. Petersburg. On the Miami run the train was scheduled for 26½ hours for 1,389 miles southward and 27 hours for the north bound run. For the St. Petersburg run the distance was 1,247 miles with a time of 24¾ hours south bound and 25 hours, 5 minutes north bound. The train was very popular and the average revenue per passenger seat was around $20.00 per trip or a total revenue of over $5,000 per trip excluding dining car and bar receipts.

The seven car train was designed especially for the long distance Florida service. Each of the coaches contained wash room lounges that equalled or exceeded to those found in the finest sleeping cars in service in 1939. Low prices prevailed in the dining car and tavern cars. Light lunches and beverages were served in the tavern. Dining car breakfast prices ranged from 50 to 65 cents and luncheons and dinners from 60 to 75 cents. Staff on the train included a registered nurse-stewardess and porter service in all passenger sections. Pillows were available at 25 cents.

As we mentioned earlier, there was a total of 280 revenue seats. In the dining car, tavern and observation lounge there was a total of 120 non-revenue seats plus a dormitory section for a crew of 14.

The first car contained a 26 foot baggage section and the dormitory compartments. The remainder of the car contained 22 reclining seats plus a conductor's desk at the forward end. The color scheme, referred to as the "green car" had a fog blue ceiling with a brown stripe, brown side walls and end doors of deeper chocolate brown. The chair upholstery was a pin stripe pattern of blue-green.

Rubber flooring was used in all of the chair car sections of the streamliner. It was dark oak in the passageways and under the seats. The aisle had a stripe pattern with inserts to harmonize with the color scheme. In the first car, the stripe was a light buff with inserts of sea foam green. On the partitions at both ends were photo murals in stainless steel frames.

The Silver Meteor coaches were designed with a continuous closed type baggage rack. On the under side of the rack were built in reading lights that could be individually controlled by the passenger. The general lighting was by recessed ceiling fixtures, in each of which was incorporated

a small blue lamp to supply a dim restful light during the late night time hours.

The seats were rotating and reclining to several positions and had a foam type rubber cushion which adjusted itself to the position of the back for maximum comfort. The seats had backs of spring construction with hair upholstery, headrest covers, stainless steel foot rail and upholstered armrests. Table positions were provided at the end facing seats by means of wall sockets, which accommodated folding type tables. The tables were stored in a locker when not in use.

Car No. 2 was a 60 passenger chair car with the vestibule forward and was equipped with large men's and women's lounges at opposite ends of the car. Referred to as the "coral car" the color scheme included brown walls, flesh brown ceiling and coral end doors. The upholstery on alternate seats was a fawn rust pattern with the chevrons pointed upward, and the remaining seats with a coral pencil stripe pattern upholstery. This alternating colors made a very pleasing appearance. Car No. 2 also contained four table positions to accommodate portable wall type tables such as described for the baggage dormitory coach.

Car No. 3 was a chair-tavern car with a 30 seat passenger section with toilet rooms and vestibule forward and a room for the hostess at the rear. This car was referred to as the "pink" car and the coach section had an orchid gray ceiling with a light tuscan rose stripe, tuscan rose side walls and end doors of a deep Indian red. The upholstery

It is interesting to note that originally a two unit Electro Motive Division FP-7 diesel electric was used to replace the streamlined Pacific on the Crusader. (Reading Railway System)

alternated again with a brown pencil stripe and a patterned chamois. The center aisle stripe was a deep red with flame colored inserts.

The tavern section contained two longitudinal settees, each with three pedestal type tables. Forward and back of these settees on either side were pairs of facing seats with a table for card playing. The upholstery in the tavern was red hand buffed leather with a light tan piping. The table tops were robin's egg blue with a white border. The oval shaped tables at the settees had fixed aluminum pedestals and the card playing tables were of the wall type with folding leg on the aisle side.

The decor of the tavern section was ocean sand and a light oyster gray and included carpeting on the floor. The bar at the front of the section included a etched gun metal back bar and side bar mirrors with diffused side lighting, glass shelves, a black rubber bar top and black molding. The bar front was stainless steel and green with a patterned multi colored stripe of orange, green yellow and mustard at the top. The bar was equipped with electric refrigeration and had a concealed radio to supply music for the patrons of the tavern section.

Car No. 4 was the dining car with olive gray walls and a three tone ceiling of medium sand panel, light stone band and dark tuscan rose stripe. The floor was carpeted with a zigzag pattern with a center of henna rust with admixture of mahogany, a dove taupe band and a side field of raisin. The chair seats were upholstered with a raisin colored pin stripe material and the backs were maroon and gray striped.

Car No. 5 and No. 6 were duplicates of coach No. 2 except for the color scheme. No. 5 was known as the brown car with a ceiling of oyster white, gray walls and the end doors, laurel brown. The seating alternated with a brown floral pattern and a fawn colored pin stripe. Flooring was a dark oak. Car No. 6 was known as the blue car with the ceiling a lemon cream, the walls a delft blue and the end doors a burnt orange. Alternate seats were upholstered in a blue pin stripe and a deep blue with a floral pattern. The flooring again was dark oak.

The last car was an observation coach car with seating for 48 coach passengers. The general scheme was yellow and turquoise with gray green walls. Alternate seats were upholstered in a brown striped pattern and a turquoise pencil stripe. As in all chair sections, the end partitions provided a setting for photo murals in stainless steel frames. The flooring was dark oak with an aisle pattern of a black stripe with blue green inserts.

The observation lounge section contained 17 movable satin finished square tubular framed arm chairs, three love seats and a desk chair. Seven of these chairs were upholstered in old rose, seven in Eiffel green and the last four chairs and love seats in Apollo gray.

Between the chair section and the lounge section was a low partition with a decorative plate glass above. Etched in each panel was a large game fish, seen as through the side of an aquariam. Against this forward partition was a writing desk on the left and on the opposite side was a magazine rack with a built in radio. Toward

The original 7 car consist of the Silver Meteor grew substantially over the years and new equipment was ordered before and after the War. The popularity of the train brought the addition of Pullmans, and that popularity continues with Amtrak. This photo shown the Seaboard's Silver Meteor departing Baltimore for Florida in 1967. (H. H. Harwood, Jr.)

the rear of the lounge were two built in side tables and on either side of the rear end doors is a built in table, one of which contained the equipment for train back-up movements. All of these tables, desk and magazine rack were in Maidon burl veneer with ebonised walnut tops. The ceiling of the observation lounge section was ocean sand with an apricot band. The floor was carpeted with inserts of dove taupe on a mahogany field, which created a restful atmosphere.

At each vestibule of the train there was a swing out sign with the car designation number for the guidance of passengers when the train is at a station.

Despite the fact that the train operated every sixth day between New York and Miami and every sixth day between New York and St. Petersburg, the Silver Meteor was extremely popular. In fact so much so that the Seaboard laid plans to expand the streamliner service. Two additional trains were purchased, one of which was a seven car train nearly identical in many respects to the original Silver Meteor while the other was a 10 car train. The 10 car train consisted of two additional coaches and a dining car. The Seaboard purchased the 17 cars from the Budd Company plus nine additional 2,000 horsepower passenger locomotives from Electro-Motive. As of 1939, the SAL operated 19 passenger diesels for the All-Coach Silver Meteor and the All-Pullman Orange Blossom Special.

With the additional equipment, the Seaboard began a daily New York-Miami operation and an every third day operation between New York and St. Petersburg. The St. Petersburg equipment ran in the Miami train from New York to Wildwood, Florida where the train was split. Between Wildwood and Miami, the standard 7 car consist including one dining car with one diesel locomotive was the standard operating procedure. The remaining three cars (two coaches and one dining car) were run with an additional standard combination coach-baggage car to St. Petersburg. It is interesting to note that the Seaboard assigned two 2,000 horsepower units to the Meteor between Washington and Wildwood. One unit continued to Miami while the other handled the St. Petersburg leg.

The popularity of the Silver Meteor could be gauged by the fact that on December 22 and 23 (weekend), 1939, there were over 2,000 unfilled reservation requests in spite of the addition of two standard all-coach trains for the Christmas holidays.

With the addition of the new equipment and expanded service, the SAL slashed running times from New York to Florida points from 55 minutes on the southbound New York-St. Petersburg run to 2 hours on the northbound Miami-New York run. The new schedules allowed 25 hours for New York to Miami; 23 hours, 50 minutes New York to St. Petersburg; 25 hours from Miami to New York and 23 hours, 55 minutes from St. Petersburg to New York.

The popularity of the trains did not wane, and in late 1940 additional equipment (two baggage-dormitory-chair cars, two 56 seat chair cars, two 48 seat dining cars and two 30 seat Chair Observation Buffet cars) went into service to provide daily service between New York and St. Petersburg.

World War II placed a heavy demand for Seaboard's passenger equipment, but after the War the popularity of Silver Meteor continued its upward climb. Post war progress included the addition of sleeping cars to the trains consist and it lost its status as an All-Coach train. The train achieved lengths from 15 to 20 cars during the winter travel season. The Seaboard Air Line Railroad, and later the Seaboard Coast Line, was proud of the Silver Meteor and it was a train of distinction until Amtrak took over. Since that time, the Silver Meteor continues to run in fine fashion providing Easterners and New Englanders with one of the finest ways to travel to Florida.

THE NEW YORK CENTRAL'S PACEMAKER

The New York Central is known the world over for the All-Pullman Twentieth Century Limited. Yet little is known about the All-Coach Pacemaker. The Pacemaker began service on July 28, 1939 with a rebuilt train consisting of standard coaches and an ex-Twentieth Century observation car. The train was scheduled for 16 hours, 30 minutes west bound and 17 hours east bound. This was only slightly lower than the Century. The train featured reclining seat coaches, reserved seats, porter service and a streamlined Hudson (4-6-4) for power. She was immediately popular as heretofore there was no such high speed service for coach passengers between Chicago and New York. She served very well through the War, and her consist was always dictated by traffic requirements. She was often a hodge podge of equipment, much of Pullman green instead of the New York Central two tone gray.

The original Pacemaker was steam powered and consisted of standard coach equipment before streamlined power and cars arrived. This New York Central photo shows the all-coach Pacemaker at Oscawanna, New York on September 5, 1939. (Ed Nowak—Penn Central)

After the war, the NYC continued to run the Pacemaker in grand manner. She was completely re-equipped in 1949 with an all streamlined consist which included a dining car, club lounge coach, Observation Tavern Lounge Coach as well as a full complement of streamlined coaches. All cars carried reserved reclining seats with radio and porter service. The Pacemarker ran as an All-Coach train from 1939 to 1957 at which time the west bound schedule was discontinued. In 1961 the east bound train was combined with the New England States between Chicago and Buffalo. However long before this pruning and

consolidation took place, the Pacemaker had more or less become an every day New York Central passenger train. This process had gone on gradually, but the Pacemaker had definitely lost its disctinctive status as a high speed New York Central run. Indeed the Pacemaker spent two hours in dead station time at Buffalo in 1966. The train was switched out of the New England States at 2:18 AM and did not depart until 4:34 AM. The schedule was a whopping 19 hours, 55 minutes, a far cry from the 1939 schedule of 17 hours and the 1953 running time of 16 hours, 45 minutes. The Pacemaker also charged a special

The streamlined all-coach Pacemaker was a highly popular train. This photo shows the 1949 version departing Chicago for New York City with a consist that more than equalled the all-Pullman Twentieth Century. (Bob Lorenz)

service charge of $1.15 for the Chicago-New York trip during the height of its career.

The Pacemaker disappeared from the schedules completely in 1966, and as of 1974 the name has not re-appeared on a schedule between Chicago and New York City. Not only has the All-Pullman Century gone the way of discontinued passenger trains, but one cannot find any "All-Coach" trains flying over the rails of the former New York Central anymore.

THE PENNSYLVANIA RAILROAD'S TRAIL BLAZER

As the New York Central placed into service the Pacemaker on July 28, 1939, the Pennsylvania Railroad responded with an equally fine all-coach train called the Trail Blazer. The PRR assembled a fleet of coaches and sent them off to the shops for complete reconstruction. An entire series of 68 seat reclining seat chair cars was built for the new Trail Blazer along with a Buffet Observation car. In addition double unit diners (Dormitory-Kitchen cars and Dining Room cars) were placed in service on the new speedster. The train, decked out in a two tone tuscan red and a gold striping, proved to be very popular and additional

coaches went into service every year until 1942. By that time the war was taxing the train to the limit, and this continued until 1946.

The original schedule for the Trail Blazer was 17 hours, a somewhat longer running time than the Broadway Limited. All seats were reserved and among the Trail Blazer luxuries were pillows and coach porter service. In 1948 the train was completely re-equipped with streamlined coaches and diesel power. However, the hand writing was already on the wall and the Trail Blazer was combined with the General in 1951. Except for separate holiday running, the Trail Blazer lost its identity as a separate train. The Pennsylvania Railroad continued to carry the train's name in the time tables through the late 1950's, but when people misunderstood the name of the train as the "General Trail Blazer" it was eventually dropped. As of 1974, there are no "All-Coach" trains, advertised as such, running over the former Pennsylvania Railroad between Chicago and New York City, although there have been rumors of Amtrak running such a train nothing has officially been announced. As for now, the All-Coach Trail Blazer has disappeared along with the All-Pullman Broadway.

The Trail Blazer was the Pennsy's answer for a competitive service with the New York Central's Pacemaker. (Harold K. Vollrath)

The Champion and Flager were identical in consist and both were powered by diesel locomotives. This touched up publicity photo shows the Champion speeding over the superb track and road bed of the Atlantic Coast Line-Florida East Coast route to Florida. The purple scheme of the ACL was a perfect color for a superb all-coach train. The scheme undoubtedly influenced Auto-Train with their color combination for a train that travels the same route as the original Champion. (Seaboard Coast Line)

ATLANTIC COAST LINE'S CHAMPION AND FLORIDA EAST COAST'S HENRY M. FLAGLER

1939 was a big year for Florida rail travelers. For not only did the Seaboard Air Line begin All-Coach luxury service from New York early in the year, but on December 1, 1939, the Champion began its daily winter schedule trips between New York and Miami via the Pennsylvania, Altantic Coast Line and Florida East Coast Railroads. December 2nd marked the beginning of new All-Coach train service on the Florida East Coast between Miami and Jacksonville. The new train, the Henry M. Flagler, provided a daily service between Jacksonville and Miami making 16 stops at east coast winter resorts. This entire service involved the use of four new seven car All-Coach trains, two owned by ACL and two by the FEC. Three of the trains protected the Champion schedules, while the fourth operated as the Henry M. Flagler. All four of the trains were alike and consisted of one combination mail and coach car, three 60 passenger coaches, one dining car, one 52 passenger coach with the hostess room and a tavern lounge observation car. Note that this seven car all-coach train is similar in many respects to the Seaboard's Silver Meteor. The big difference being the placement of the tavern lounge.

The 28 cars were constructed by the Budd Company, and the four 2,000 horsepower diesel locomotives were built by Electro Motive Corporation.

THE CHAMPION

The first car of each train was a combination mail storage and coach car plus sleeping quarters for a crew of 12 and a compartment for the steward. The passenger compartment furnished accommodations for 22 passengers and was decorated in tones of blue and tan. The upholstery repeated the same motif.

The next two 60 seat passenger cars contained adjustable revolving reclining seats. The walls were of red brown and were combined with a ceiling in flesh drab with light green ceiling stripes. The upholster was a warm brown. The men's and women's lounges and washrooms were of sleeping car designs and the latter contained complete powder room facilities and deep divan chairs.

The dining car contained table seating for 48 people and was decorated in gray browns with pink and light orchid tints. The dining car seats were upholstered in blue. The kitchen interior was of stainless steel and completely equipped with refrigeration units, ranges, sinks, work tables and storage space. A service door on the side of the car permitted loading of supplies directly into the kitchen.

The fifth car was another 60 passenger chair car and duplicated the other 60 seat cars. The upholstery was green and the walls were finished in gray green and the ceiling in yellow white with ivory stripes.

The sixth car was a 52 passenger chair car and included men's and women's lounges as well as a compartment for the hostess. The color scheme was light brown with gray whites and ivory tans. Amber rose upholstery rounded out the color ensemble.

The seventh car was an observation lounge and tavern car. It seated 57 passengers in its various accommodations. The tavern section, in the forward end of the car, seated 36 people. The two lounges were equipped with curving divans facing the center of the car. These were divided by a series of booths. The color effect was designed to carry out this theme with deep blue wainscoting, upper side walls of light tan giving way to a deep tan drab ceiling. The bar was decorated in a marine motif and extended into the car from the after end of the tavern. It was backed by plate glass with shelves conveniently arranged for beverages and glassware.

The observation lounge was framed in a rounded and streamlined rear end, the rounded effect being carried out also in the forward end to produce an oval room. Here broad windows provided an unobstructed view while deep lounge

chairs and divans were arranged to provide a maximum comfort index. A writing desk was located at the forward end of this lounge.

During the night running, soft blue lights could be turned on in all of the cars. It is interesting to note that sometimes the coaches on the Champion were referred to as "sleeper-coaches."

The Champion was a very popular train and sleeping cars were added later in its career. In fact new coaches were added to the Champion within a year of its initial service. After the war, sleepers and a splitting of the Champ into two trains, the East Coast Champion and West Coast Champion demonstrated its popularity. Although it had lost its All-Coach status, the two trains grew to 20 cars and the Champion continues the tradition of fine service in 1974 for Amtrak.

THE HENRY M. FLAGLER

The Flagler was virtually identical to the ACL Champions. The first car was the combination coach with a decorative scheme of soft gray. Upholstery was in blue.

The second car was a 52 passenger chair car with the compartment for the hostess. The color scheme of this car was identical to the first with the exception of the upholstery which was in warm brown tints. The end paneling, as in the other cars of the train, was of figured woods decorrated with two sea gulls in flight in metal relief.

The entire consist of the Henry M. Flagler was transferred to the Chicago-Florida run, and the cars retained their Florida East Coast lettering. The Dixie Flagler is shown here at speed on the Louisville & Nashville Railroad. (Louisville & Nashville Railroad Co.)

The third car was a 60 passenger coach with a color scheme of gray, green and blue on the walls and ceiling complemented with a wine rose upholstery.

The dining car seated 48 passengers and was decorated with walls of deep blue and a ceiling in mist white and buff tan. The dining chairs were upholstered in blue.

The fifth and sixth cars were duplicates of the third car with the exception of the color schemes. In the fifth car the decorations of soft grays, greens and blues set off the rose and tan upholstering. The sixth car contained blue green upholstery with walls finished in deep grey and the ceiling of robin's egg blue. The observation lounge car was identical to the ACL equipment. The color scheme was light gray brown wainscoting, upper side walls of grayed white and a ceiling of burnt yellow. The bar was decorated in a "drum" motif and extended into the car from the after end of the tavern. It was backed by plate glass.

THE SCHEDULES

The original all-coach Champion departed New York at 12:30 PM and arrived at Miami at 1:30 PM the next day. Northbound the Champ departed at 8:15 AM arriving in New York City at 9:15 AM. The Flagler departed Jacksonville at 8:00 AM and arrived in Miami at 2:15 PM. The train had but a 45 minute lay over in which to be turned and cleaned before departing for Jacksonville at 3:00 PM. She arrived in Jacksonville at 9:15 PM and was serviced at that point.

The Flagler lasted but a year on its fast daylight schedule on the East Coast of Florida. In late 1940, the train was shifted to a Chicago-Miami schedule as the Dixie Flagler.

THE CHICAGO-FLORIDA ALL-COACH STREAMLINERS

On December 17, 18 and 19, 1940, three luxury coach streamliners, the Dixie Flagler (the ex-Henry M. Flagler), the City of Miami and the South Wind were placed in operation between Chicago and Miami, Florida. Nine railroads participated in the operation of these three trains that individually ran every third day, thereby providing a daily streamliner service. Up to 1940, this was the fastest daily service ever operated in this territory; and was much faster than trains operated in the territory since that time.

The three trains offered soft individually adjustable reclining seats, a charming tavern lounge observation car and delicious low cost meals in the dining car. The operation represented a unique plan of pooled service which afforded a substantial saving in train miles and equipment. It was a concept that could and should still be used today, not only in the Chicago-Florida market, but in other districts as well.

The new trains were designed to challenge the highway competition. (Does this sound familiar?—and remember this is 1940.) It was estimated that travel between Chicago and Florida in 1939 was 73% highway by private automobile and bus. Although the trains were intended to capture long haul Florida travel, the schedules included numerous intermediate stops to capture local business.

The three routes over which these trains traveled traversed different sections of the middle west and south with the result the new service blanketed a large area without duplication. The Dixie Flagler (owned by the Florida East Coast) operated over the Chicago and Eastern Illinois to Evansville, Indiana; the Louisville and Nashville to Nashville, Tenn., the Nashville, Chattanooga and St. Louis to Atlanta, Georgia; the Altanta, Birmingham & Coast to Waycross, Georgia; the Atlantic Coast Line to Jacksonville and the Florida East Coast to Miami. The City of Miami (owned by the Illinois Central) operated over the IC to Birmingham, Alabama; the Central of Georgia to Albany, Georgia; the Atlantic Coast Line to Jacksonville and the Florida East Coast to Miami.

The South Wind (owned by the Pennsylvania Railroad) operated over the Pennsy to Louisville, Kentucky; the Louisville and Nashville to Montgomery, Alabama; the Atlantic Coast Line to Jacksonville and the Florida East Coast to Miami.

Under the plan of pooled service that was developed, a train departed Chicago each day over one of the three routes, the Dixie Flagler departing Dearboarn Station on one day, the City of Miami from Central Station on the next day and the South Wind from the Union Station on the third day. Although revenues were not pooled, tickets were interchangeable and passengers had complete freedom in the selection of routes, going and returning. With this arrangement, a passenger on his going trip did not have to secure a refund if after purchasing his ticket he decided to change his day of departure or to take another route. He also had a choice of routes returning.

To make the service uniform each train was similar in design and location of cars and all seats were reserved. Each train provided table d'hote as well as a la carte dining car service at popular prices for 1940. For example, breakfast was served for 50¢ and luncheons and dinners for 60¢.

This fleet of streamliners provided the fastest service ever offered between Chicago and Florida —29½ hours. Prior to the new All-Coach trains, the fastest time was 31 hours, 40 minutes for the Dixieland of the Chicago & Eastern Illinois. The new trains departed Chicago around 9:40 AM and arrived in Miami the next day at about 4:10 PM. Returning from Miami the trains departed Miami at 6:25 and arrived at Chicago at 10:55 PM the next evening. With this schedule the trains laid over only 2 hours, 15 minutes at Miami and 10 hours, 45 minutes in Chicago. This resulted in the trains being in revenue service 82 per cent of the time. This type of schedule required a high average speed and exacting operations, especially at the station stops. The Dixie Flagler averaged 48.6 miles per hour for its 1,434 mile run with 17 intermediate stops; the City of Miami averaged 50.6 mph for its 1,493 miles with 25 stops and the South Wind averaged 52.8 mph for 1,559 miles with 16 stops.

Special ceremonies were arranged for the inauguration of these trains by the railroads and the car builders. The press rode the Dixie Flagler from Miami to Chicago, which was greeted by bands and chambers of commerce along its route. A beauty queen group from Florida and Georgia, the Sun Queens, participated in the christening ceremonies in Chicago. This event took place, along with dinner and the public exhibition on December 17th. The train was christened by the "Theme Girl of the Orange Bowl Festival," who broke a bottle of orange juice on the observation car.

The City of Miami was christened with water from Biscayne Bay after a public showing on December 18th.

The South Wind was exhibited in the Union Station on December 16th amidst orange branches and the perfume of orange blossoms. On its first trip south, the train was met by bands, mayors and chambers of commerce.

With the completion of the ceremonies, the trains went into service on one of the hottest assignments in history.

THE DIXIE FLAGLER

The Dixie Flagler was the Henry M. Flagler which had an unsuccessful operation over the Florida East Coast. The schedule virtually duplicated the Champion, and since the train was providing only a Florida service, it was withdrawn to be placed on the Chicago run which was far more successful. The interior of the train was changed very little for the new service, however the motive power came in the form of streamlined steam power. (The interior of this train is described in the section on the Henry M. Flagler.) Pacific type steam power was spruced up and streamlined for the entire route from Chicago to Jacksonville. At that point, the Florida East Coast changed motive power and added the diesel originally built for the train.

The Dixie Flagler proved to be a popular train and profit maker for the roads involved. However, Sleeping cars were eventually added by 1949. The train was discontinued in 1957, and the C&EI no longer participated in high speed streamliner service between Chicago and Florida.

THE CITY OF MIAMI

The Illinois Central's City of Miami was noted for its beauty of line and color, as well as for the provision of comfort and convenience features designed to appeal to the most exacting passenger requirements. The train was designed and constructed by Pullman Standard Car Manufacturing Company. The seven car All-Coach

The City of Miami was one of three all-coach streamliners operated by the Illinois Central. Besides the City of New Orleans (also covered in this book), the IC ran the all-coach Land O' Corn on the Iowa run. (Bob Lorenz)

The City of Miami barrels along at 80 miles per hour near Tuscola, Illinois on May 27, 1942. (Harold K. Vollrath)

streamliner consisted of one baggage-dormitory-coach, one women's coach with nurse's room, three coaches, one dining car and one lounge bar observation car with a total of 254 revenue seats and 135 non revenue seats.

Motive power was supplied by a 2,000 horsepower diesel electric locomotive purchased by the Illinois Central from the Electro Motive Division of General Motors. This engine handled the train from Chicago to Jacksonville. From that point, the Florida East Coast assigned the locomotive from the Henry M. Flagler.

The train received a distinctive decorative treatment by Pullman Standard. Typifying Florida's vibrant colors and tropical background, the exterior was done in orange, palm green and scarlet. The green was also used on the roof and the skirt coloring, separated from the orange of the car body by scarlet stripes placed at the eave and lower edge of the girder sheets. The structure and styling of the power unit was emphasized by a streamline wave effect of green, giving an effect of speed and driving power with the train name lettering in a graceful curve on both sides of the nose. The brilliant flash of the orange, green and scarlet was carried throughout the train to the tail end of the observation car, where the roof color was carried in sweeping lines down to the tail sign.

The interior of the train was decorated with Florida in mind with the use of native woods such as bamboo and sheet cork. In each chair car large photomurals decorate each bulkhead of the main coach compartment. The subject matter was carefully selected for its artistic merit and from a view of creating further interest in that part of the country to which the passenger was going or which he had just left. Comfortable reclining seats were installed and a new style of individually controlled glareless lighting assured further comfort. A twin lens type of fixture was used on the basket rack so arranged that one occupant could read or sleep independently of his fellow traveler. The center lighting was arranged to light only the aisle. Draperies at the windows were in the palm leaf design. Four color schemes

were used in making the coaches different. One was yellow, blue and coral for its major tones, another was green, copper and gold; another was tan, blue and gold; and the last was blue, copper and tan.

The dining car was beige, green and rose as its color scheme and complemented by photomurals, etched mirrors on pier panels and a specially designed carpet in a bamboo pattern.

The observation lounge car, because of its unique floor plan arrangement loaned itself to an unusual decorative treatment. Semi-secluded cocktail sections were placed on either side of the entrance and upholstered in coral leather with yellow piping. This section was separated from the main lounge by bamboo grilles. The main lounge had frieze panels and wainscoting of sheet cork, pier panels of zebra wood and furniture coverings of green, coral and gold with a burgundy colored carpet in a bamboo pattern. The bar section was the real decorative keynote of the train with a natural bamboo bar and canopy against a photomural background and artifical palm tree, fibre floor covering and carved cocoanut masks. The walls opposite the bar are lined with flesh toned mirrors and by, reflection, made this section seem many times larger than it actually was. The back bar had an indirectly lighted mirror on which was sand blasted a tropical fish design in full color and was framed with scarlet and yellow leather matching the under part of the canopy. At the bar was a mural route map of the territory through which the train traveled. It was so arranged that by means of illumination, the progress of the train and the scheduled time of the next stop could be shown.

The observation room had frieze panels of faux-satine flexwood, pier panels of sheet cork and wainscoting of imitation leather. The seat coverings were in blue, coral, and gold, the draperies in blue, tan and gold and the bamboo pattern carpet combined all of these colorings giving the foundation to the color effect. The seating arrangement at the observation end allowed flexibiity for bridge groups to be formed or for placing chairs to suit their individual comfort for reading

The South Wind departs Louisville, Kentucky during the days of steam with one of the L&N's streamlined steam engines that was assigned to South Wind service. The stainless steel consist was painted Tuscan Red by the Pennsylvania Railroad, the owner of the South Wind. (Louisville & Nashville Railroad)

The Delta Eagle can lay claim to being one of the shortest all-coach streamliners. Operated in a sparsely settled territory, the train ran with two cars constructed specifically for the run. The Delta is shown here at Marianna, Arkansas. (Missouri Pacific)

or observing the passing scenery. The writing desk, magazine table, table lamps and tables were all carefully worked out to blend in with the cork and bamboo treatment of the room.

The All-Coach City of Miami was a very popular train and received sleeping cars by 1949. She continued to run on a one night schedule to Florida from Chicago, although not quite as fast a schedule, until the advent of Amtrak. By May 1, 1971, she was the only through Chicago-Florida train left of the original three. However, she was not selected for Amtrak service and the superb Illinois Central service came to an end on that day.

THE PENNSYLVANIA RAILROAD'S SOUTH WIND

The Pennsylvania's contribution to the new Chicago Florida service was the South Wind. Operations began on December 19th, 1940 and it was decked out in the famous Pennsylvania tuscan red with gold striping and lettering. Two K-4s Pacific type steam locomotives were streamlined at the Altoona works of the railroad and finished in a green black with a trim of chromium and gold. The make up was the usual 7 car consist of a combination passenger dormitory baggage car, four coaches, one dining car and an observation lounge car.

The first car of the South Wind contained a 24 foot baggage section, the dining car crews' quarters with 15 berths, a complete washroom with showers and lockers, the steward's room with an upper and lower berth and a passenger compartment with 18 seats (12 reclining). The interior motif was the same as used in the 60 passenger coaches.

The 60 seat cars contained rotating chairs with individual reclining seats and folding center arms.

Each car contained large men's and women's lounges and decorative features were designed by Raymond Loewy. Throughout the train soft gray was used as the unifying color in the interior. In varying tones it appeared on the fascia and pier panels of the coaches and in the cove and dado of the dining and observation cars. Accents of wine, burgundy, blue, and yellow gave character to the neutral background.

The upholstery in the coaches was a soft shade of brown with diagonal striping. The floor was linoleum, sand jaspe with terra cotta striping.

The dining car seated 48 passengers and had an overtone of gray, shades of which were used on the wainscoting and ceilings. The burgundy carpet and patterned draperies gave character to the interior and a luminous note was added by the use of opalescent gray lacquer for the venetian blinds and bulkheads. Other striking centers of interest in this car were the brilliantly colored and amusing cartoons of scenes peculiar to the south, particularly to the Florida resort region.

The Observation lounge car contained 35 deeply cushioned roomy chairs. They had light satin finish aluminum frames and the passengers could move the seats for their convenience. The car contained a radio that could be controlled by the passengers. Forward of the lounge was a club section seating 16 passengers at four tables. Adjoining it was a small but completely appointed kitchen buffet in which there was a small coal range. From this light meals and refreshments of all kinds could be served. It supplemented the dining car service and remained open as long as was required after the dining car closed in the evening. The entire car was very attractive with light blue draperies and the chairs upholstered in mohair fabrics. The carpeting was a deep mulberry patterned in a lighter shade of the same color. The lower walls were a medium gray topped by a light gray on the upper walls.

The train was steam powered all the way from Chicago to Jacksonville. Power was changed at Louisville and Montgomery, Alabama and the FEC's diesel for the Flagler went on the point for the Florida leg into Miami.

The South Wind became a coach-Pullman train by 1949, and was selected by Amtrak. It has since been replaced by a new train called the Floridian on a schedule far slower than the original South Wind.

MISSOURI PACIFIC'S DELTA EAGLE

Of all the Eagles, the most unusual one of them all was the Delta Eagle. It had the shortest regular consist of any of the fleet—just two cars. It served an area that was very sparsely populated between Memphis, Tenn. and Tallulah, La., a distance of 259 miles. It went into service on a route that had not had any previous through train or bus service and could be considered a traffic experiment by the MoPac. And in the beginning, before World War II broke out, the little train was a whopping success.

In early 1940, the Missouri Pacific was deeply involved in plans to expand the Eagle train service that would begin in March, 1940. By mid-1940, the railroad was ready to place an order for a most unusual train. The order went to Electro Motive Corporation for a 1000 horsepower diesel passenger locomotive with a baggage compartment, and to St. Louis Car for two passenger cars. At the same time, the railroad conducted a contest among the employees for a name for the new train. By August, 1940, 313 employees had submitted 117 possible names for the new pocket streamliner. During that month the MoPac selected the name "Dixie Eagle" which had been suggested by 28 people.

As one might guess, more planning needed to be done before the train went into operation. In January, 1941, the railroad changed the name from Dixie to Delta because the new name was more closely related to the rich alluvial country —referred to as the Delta country—through which the train would operate.

The train was placed in service on May 11, 1941, and the MoPac was very pleased with the new traffic the train generated. What made the train service so unusual was the type of territory served. Between Memphis and Helena, a distance of 76 miles, the land was used mostly by cotton plantations and fairly populated. The highways in the area were all-weather roads. The principal towns were Marianna and Helena, with populations of 5,000 and 8,500 in 1940.

South of Helena, a hard surfaced highway paralleled the railroad as far as Snow Lake, a distance of 52 miles. In this section the population was considerably less dense. Beyond Snow Lake, the railroad goes through the delta country of the White and Arkansas rivers. This area was a swampy and inaccessible region in 1940, and did not contain any towns or roads at all. Thirty nine miles south of Snow Lake is McGehee, a railroad junction which had a population of 4,000 people at that time. From McGehee to Tallulah, a distance of 91 miles, the railroad was, and is, paralleled by a trunk highway. Tallulah is located 22 miles west of Vicksburg, Mississippi; and the population was 3,500 in the 1940 census. There were but three principal towns between McGhee and Tallulah in those 91 miles: Lake Village, Eudora and Lake Providence. This gives one an idea of the type of territory the train ran through during the time it was placed in service.

The train itself consisted of three units. The locomotive was a special design 1000 hp diesel electric unit built by Electro Motive Corporation. It was actually delievered to the MP in September, 1940 and was used in regular passenger service between Memphis and Wynne until the new Eagle was placed in service. This special unit contained a 19½ foot baggage section at the rear, and was so built that it could be converted to a 2000 hp passenger if the occasioh should arise.

The two air conditioned passenger cars were designed specifically for the Delta Eagle by the St. Louis Car Company. The equipment was built of low-carbon, high tensile steel and the interior and exterior decorative design was similar to the Missouri River Eagle. The first car was a combination mail and coach car. The front end of the car contained a 15 foot mail compartment. The seating capacity of the car was 60 passengers and included rest rooms for men and women. The second car contained 48 passenger seats and had two lounge rooms. The forward section of the car included a lunch counter grill and two tables seating four each. The counter served three people. The grill not only provided table and counter service, but also provided tray service to individual seats. Despite the small size of the cooking and serving area, the equipment was so arranged that anything from sandwiches to steak dinners could be served.

With the delivery of the new coaches in 1949, the N&W posed a number of the cars with a "J" class Northern type steam locomotive for this publicity photo. (Norfolk & Western Railway)

Prior to going into service, the train was put on display for five days during the period April 30th to May 10th. In most of the towns and villages along the route, the entire population turned out to inspect the new train. The train also made six trips into Memphis carrying good will tourists from various towns along the line. The MoPac commented that business men of the area reacted very favorably to the new train, and the company felt that the public relations benefits of the six trips and displays were very great.

After the good will tours and exhibitions, the train was placed in service on May 11, 1941. The single train made one round trip per day with a mid-day layover of several hours for servicing in Memphis. Her round trip mileage was 518 miles (259 miles one way) and the average speed for the initial time schedule was 40.3 miles per hour. The train was not a speedster, shall we say in terms of a Zephyr or a Hiawatha, but for the type of railroad line it operated over and the type of service provided, it did very well. Initially, the MoPac set the top permissive speeds as follows:

Rock Island Jct. to Marianna	60 MPH
(RI Jct. is located just outside Memphis.)	
Marianna to Lexa	65 MPH
Lexa to McGehee	55 MPH
McGehee to Tallulah	50 MPH

The schedule of the train was arranged to be of the most convenience for the local towns as possible, and also in regard to connections with other MP trains. Leaving Tallulah and the other towns served in Louisiana and Arkansas, the Delta Eagle arrived in Memphis at 12:35 PM. It did not depart on its southbound trip until 4:30 PM and arrived back in Tallulah at 10:55 PM. The residents of the 33 towns served could leave home in the morning, spend four hours in Memphis, and return home that evening.

The new Delta Eagle was tied in with through schedules. On the northbound trip, the MP train from New Orleans, Alexandria and Monroe made close connections with the Eagle at McGehee. At the same time the train gave Eagle passengers a connection for Pine Bluff, Little Rock, and other points. On the southbound trip, the Eagle exchanged passengers with a southbound train from Little Rock to New Orleans at McGehee.

The Delta Eagle also made connections with the Missouri Pacific Transportation Company bus to and from Greenville, Mississippi, a town with a population of about 15,000 (1940 census) on the east bank of the Mississippi River. This connection enabled people in Greenville to board an air conditioned bus at 7 AM and to make a connection with the Eagle at Lake Village. A similar service was offered southbound which enabled travelers to return home to Greenville at 10:25 PM. This bus service, by the way, also extended to Dermott and McGehee. This arrangement enabled passengers to transfer at Dermott to MoPac trains to and from Monroe, Alexandria, New Orleans, Pine Bluff, Little Rock and St. Louis. Thus the new Eagle service to the Delta country opened up a whole new travel arrangement, which heretofore had not been available.

A five car Powhatan Arrow whips along the double track main line near Blue Ridge, Virginia in September, 1951. (Bert Pennypacker — Harold K. Vollrath)

World War II curtailed much of the supplementary service on the Delta Eagle. The train was slowed down, and meal service was discontinued. The period after the war did not actually show a come back. In 1949, the train departed Tallulah at 4:30 AM and arrived in Memphis at 11:30 AM. Southbound, she departed Memphis at 4:00 PM and arrived at Tallulah at 11:20 PM. Instead of a 6 hour, 25 minute schedule, it was a 7 hour, 20 minute run. By 1952, the train's run had been shorted or cut back to McGehee, a distance of 168 miles from Memphis. The train departed Memphis at 4:00 PM and arrived at McGehee at 8:40 PM. Northbound, she departed McGehee at 5:30 AM and arrived at Memphis at 10:15 AM.

Later in the 1950's, the train was discontinued as an Eagle altogether. She was reduced to a local plug run between Helena and McGehee. Even that local disappeared by the early 1960's. All remnants of the once sparkling and snappy Delta Eagle had disappeared.

THE POWHATAN ARROW

The Norfolk and Western Railway placed a daylight all-coach train in operation between Norfolk and Cincinnati on April 28, 1946. The original train, named the Powhatan Arrow, ran as a companion train to the Pocahontas through the same territory. She was equipped with a mixture of 1941 constructed streamlined coaches and rebuilt heavyweight dining, lounge and other coach equipment. However, the N&W was not satisfied with that type of a consist and the train was totally re-equipped in 1949.

The new equipment comprised of two 10 car train sets, built by Pullman-Standard. Each train consisted of one combination coach-locker car, one two-compartment coach, five full coaches, two dining cars and one observation lounge coach car. (Two dining cars did not become standard operating procedure, although that was the original intention.) Power for the new train came in the form of a Class J, 600 series 4-8-4 streamlined steam locomotive. These locomotives were designed by the N&W to haul heavy passenger trains in mountainous territory and were capable of high speeds on straight level track. The streamline effect of these locomotives was enhanced by their high-gloss black color set off by a rich Tuscan red stripe running the entire length of the locomotive and tender. Lettering and borders on the stripes were of bright gold. These locomotives maintained exceptional availability records and were highly dependable. The N&W normally assigned about 15,000 miles to each locomotive per month. The actual utilization averaged about 60% and the maintenance cost in 1949 dollars was about 20 cents per mile. The Class J developed 5300 horsepower and were able to handle trains up to 15 cars unassisted over all parts of the N&W with the exception of the 2% grades between Williamson and Bluefield, West Virginia.

Five of the seven coaches had a seating capacity of 58 people, while the other two were divided, one to provide space for a smoking area, steward's quarters and a locker for the dining car crews, and the other to provide two passenger compartments. This car provided 42 seats in one section with 24 in the other area. The combination car featured a smoking room with individual chairs for 8 people and sat 40 passengers in the main coach section.

There were spacious men's and women's lounges in all of the coaches and all lighting was flourescent with individual lights conveniently located in the overhead baggage racks.

Heavy baggage was stored in baggage compartments near the vestibule entrance of each car, while the overhead racks were available for hand baggage and hats and coats. Electrically cooled drinking water was available at the end of each car.

The main passenger section in the combination coach had a ceiling of light tan and wall tones in a medium green. The window shades were a gold tone textured material and seat coverings were deep brown with a chevron pattern. The floor under the seats was mahogany brown rubber tile. The main aisle strip was green marbleized tile.

The general colors were tan and brown in the two-compartment coach. The bulkheads in this coach were covered in a beige corded synthetic leather and photomurals worked out in gold tones were used on either side of the entrance doors. These murals were interesting photos of scenes along the N&W.

The N&W purchased a fleet or coaches prior to the Second World War for general service, and were assigned to the Powhatan Arrow in 1946. This particular coach, as well as seven others, has been rebuilt into 82 seat cars for the Chicago-Orland Park service. (Pullman Standard)

A second group of streamlined cars was built in 1949, this time specifically for the Powhatan Arrow. This photo shows a 68 seat divided chair car. N&W passenger equipment was truly superb with its Tuscan Red and gold color scheme plus a glossy black roof. (Norfolk & Western Railway)

The other five coaches contained three different color schemes. One was finished in tan and brown, two were done in a gray and cedar combination and the others in a blue and brown combination.

The lounge rooms in these five cars were done in tan and blue with light tans on the ceilings. The walls were medium tan and the window shades were light blue. Chairs were upholstered in brown and the floor covering was a blue marbleized rubber tile.

All coach seats were rotating and reclining and spaced on 41 inch centers. Individual free-turning foot rests, covered with rubber, were provided on the back of the seats to give the ultimate in foot comfort in any of four different adjustments.

All coach end doors were electro-pnuematically controlled. Slight pressure on the door plate on the outside or a slight pull on the door handle on the inside opened the doors automatically. Door action was timed to conserve conditioned air within the coach.

The dining cars could seat 36 passengers each and were finished in a combination of yellow, gray and red. The seat coverings were done in a special red needlepoint material and the carpet was a deep red tone Hooksett type. A striking effect was introduced in the dining room by the use of flesh tinted mirrors on the backs of which were etched designs in gold. Colorful Venetian blinds added to the overall decorative designs. Kitchen equipment included ranges, steam tables, broilers, electric dishwasher and garbage disposal unit, frozen food lockers and cup and plate warmers.

The Observation lounge tavern car was divided into a number of sections: a lounge, seating 12;

Interiors of the 1949 group of cars featured picture windows, reclining seats, and soft pastel colors. (Norfold & Western Railway)

Interior of Powhatan Arrow dining cars featured table seating for either two or four, picture windows and a complete selection of meals. (Norfolk & Western Railway)

Exterior of dining car No. 491, constructed in 1949 for the all-coach Powhatan Arrow. (Norfolk & Western Railway)

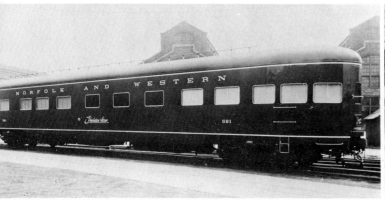

Observation lounge cars brought up the markers end of the superb streamliner and added a graceful end to a totally streamlined train. (Norfolk & Western Railway)

Table and lounge seating permitted passengers to play cards, write letters, enjoy one another's company, or just watch the scenery pass by. Such club lounge facilities were still rare for coach passengers in 1949. (Norfolk & Western Railway)

tavern lounge, seating 24; bar; pantry; hostess room; and a observation lounge, seating 16 for a total capacity of 52 passengers.

The lounge section was divided from the tavern lounge in the middle of the car by using wing partitions in which Lucite was used to separate the sections. The ceiling was done in light apricot and the walls in gray rift oak. Wall coverings were a synthetic leather in a corded design. The seat covering was in blue with darker blue carpeting. Table tops were in a blond wood Formica with inlays done in red and black.

The open bar featured the tavern section with the bar front worked out in a diamond design of red leather with a yellow leather piping. The bar top was in yellow Formica and ornamental flesh tint mirrors were installed at the back bar. A photomural depicting an N&W scene was also used on the back central portion of the bar.

The observation lounge could seat 16 passengers in individual chairs. This section had ceilings of light apricot and walls of medium blue.

The bulkhead at the forward end of the lounge featured two water color paintings with the sea as the subject. The same dark blue carpet used in the forward end of the car was used again in this section. Lighting was of the direct and indirect type for reading and general illumination. This section also featured a writing desk and a magazine rack.

One would normally expect to find a car such as this one available to Pullman passengers only. Not so on the N&W. The car ran on the Powhatan Arrow for a number of years before being placed in storage because of declining patronage. The diner was later modified to include a small lounge. The Powhatan Arrow became a Domeliner with ex-Wabash Railroad dome coaches in the late 1960's (see *The Domeliners*, Superior Publishing Company, 1973). The train remained an all-coach streamliner, despite the inclusion of standard head-end cars, until it was discontinued in 1969. The "Arrow" goes down in history as being one of the finest all-coach trains in the east.

THE PERE MARQUETTES

In August, 1946, the Pere Marquette (part of the Chesapeake & Ohio System) operated a pre-inaugural run of a new all-coach streamliner, The Pere Marquette. People turned out in large numbers between Grand Rapids, Lansing and Detroit to watch one of the first post war streamliners go by. Following a newspaper trip and christening ceremonies at the Fort Street Union Station in Detroit on August 6th, the train made several trips over the next three days carrying business men and state officers of Grand Rapids, Detroit and Lansing. The trains were placed on display in those three cities prior to regular service, which began August 10th.

The trains began service with a time schedule of 2 hours and 40 minutes for the Detroit and Grand Rapids on their morning and evening runs from both terminals including stops at Plymouth and Lansing in both directions. The distance from Detroit to Grand Rapids is 152 miles. The mid-day run of the new streamliner was made in three hours with eight intermediate stops.

The Pere Marquettes featured a number of new things not normally found on trains. For example, attractive waitresses formed the staff of the dining cars. No tipping was permitted in the dining cars which was an experiment originated by Robert R. Young, chairman of the board of the Chesapeake & Ohio.

Another innovation on the Pere Marquettes was that passengers could make advance reservations and pick up tickets and seat accommodations on the train without waiting at station ticket windows. All the passenger had to do was

The Pere Marquette Railroad was named after the Roman Catholic priest who was both missionary and explorer in the Great Lakes Region. Therefore it was most appropriate that the Pere Marquette (later the C&O) would name their new streamliners the Pere Marquettes. The trains had one thing in common with the Crusader — an observation car at both ends of the train. (Chesapeake & Ohio Railway)

to telephone any Pere Marquette office and make the reservation in advance.

Passenger representatives aboard the train saw to the seating of the passengers in accordance with the reservations shown on the diagram and sold the necessary tickets. When requested, the representative could make arrangements for return reservations on the same basis.

The Pere Marquette, by the way, was and is the only streamliner to run entirely within the state of Michigan.

Dining car rooms were equipped with the triangular seating arrangement, which has proven very popular over the years. The C&O (Pere Marquette) employed waitresses in the dining cars instead of the usual male waiter. The unusual table arrangement was very comfortable to sit in, and was one of the points that made Pere Marquettes so very popular in the late 1940's. (Chesapeake & Ohio Railway)

Coach accommodations were of the sleepy hollow type. Tables for coach seats were available. This photo shows the observation room at the rear of the two end coaches, which contained both table and sofa seating. These were highly unusual coaches, and were seldom duplicated on other lines. (Chesapeake & Ohio Railway)

An Electro Motive Division diesel locomotive, with a horsepower rating of 2000 and a top speed of 117 miles per hour, was assigned to the seven car all-coach streamliners. The first car was a mail and baggage car, and a full baggage car was next in the consist. The third car was an observation lounge coach with 56 passenger seats plus 10 in the lounge. The fourth and sixth cars were full coaches, while the fifth car was a dining car and the last was an observation lounge coach. The observation cars were operated in the same way as the Crusader, and therefore, turning of the train was not necessary at either Detroit or Grand Rapids. The mail and baggage cars were simply switched from one end to the other, the locomotive turned and the train was ready to go.

Each coach was equipped with a spacious powder room and lavatories as well as a luggage compartment and electrically refrigerated drinking fountain. A loud speaker outlet could be used to transmit programs from a master radio in the dining car or, by simply turning a switch could become a public address system for making announcements to passengers.

The interior decorative treatment for the two full coaches utilized tones of tan, while the other two coaches were painted with tones of green with window drapes, upholstery and carpeting harmonizing. Large photo murals, depicting actual scenes along the right-of-way were finished in a gray-green monotone to harmonize with interior color schemes. These murals were displayed on bulkheads between passenger compartments and lounge sections of all coaches. The exterior decoration included the roof, window bands, and the trucks finished in blue. Below the windows and in the center of the car above the windows were car length stainless steel bands. The name "Pere Marquette" was blazoned on maize color letter boards in stainless steel script letters. The coach seats were of the Sleepy Hollow type spaced 41½ inches on centers to give ample leg room and providing for a wide range of adjustments of back and foot rest positions. This seat was developed as a result of studies of 3,867 people who were measured to determine the scientific seating requirements and postures of the average man and woman passenger. Eight measurements were taken of each person and then checked against experiments with three chair forms in which people were invited to sit. Lighting was provided by both ceiling lights over the aisle and reading lights in the baggage racks over the seats. Dim blue lights were incorporated in the center ceiling fixtures for night operations.

The Meadowlark began as a four car streamliner, but its consist often expanded to six or more cars. When that happened, a standard car would be part of the consist breaking the otherwise fully streamlined all-coach train. The Meadowlark is shown here passing Englewood, Illinois in September, 1949 with 7 cars. (Harold K. Vollrath)

The C&EI operated a companion streamliner to the Meadowlark, which served the Indiana side of the railroad. This train, the Whippoorwill, began operation between Chicago and Evansville, Indiana on November 10, 1946, a little more than a month after the Meadowlark began service. The 7 car streamliner is shown here at Vincennes, Indiana. The consist included a mail-baggage-tavern-coach, four 60 seat coaches, one 36 seat dining car and one parlor observation car. (Chicago & Eastern Illinois Railroad)

The Whippoorwill too carried a larger consist than originally intended, and lost her streamliner status. Despite her fast schedule, the traffic was not to be had and the deluxe coach-parlor car train was discontinued in late 1949 on the Evansville run. (Harold K. Vollrath)

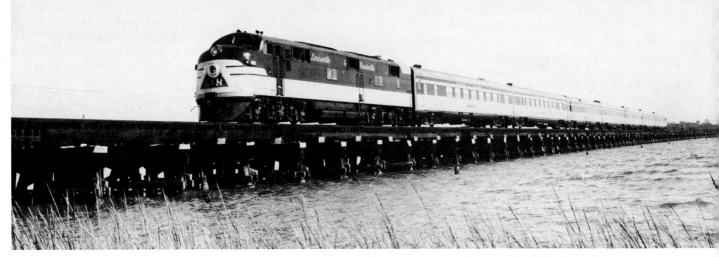

The All-Coach Humming Bird crosses Biloxi Bay during its first year of operation in early 1947. (Louisville & Nashville Railroad)

The dining car contained a number of unusual features. For example, the kitchen was centrally located and flanked by the dining rooms, each for 22 people. The seating arrangements were also triangular instead of the usual type of seatings.

The original plan for three round trips was reduced to two, although by the late 1950's, the C&O did run three round trips daily. However, the late night run was actually a mail run. The C&O added parlor car service to the Pere Marquettes by 1950, and the trains lost their all-coach status. The original Pere Marquettes were withdrawn from service with Amtrak.

THE MEADOWLARK

The Chicago & Eastern Illinois Railroad placed in service a high speed all-coach streamliner on October 6th, 1946 between Chicago and Cypress, Illinois. This four car train provided fast daily service between Chicago and southern Illinois and made it possible for residents of the latter to travel to Chicago in the morning, have plenty of time for shopping and business and return home in the evening.

The four car streamliner consisted of one 2,000 horsepower diesel electric locomotive built by Electro Motive Division of General Motors, one combination mail, baggage and grill-room car and three coaches. The grill was designed to serve 20 people at a time, while each of the 60 seat coaches featured reclining seats, individual seat-lighting, wide-paned windows and mirrored or muraled partitions.

The train was exhibited at 13 cities and towns in southern Illinois from October 2 to October 5th.

Following the close of exhibition at West Frankfort at 9:30 PM, October 5th, the train ran as an extra to Cypress to start the initial trip of its 345 mile run to Chicago on October 6th.

Originally, the Meadowlark was scheduled as trains 25 and 26 and departed Cypress at 5:15 AM and arrived in Chicago at 12:25 PM. South bound the train departed Chicago at 5:10 PM and arrived in Cypress at 12:20 AM. The train was scheduled to make 19 intermediate stops between terminals in each direction including two flag stops. In 1956 an RDC car was assigned to the run and the train was discontinued in 1962.

THE HUMMING BIRD AND THE GEORGIAN

In November, 1946, the Louisville & Nashville and the Nashville, Chattanooga and St. Louis Railroads joined the ranks of post-war all-coach streamliner operators. On the 17th of that month, the two roads placed in service the Humming Bird between Cincinnati and New Orleans and the Georgian between St. Louis and Atlanta. And as one might expect, the two trains were again the ever popular 7 car all-coach train sets.

These two trains were the first of new post-war streamliners to be run in the southeast. They were, in a way, symbolic of the faith of the managements of the L&N and the NC&StL in the future of the south at that time.

World War II brought many military encampments to the area because the mild climate was more conducive to intensive troop training. The war also brought a large number of industries and people to the area, and the railroads had to make

The Georgian consisted of equipment identical to the Humming Bird with the only differences being in the road names on the diesel power and passenger equipment. This photo of the Georgian shows the initials of the L&N and N.C. & ST. L on the nose of General Motors E-7 passenger diesel, and also on the letter board of the passenger cars. To this writer's knowledge, this is the only case where a joint operation displayed car ownership in this manner. (Louisville & Nashville Railroad)

changes to accommodate the shipping and traveling public. The new streamliners reflected that ability to change.

The Georgian operated over the L&N between St. Louis and Nashville and over the NC&StL (now merged into the L&N) betwen Nashville and Atlanta. The total distance between terminals is 611 miles. There were morning departures and evening arrivals at both terminals on a schedule of approximately 13 hours. The fastest previous service was 18 hours and 5 minutes. The Georgian supplied not only the first through daylight schedule, but also cut more than five hours from the running time.

The Humming Bird operated over the L&N between Cincinnati and New Orleans, a distance of 922 miles. The Bird departed each terminal about noon and arrived in the opposite terminal early the next morning. Including 13 intermediate stops in each direction, the scheduled running time was 19 hours compared to 23 hours, 30 minutes for the fastest train up to that time.

Each train consisted of five coaches, one dining car and one tavern lounge car. The total revenue seating capacity was 298 passengers with 48 seats in the diner and 52 in the tavern lounge. The exterior color treatment was royal blue.

Each coach could seat 60 passengers with the exception of one coach which could accommodate 58 people. This particular car was equipped with a 10 passenger smoking lounge at one end of the passenger section. This section replaced 12 regular seats. All seats were individually reclining and revolving so that passengers could take full advantage of the full vision 60 inch picture windows. A loud speaker system for music and announcements was provided in each of the seven cars. There were large and spacious lounge rooms

for men and women including stainless steel encased twin lavatories with soiled towel space beneath large mirrors and a vanity for women passengers.

The interior color schemes of the coaches was developed in varying shades of red and brown. Soft henna was in the upholstery, working into a plum shade at the wainscot, and rose bulkheads were set off by a pale ivory ceiling. The window panels were of anodized aluminum with delicate beige drapes between the windows. Soft shades of green were used in the men's lounge and salmon in the women's lounge with dark green curtains lending added privacy. Each lounge was equipped with a deep-cushioned sofa, the men's upholstered in a reddish brown and the women's in chartreuse.

An electric water cooler was recessed in the end partition of the men's lounge at one end of the passageway. Nearby was a roomy compartment for the storage of luggage with pillow storage space immediately above. Photo murals of points of interest along the L&N System were located on the partitions at each of the passenger compartments. Each mural had a caption and was bordered by an aluminum molding.

The dining car contained seats for 48 people at 12 tables adjacent to the wide full-vision windows. In the partitions at each end of the dining room were full-length plate glass mirrors. The color scheme was built around harmonious and varying shades of reds and browns with fawn colored upholstery and rich-hued dark maroon carpeting. All of these blended into ivory walls and ceiling. There were cocoa drapes at the sides of the windows.

The tavern lounge cars were arranged in two sections, the lounge section seating 28 passengers

The City of New Orleans was one of three all-coach trains on the Illinois Central. This particular train ranked high in the luxury class of long distance trains, and was just as popular as the overnight All-Pullman Panama Limited on the same route. This photo was taken during the late Fall of 1970 on a Wednesday and the short 7 car consist reflects the middle of the week traffic demands. Train No. 1 is shown here at Homewood, Illinois. (Patrick C. Dorin)

and the tavern section with accommodations for 24. These two areas were separated by a completely equipped curved bar. At the tavern end were men's and women's rest rooms and lockers as well as the train conductor's office which housed the train loud speaker and amplifier-system controls.

The lounge presented an interesting grouping of deep lounge chairs and two place sofas. The room was divided into three intimate groupings by glass partitions.

The tavern section included four built in brown-leather-upholstered horseshoe shaped seats at each end, and seats for four passengers arranged around tables on each side of the car. This area was set apart from the bar section by an etched figured glass partition.

The color scheme was warm and pleasing to the eye including shades of red in the carpeting with chartreuse and rust in the lounge chairs. The wainscot was light green working into a lighter green at the piers and frieze and terminating in a cream ceiling.

One of the interesting things about the Humming Bird and Georgian was that neither train was successful as an all-coach train. By 1948, the Georgian was rescheduled to operate between Chicago and Atlanta as a coach-Pullman train. The train then began turning in a profit, not only for the L&N but also for the Chicago & Eastern Illinois who handled it between Chicago and Evansville. For awhile, it was the best money maker for the C&EI, but it too eventually fell prey to the automobile and was discontinued from Chicago in 1968, and the St. Louis connection came off in 1971. The Georgian ran as an all-coach train for a scant two years.

Meanwhile the Humming Bird did not turn a profit either on its Ohio-Gulf of Mexico run. The

L&N added a Pullman Sleeping car, but the train did not achieve black ink status until moved to a Chicago-New Orleans routing via the C&EI to Evansville in August, 1951. The Humming Bird also had a very short career as an all-coach train. She was discontinued on the Chicago run in 1968 and she finished her days in 1969 running on the same route, Cincinnati-New Orleans, where she began her career as an all-coach train.

These two trains can probably claim a world's record for their brief operation as a high speed all-coach streamliner. Neither train is known for its all-coach operation, but it is significant that each train did not become a profit making venture until Pullmans were added. This is the exact reverse of most operations where all-Pullman trains had coaches added to them to improve their financial standing. It is for this reason that the all-coach Humming Bird and Georgian should be remembered.

THE CITY OF NEW ORLEANS

On April 27th, 1947, the Illinois Central placed in operation a new all-coach streamliner with equipment so comfortable, convenient and interesting that even a full day's journey would not be tedious. The new train operated on a daylight schedule between Chicago and New Orleans on a record all day run of 921 miles in 15 hours, 55 minutes, which was 35 minutes less than the overnight companion train, the all-Pullman Panama Limited. The new all-coach streamliner also made available equally fast service between St. Louis-New Orleans and Louisville-New Orleans. There were a total of 19 regular intermediate stops in the run between the Windy City and Gulf Coast.

Train No. 1, the City of New Orleans, arrives at Homewood, Illinois just moments before a cloud burst. As the train departed the clouds let loose with a real down pour. Yet the train departed and continued on its way — ON TIME — demonstrating the all weather dependability of railroad transportation. (Patrick C. Dorin)

The City of New Orleans consisted of two 14 car trains powered by three 2,000 horsepower diesel electric locomotives. The make up of the train included one mail and express car, one baggage-dormitory car, two 48 seat coaches, seven 56 seat coaches, one dining car, one diner lounge car and an observation tavern lounge car. Departing Chicago the train carried 11 cars and picked up one coach from St. Louis at Carbondale and two more from Louisville at Fulton, Kentucky for a total of 14 into New Orleans. The reverse operation was followed on the northbound trip.

All of the coaches for the train were constructed by Pullman-Standard, while the other cars were out shopped by the Illinois Central's Burnside Shops (Chicago). The exterior color scheme consisted of the now *world famous* orange-brown-yellow combination which identified the Illinois Central. These brilliant colors could be seen at a great distance and provided additional safety factors in the high speed operations.

The train was powered by diesel locomotives, built by Electro Motive Division of General Motors, which were geared for 117 miles per hour. However, the high maximum speed was not as important to the maintenance of the scheduled running as was the ability to accelerate rapidly, to travel long distances without stops for fuel and/or servicing and to take curves faster with safety.

The coaches were equipped with unusually wide, 62 inch windows of double thermopane, shatterproof glass being used. All cars were insulated with fiberglass and stonefelt.

It is interesting to note that the coaches for the City of New Orleans were equipped with high-speed electro pneumatic air brakes including a governor and decelostat control for the prevention of wheel slippage. Cars were provided with air controlled sanding equipment which was operated automatically in conjunction with the wheel slide control. This resulted in a substantial savings in flat wheels caused by excessive brake applications.

The coach seats in the 56 seat cars were spaced 41½ inches apart between centers to give ample leg room and to provide a wide range of adjustments for back and foot-rest positions. A button adjusted the back of the seat to nine different positions. The foot rest on the seat ahead could be adjusted to four positions.

The two 48 seat coaches in each train were constructed with Day-Nite features which provided many of the comforts and conveniences of first-class travel. For sleeping comfort, the seats were spaced 52 inches apart between centers giving passengers an opportunity to stretch out with their feet and legs supported at seat level by an upholstered leg rest pulled down from the back of the seat ahead. Spacious women's lounges with double toilet facilities were located at one end of each coach with an equally large men's lounge at the other.

Reading lights were in the overhead baggage racks and were equipped with two lenses over each cross seat. One was designed to give light for the window passenger, the other for the aisle passenger. Each lens supplied a high-intensity beam at the reading level for one passenger without overlapping to the adjacent passenger or others seated to the rear or forward. Each light had an individual switch so that passengers could read without disturbing any neighbor.

In order to obtain maximum light in the aisles without disturbing passengers or causing conflicting light beams, magnifying prism-lens glass was employed in the coach ceiling lights which projected a narrow beam of light the width of the aisle. This fixture also gave a soft, diffused light for the ceiling and upper portion of the car.

At night when the main ceiling lights were turned off, night lights incorporated in the aisle side of the seats near the floor threw a dim light on the aisle way which was sufficient so that people could move about without any difficulty, yet not bright enough to interfere with sleeping.

The dining cars of the City of New Orleans were richly decorated in natural wood backgrounds. One diner contained walls finished in walnut while the other was done in mahogany. The seating capacity of each diner was 36 people. The diner lounge car contained a lunch counter for ten passengers, cocktail booths for eight and a large open section for 22 passengers. The diner lounge car also contained quarters for the train stewardess.

Background colors of the observation-tavern-lounge cars were predominantly blue and yellow. Chairs and seats, with a total seating capacity of 48, were upholstered in both fabrics and leatherette and informally arranged. Windows were 62 inches wide. Murals depicting levees, docks, cotton fields, battle scenes and picturesque New Orleans decorated the observation-tavern-lounge and the dining cars.

Radios, installed in the observation and diner lounge cars provided music and other entertainment. A public address system was installed throughout the train and could be used to make announcements. Broadcasts from the master radio could also be heard in all cars over the public address system. The dining car, dining lounge car and observation were rebuilt from heavy weight equipment.

Other cars included a baggage dormitory, which by the way included a 25 foot baggage section, a 6 foot linen room and a 29½ foot dormitory with lounge, locker and wash room facilities for a 20 man dining, diner lounge and observation crews. The car also contained a 6½ foot stewards room and a 7 foot conductor's room with wash and toilet facilities. The dormi-

tory, steward's and conductor's room on this car were air conditioned.

The Illinois Central maintained high standards for the City of New Orleans from its beginning to Amtrak. Although in the last few years the train lost its observation car, the train carried dome coaches for a short while too. The final scheduled running time southbound was 17 hours, 30 minutes, and northbound it was 17 hours, 35 minutes. The train was selected by Amtrak but was later retired in favor of the new Panama Limited. The City of New Orleans ranks as one of the nation's finest trains, a fine tribute to the Illinois Central management.

THE CITY OF MEMPHIS

On May 17, 1947, the Nashville, Chattanooga and St. Louis Railroad placed in service a shining new blue and grey "City of Memphis" between Nashville and Memphis, a 239 mile run. The train was scheduled to make a daily round trip making the run in five hours in each direction. This was faster by 1 hour, 50 minutes than any previous eastbound train, and 1 hour and 25 minutes for any westbound operation.

Like the Powhatan Arrow, the new all-coach streamliner departed from the usual 7 car set-up. This steam powered speedster consisted of one mail and baggage car, one coach-lounge dinette, one dining-tavern car, two coaches and one coach-lounge-observation car. The train provided coach seats for 194 passengers not including 48 seats

The City of Memphis was one of a small number of all-coach streamliners that were powered by steam. Here the City picks 'em up and lays 'em down with a seven car consist (one more than usual with a rebuilt standard coach behind the mail and baggage car) near Nashville, Tenn. (Louisville & Nashville Railroad)

The Hi-level El Capitan, the Santa Fe's most modern all-coach streamliner, departs Los Angeles for Chicago. Note the dormitory-baggage car which has been rebuilt for hi-level service. (Santa Fe)

in the dining-tavern car, 18 in the lounge-dinette and 21 in the observation-lounge section. No seats were reserved.

The entire train was designed and built by the company's Nashville shops. The locomotive was a Pacific type with a streamlined shrouding.

The coaches featured air conditioning, wide vision windows matched to pairs of reclining seats with foam rubber cushions, foot rests and individual lighting. Baggage compartments at each end of the coaches supplemented the steel

Trains are a great place to hold parties and business meetings. Here a business firm holds a dinner meeting aboard the Starlight. If one stops to think about it, what better place to hold a meeting, with no phones ringing or other interruptions. In this case, the dining car tables were rearranged for a more business like meeting arrangement. (Southern Pacific Company)

and aluminum overhead baggage racks. Washroom facilities included wash basins, dental basins, and illuminated mirrors with electric razor outlets. A sectionally controlled public address system was used for announcing stations, pointing out scenic areas, meal times and radio programs. A number of the cars carried photo murals depicting scenes along the City of Memphis' route.

The schedule of the train was enhanced by its connections at both terminals. For example at Nashville the train connected with the all-coach Georgian to and from Chattanooga and Atlanta; and with the Louisville & Nashville's Pan American. The train also connected with the Rock Island's Choctaw Rocket, Missouri Pacific's Sunshine Special and the Cotton Belt's Lone Star at Memphis. Despite the daylight and extra fast schedule, and the numerous connections, the City of Memphis was not particularly a successful train. She is significant because of being an entirely new schedule with rebuilt equipment and for the type of service offered. She was discontinued in 1958 after serving the traveling public for 11 years.

THE STARLIGHT

Southern Pacific placed in service a first class overnight coach service between San Francisco and Los Angeles in 1949 with a new train, "The Starlight." Equipped with the 1937 Daylight consist, she departed San Francisco as train No. 94 at 7:45 PM and arrived at her destination the next morning at 6:45 AM. Her northbound running mate, train No. 95 carried an identical schedule for the 470 mile run.

All seats were reserved and a special service charge of $1.00 was made for each chair car seat occupied by an adult or child of any age. A passenger agent was assigned to the train as well as porter service for all chair cars.

The consist of the train included a Coffee Shop Snack car which remained open all night for the convenience of passengers. Today (1974) Auto-Train offers a comparable all night type of service. A tavern car offered passengers club lounge service as well as place to play cards and enjoy companionship.

The Starlight was a fine way to travel between San Francisco and Los Angeles, but by 1957 not enough coach passengers were making the trip. It was decided that year to combine the All-Pullman "Lark" with the Starlight, and the train lost its identity as a separate train. The Starlight was not alone with this type of combination procedure. The B&O's Columbian lost its all-coach status in the same way.

Although the Starlight ran for only about eight years, she will be remembered by Californians (who were not addicted to the automobile) as the companion train to the Lark. It is interesting to note that the Starlight's name was selected by Amtrak for the new San Francisco (Oakland) — Seattle train service — another Southern Pacific Route.

THE HI-LEVEL EL CAPITAN

The Santa Fe placed in service the hi-level El Capitan in 1956, and although there have been many beautiful all-coach trains, the hi-level El Capitan must rank as one of the finest, if not the finest, all-coach train ever operated. It was born during the so-called light weight, low center of gravity era. Many railroaders felt that the Santa Fe was barking up the wrong tree with a hi-level train. However, the Santa Fe has a reputation for making wise decisions with its transportation services, and the Hi-level concept was very sound.

As we pointed out in chapter 1, the Santa Fe experimented with two hi-level coaches in 1954. Passenger satisfaction led to the construction of a complete train.

With the double deck arrangement, and the elimination of vestibules, each car could seat as many as 28 more people than in a regular single level transcontinental Santa Fe coach. Seven hi-level coaches can seat approximately 496 passengers where as eight single level El Capitan coaches could accommodate only 350 passengers.

Entrance doors are located on both sides of each directly in the center of the car. As a passenger enters he or she can place their luggage in the space adjacent to the door way, or the porter can handle it for them. There is just a short stairway to the coach compartment which extends the full length of the upper level. The lower level also includes the washrooms, air conditioning equipment and auxiliary power units.

All coach seats were, and are, leg rest reclining seats of foam rubber and covered in a handsome blue needlepoint. However many of the cars either have or will have new upholstery under the Amtrak service, and the passenger may not find the blue needlepoint. Carpeting, under Santa Fe's direction, was a special cactus design and colors of the Indian Southwest prevailed in the new hi-level cars. This carried on a tradition from the original El Capitan born in 1938, which incidently was a five car train rather than the usual seven car all-coach streamliners of that time. All cars carried a fully equipped public address system for recorded music, radio programs and train announcements.

The dining car was a masterpiece of construction. All kitchen work was confined to the lower floor and food and beverages were delivered by means of a dumb waiter elevator. The hi-level dining car combined all of the advantages of a double unit or an articulated dining-kitchen car into one compact car that could serve up to 80 people at one time. This is another reason why the hi-level design or concept is such a strong one. The lounge car was described in *The Domeliners*. However, this lounge can serve eighty six passengers on her two levels. The lower level is known as the Kachina coffee shop which is named after religious activities of the Hopi Indians of the Southwest. Part of these festivities included an all night bean dance. This area includes seats for 26 passengers and contains a refreshment bar, newsstand, and rest rooms.

The Santa Fe placed the new hi-level El Capitan in a public exhibition from June through July, 1956. The train was displayed not only on Santa Fe points from Chicago to Los Angeles, but also in Washington, D.C., Pittsburgh, Youngstown, Cleveland and Detroit.

The new train went into service "officially" on July 8, 1956 when trains 21 and 22, the westbound and eastbound El Capitans, met at Albuquerque, New Mexico during the 250th anniversary celebration of that city.

The hi-level cars are exceptionally quiet riding. Part of this was accomplished through the use of sound-deadening materials in the linings of the side and end walls of each car. This was a selling point for passengers that returned time and time again to ride the El Capitan between Chicago and the Southwestern United States.

Originally the El Capitan consisted of a storage mail car, baggage car and a dormitory baggage adapter car. This particular car included a built up roof line for the purpose of smoothing out the lines of the train. A 68 seat Hi-level chair car with step down stairway at forward end, Two 72 seat cars without step down stairs,

one hi-level dining car, one hi-level lounge car, three 72 seat chair cars without step down stairs and one 68 seat car with step down stairs at rear end. Later the mail storage car was removed from the consist. Trains 21 and 22 continued to operate separately until 1958, when the El Capitan was combined with the Super Chief except during peak travel periods. However there was one great difference with this combination. The El Capitan section remained intact with its own dining and lounge facilities, and the same held true for the Super Chief. Consequently, the El Capitan continued its own operation and did not lose its identity. This system of operation continued with Amtrak, although the name El Capitan no longer appears in the time tables. The Santa Fe was proud of its train service, and never allowed it to deteriorate. Because of the Santa Fe's positive attitude, one could say that it was entirely expected that the Company would develop the World's most luxurious *All-Coach* train.

The Hi-level El Capitan represents Santa Fe's finest efforts for long distance coach service. The Santa Fe Railway has long been known for being one of the nation's finest railroads, and the El Capitan reflected that image until Amtrak day in 1971. To this writer it is a bit sad that Santa Fe no longer operates the El Capitan (indeed the name is no longer in the Amtrak time tables) as it is shown here climbing toward the crest of Raton Pass in colorful southern Colorado near the famous Wooton Ranch. The Santa Fe certainly deserves the distinction and the recognition of having operated the finest all-coach streamliner in the World. (Santa Fe Railway)

CHAPTER 6

Local Trains

The turn of the century could possibly be considered the peak of local train travel. These trains were in operation over every rail line, to every town and hamlet and there were no locations without rail service. A village had to be very small to rate only "flagstop" status for a local passenger train.

The local train provided service for everybody. In those early days, salesmen by the score rode the trains to every village and town to sell their goods. Often the hotel was right across the street from the depot, and the salesman did not have far to go. The local was also the way to travel to Grandma's house or to the farm for the day, weekend or over the entire summer. The local was dependable and carried with it an atmosphere that no other form of transportation could equal. That atmosphere could be summed up in just one word, "friendly." Everyone knew each other in the local's territory. The conductor and trainmen were often carriers of various bits of news and gossip. For example, if Martha Jones was going to get married, the train was the vehicle on which the news would travel from one part of the county to the other. If the conductor knew that someone was going to ride the train on a certain day, and that person was late, the train would wait. Can you imagine that? The railroad local passenger train, and the depot in each village, were literally the center of life — next to the family, church and barber shop and somehow they were all intertwined. People rode the local to church, school, picnics, parties (indeed, even parties onboard the train), shopping and sometimes just for the heck of it. No one could know that the automobile would change all that.

Local trains could be classed in three ways: branch line runs, connecting trains for thru services and main line locals. To further complicate the picture, many limited trains were reduced to local status after numerous consolidations took place on a given section of railroad. An example of this phenomenon would be the Soo Line's Atlantic Limited.

Most local passenger trains consisted of steam locomotives of the ten wheeler, Atlantic or light Pacific types (4-6-0, 4-4-2 or 4-6-2 respectively),

a baggage car or mail and baggage car and a coach. There were numerous variations of the theme and trains often included a combination coach and baggage car, several head end cars or coaches and possibly a cafe coach if the train ran any distance. Other locals, especially later in the 1930's and 1940's and even the 50's, consisted of gas-electric doodle bugs and Rail Diesel Cars. The consists were always simple and the atmosphere unhurried and friendly. It felt good just to ride those trains, an aspect of American life that may be lost forever.

Many branch line locals were totally independent of other trains or bus runs. An example of such a service was trains 183 and 184, branch line locals between Ashland, Wisconsin and Bayfield. These daily except Sunday trains of the Chicago, St. Paul, Minneapolis and Omaha Railroad made 6 stops in each direction over the 25 mile route. They simply provided a service between Ashland and Bayfield for passengers on the line. They did not connect with trains for Chicago or Minneapolis or from any point. This pair of trains, and others like them, can be called independent branch line locals.

The second type of local was the connecting train for thru runs. This was simply a train that ran to and from a junction providing a connection between secondary main or branch line points and main line points. One such branch line operation was the New Lisbon-Woodruff, Wisconsin Hiawatha-North Woods Service of the Milwaukee Road. Although during part of the history of this particular train through cars were handled, most of the time it was simply a connecting train. At times the train even included cafe and parlor car service. Another example was the Northern Pacific gas-electric runs throughout North Dakota and Montana. These trains ran from main line points over various branches after connecting with main line trains, such as the North Coast Limited. There were hundreds of such connecting trains, not only on the Northern Pacific, but on every railroad in the country.

Mixed trains too sometimes provided a connection service. Frequently they not only made a connection with a main line passenger train, but also with a freight that operated about the same time as the passenger run.

A few railroads operated Rail Diesel Cars over branches. The NP operated one out of Spokane and the New York Central ran such a car to Bay City and Saginaw in Michigan.

Every railroad operated main line local trains. One of the longest runs this writer can think of was trains 1 and 2 on the Canadian Pacific Railway between Montreal and Vancouver. This train operated before the Domeliner Canadian was placed in service, and provided local coach, mail and express service over the entire route of the Dominion. Another such run was trains 13 and 14 on the Santa Fe between Chicago and Kansas City. This pair of trains literally made every stop in the 451 mile overnight run. Very few through passengers would elect to ride this train.

One might be asking what purpose did these main line local trains have? Basically, it was two fold. First, it relieved the limited trains of burdensome head-end traffic. The second reason is succinctly stated in the November 5, 1948 issue of the Soo Line Passenger Train Time Tables.

"IMPORTANT NOTICE — Passengers using Soo Line Limited trains, holding tickets to destinations at which such trains do not stop, must leave fast train at last scheduled stopping point of such train short of destination, and use local train to destination."

The Soo operated locals with the Soo-Dominion, Mountaineer and Winnipeger along the entire route from St. Paul to Noyes, Minnesota and Portal, North Dakota.

Short distance main line locals often provided the same type of service. These were locals that ran for 100 miles or less, and were shorter in consist than the long distance boys. Where the

One of the last purely local trains of the older style (that is not downgraded through trains) to operate from Chicago was Rock Island 21 to Peoria, shown ambling into South Side Englewood Union Station in August, 1949 behind a clean medium sized Pacific of the type also pulling most of the Rock Island's suburban trains of the era. (Jim Scribbins)

The New Haven was literally loaded with local passenger trains. Many looked like this one barreling through the snow with an Alco road-switcher, one mail and baggage car and four coaches. (J. W. Swanberg)

Chicago Great Western motor car 1009 burbles away from Grand Central Station beginning its stop infested trip to Oelwein, Iowa. The red and maroon color combination arrived with the diesels and the baggage cars were the only streamlined equipment purchased new by the Great Western. This motor train was CGW's last Chicago passenger service and was one of the few doodle-bugs to operate from the Windy City, others in the 1940's being the Santa Fe Pekin branch train and a CB&Q run to Rockford which was handled on the rear of steam-powered suburban trains east of Aurora. The date of this photo is September 15, 1949. (Jim Scribbins)

A few locals carried names even though they were never anything but a local run. Here the Western Pacific's Feather River Express, with a short four car consist, rolls through Sacramento behind ten wheeler No. 83 in July, 1942. Only a wisp of smoke comes from the stack as the little steamer makes easy work of the train which does not have a troop movement on this beautiful but WAR torn July day. (Harold K. Vollrath)

110

GM&O train No. 9 operating from Bloomington, Illinois was the former Alton Route's last passenger schedule across its Kansas City line. The rear of the motor car had once carried coach accommodations, while the trailer was a combination RPO-coach. The coach section had large rear windows with facing seats and an open platform in the best "limited" observation style. Here the two man crew examines their train orders during the Jacksonville, Illinois stop; and later on in Missouri, through passengers will have the opportunity to enjoy good box lunches specially catered to the bright little train. April 14, 1959. (Jim Scribbins)

long distance train would include several head end cars and two or three coaches, and perhaps even a sleeper, the short distance brother normally carried only one or two cars, with three being the very most. However, there were exceptions to every rule. For example, the Western Pacific's Zephyrette, a long distance local between Salt Lake City and Oakland, ran with a single RDC-2 combination baggage coach car. On the other hand, some short distance locals on the Chicago and North Western and Pennsylvania Railroads carried a substantial number of head end cars. The traffic requirements dictated the consist.

The coaches operated on these trains were usually cars that had been bumped from the limiteds. The cars were nearly always equipped with straight back seats, and reclining seat cars were the exception rather than the rule. Nevertheless the trains provided a service over thousands of miles of railroad that is no longer available in the United States. To find such service in 1975, one must travel to Canada or Mexico.

There are two other types of local passenger trains of major significance. These locals would be more appropriately called a hybrid instead of a pure local. As passenger patronage declined over the years, equipment and service requirements also diminished. The result was a combination or consolidation of trains. Some locals were combined with a freight train and the result was

Pretty little Pacific 1107 of the Duluth, Missabe & Iron Range hustles train 6 from Winton to Duluth a mile south of Lakewood, Minnesota in the near dusk of May 30, 1947. The rear coach had a solarium and illuminated signs designating the railroad and train. (Jim Scribbins)

Pacific No. 402 powers train No. 2, from Hibbing to Duluth over the Missabe Division of the DM&IR in March, 1957. The train is passing Garfield Avenue en route to the Duluth Union Depot and is operating over Northern Pacific Railway tracks at this location. (Wayne C. Olsen)

The steam powered local was replaced by an RDC-3 purchased by the DM&IR in December, 1952. Train No. 6 is approaching Duluth in July, 1953. (Harold K. Vollrath)

The RDC-3 was also assigned to the Duluth-Hibbing run, and on Sunday evening August 11, 1957, the car had some modest trouble. So on Monday morning, a stream train substituted for train No. 2 between Hibbing and Duluth. Up ahead was heavy 4-6-2 No. 400 and the Solarium and signs more than made up for the lack of air conditioning. The DM&IR maintained this train at Hibbing in the event of difficulties with the RDC, which had a rather tough assignment with daily round trips between Duluth and Winton and Duluth and Hibbing. (Jim Scribbins)

111

The DM&IR operated connecting local trains for main line runs 1 and 2 from Iron Junction to Virginia and Eveleth. The train made two round trips per day. Numbers 12 and 11 connected with south bound No. 2, while 13 and 14 met No. 1 at Iron Jucntion. Here Pacific 1110 wheels a wooden combination car and a coach as train No. 12 en route to Iron Junction from Virginia in October, 1947. (Harold K. Vollrath)

The Northern Pacific operated connecting trains for the North Coast Limited between Logan, Helena and Garrison, Montana while the North Coast itself operated via Butte. Here the west bound train awaits the arrival of the North Coast before departing for its local run to the Montana State Capitol. The train is a typical local in every respect. (Harold K. Vollrath)

a mixed train. Although this generally occurred on branch lines, it frequently took place on the main line. Again it was traffic requirements that governed the choice. On the other hand some locals were consolidated with fast or limited trains. Usually this meant that the limited train assumed the local's head-end work and schedule. Often the train retained the name "Limited" although it no longer could be considered such a train. The result was that the former fast train became a much slower train, which in turn drove more passengers to the automobile, airline and bus services. Most of these consolidations took place during the Depression in order to save on train miles, engine and train crews and equipment requirements. There are literally countless examples of these hybrids. When the Chicago & North Western's Ashland Limited between Chicago and Ashland took over the local work, her schedule lengthened from 12 to 15 hours — a three hour addition almost all of it sitting at various stations. With the Depression being what it was, it was about the only

Another connecting train was the Rock Island's Rocket Jr. This car was rebuilt from a standard gas-electric motor car to a diesel electric, painted a maroon, red and aluminum color scheme to match the regular Rockets, and the interior was fitted with comfortable seats, air conditioned and painted with soft pastel colors. The car ran a vigorous schedule by making three round trips daily from Peoria to Bureau, 47 miles, where it connected with main line trains. In the photo engineer Ted Scott waves a friendly greeting as he wheels by at 70 miles per hour. (Paul H. Stringham)

At the final stage of its career, the Will Rogers had become the daytime local between St. Louis and Oklahoma City on the Frisco. University City is one of the post-war coaches built for the Meteor and other important trains, and on the head end is named diesel unit No. 2007 "Whirlaway." The photo was snapped on May 20, 1955 at Newburg, Missouri, the location of Fort Leonard Wood. The train carried no brakeman or flagman. When asked if he had to do his own flagging, the conductor replied that they did not flag in CTC territory. (Jim Scribbins)

Northwestern Pacific's SD powered local "Redwood" train No. 4 is stopped briefly by a slide in the rain-soaked Eel River Canyon north of Spyrock, California in February, 1957. The baggage car also contained a large coffee maker and the attendant had enough sandwiches and pastry to keep the riders from becoming hungry. (Jim Scribbins)

alternative the railroads had in reducing costs especially in low density traffic areas.

The mixed trains generally carried a single combine, or a baggage car and a coach either on the head-end or rear end of the freight section. If the passengers were carried behind the engine, a caboose usually brought up the markers end. Head end operation was generally an inconvenience to train crews because it meant that the passenger equipment had to be set out at the depot before they did their freight work. If they kept the passenger cars coupled to the engine, the passengers were jostled and shaken during the switching operations at each stop. It was far easier to carry the passengers on the rear end of the train.

The hybrid-local/limited, on the other hand, benefited with improved coach accommodations. In some cases this meant reclining seats or bucket type seats, depending upon the railroad. It also meant improved washroom facilities, not to mention a dining car or a Depression style cafe lounge car.

Under the present Amtrak operation, there are no hybrid local/limited trains in operation. They had all but disappeared from the scene by May 1, 1971 when Amtrak went into operation. Such trains are, however, still in operation on the Canadian National in eastern Canada. As for mixed trains, with the exception of the Georgia Railroad in the United States, one must also travel to Canada for such train service. Indeed, one Canadian mixed train is a tour in of itself and even has a name. (See Chapter 12)

Although many people grumbled at the slowness of the local, these trains seem to say "take it easy," "slow down, the world will not run away." But Americans were in a hurry, too much of a hurry for the local. The local became part of American History, and we lost it because we wanted to go faster and faster in our daily life. The family no longer can ride the "local" to a picnic. We will never know what we truly lost — until we have no gasoline to run our automobiles.

The Lehigh Valley Railroad took advantage of the RDC for local passenger runs. By the time this photo was taken in the late 1950's, the local had but all been deserted for the automobile — except for days like this one when the snow came down thick and fast. The photo was taken at Hazletown, Pennsylvania by Bob Lorenz.

Southern Pacific, often accused of downgrading passenger service by the late 1950's still cared enough to operate an ex-Sunbeam/Hustler Pullman Standard built divided coach (in which the smokers and non-smokers were effectively separated) on its subsidiary Northwestern Pacific. In the style of the much more important "Daylights," the name of the three trips per week isolated local was applied to the coach. (Jim Scribbins)

Built by St. Louis Car and powered by a 600 HP EMD engine, Seaboard Air Line 2028 was handling the Bocca Grande local round trip in March, 1959, when it was snapped awaiting departure from Tampa as train 321. It survived the SCL merger and was the power for the Lakeland-Naples, Florida Champion connection until Amtrak day, May 1, 1971. It was constructed in 1936, and at the time of this photo it supported the attractive SAL alligator green and yellow with red trim — freight diesel colors. (Jim Scribbins)

The Northern Pacific equipped trains 55, 56, 57, and 58 between Duluth and Staples, Minnesota with RDC-3 cars. The B-41 is shown here at Staples after completing the day time run from Duluth. This particular train connected with the west bound Mainstreeter and also provided through connecting trains, a day time run between Duluth and Winnipeg. The same arrangement held true with the east bound operation. The night runs 57 and 58 connected with the North Coast Limited. (Bob Lorenz)

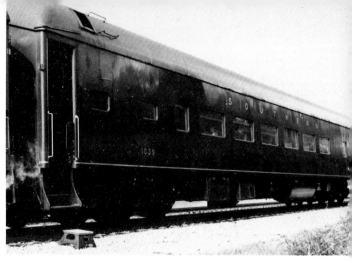

Local branch line connecting trains could be complicated at times. Here it is just past 8:35 AM on a drizzly damp morning in Jamestown, North Dakota in the mid 1950's. In the background we see train No. 3, a head-end traffic accommodation run en route from St. Paul to Glendive, Montana. In the foreground, we have the B-19 which will depart at 9:05 AM as train No. 157 en route to Leeds, North Dakota. The gas-electric in the rear will depart at 9:20 AM as No. 147 en route to Wilton. The Wilton branch leaves the Leeds line at Pingree. East bound, trains 148 and 158 connect with train No. 4 at Jamestown. It is also interesting to note that the NP operated a mixed train on the Turtle Lake Branch (Which leaves the Leeds line at Carrington) that connected with train No. 157. The NP also operated another pair of local trains to and from Oakes, North Dakota, Numbers 154 and 155. These also connected with No. 3 and 4. (Bob Lorenz)

The Southern Railway's Royal Palm is another example of a limited train that eventually evolved into what might be called a quasi-local primarily for mail and express. Originally a Detroit-Florida streamliner in 1951 with thru service to Miami and a Hostess-Train Passenger Representative for coach passengers; the full consist of the 1967 version carried but one coach. Further trains 3 and 4 had lost their name. This photo shows Southern rebuilt standard coach No. 1039 bringing up the rear of train 3, which ran only between Cincinnati and Atlanta in 1967. However, the train carried a coach porter for the single coach in addition to the conductor and brakeman. Good box lunches were ordered in advance while on the train and placed aboard at an intermediate station. Thus despite the loss of business and downgrading of the train, the Southern still offered First Class coach service. (Jim Scribbins)

Duluth, South Shore & Atlantic Railway train No. 2 arrives at St. Ignace with its RDC-1, which was not only number 500, but also named the "Shoreliner." To this writer's knowledge, the DSS&A and the WP were the only two roads to name their RDC's. The DSS&A RDC-1 now operates for parent Canadian Pacific Railway. (A. Robert Johnson)

The Soo Line operated a number of trains that were once Limiteds and evolved into locals. Even the mighty Winnipeger was a local for a good deal of its run. Other thru trains that became locals ran on the Minneapolis-Chicago run (5 and 6), Chicago-Duluth (17 and 18), Minneapolis-Sault Ste. Marie (7 and 8) and Minneapolis-Portal (13 and 14). (Harold K. Vollrath)

One of the more unusual local passenger services was offered by the Western Pacific prior to the 1960's. All freight trains except symbol freights SWG (154), or CAL (155) would handle passengers between Keddie and Bieber or to and from intermediate points. The above freight trains would not handle passengers to or from intermediate points. This photo shows train 153 at Halls Flat, California in the late 1950's. As only 145 passengers rode the trains from 1953 thru 1959, the California Public Utilities Commission authorized the discontinuance of the passenger tariffs on October 26, 1959. (Bob Larson)

The interior of Southern 1039 was fully the equivalent of any non leg rest streamlined coach and rode very well. (Jim Scribbins)

Passengers on WP freight trains generally rode the caboose. Although passengers were carried only on the Fourth Subdivision of the Western Division, the trains originated at Stockton Yard on the Second Subdivision of the main line. Here Baldwin switch engine No. 581 puts the caboose on symbol freight NCX, which will run as train 156 on the Fourth Sub and perhaps even a passenger may board the train at Keddie. (Collection of Patrick C. Dorin)

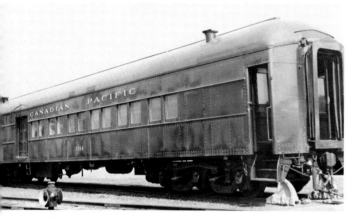

The most typical type of passenger equipment found on the mixed train was the combine, such as Canadian Pacific No. 3314 shown here at Penticton, British Columbia in August, 1960. (Stan F. Styles)

The Soo operated combines with vestibules at each end and equipped with caboose hand rails for mixed train service. (Patrick C. Dorin)

The more customary way that passengers rode freight trains was the "Mixed Train" which was really in a class all by itself. They came in different consists depending upon what part of the country you were in. In the North Woods you would see something like Chicago & North Western mixed train Extra 899 east rolling toward Antigo, Wisconsin. This train on the day the photo was taken, carried four cars of pulpwood and one combine after completing a turn on the Crandon Branch. The train originated at Antigo at about 5:30 AM and ran as an extra west to Pelican Lake. It departed Pelican Lake for Crandon at 6:30 AM as train No. 711. The running time to Crandon was one hour for the 17.5 mile run. The crew was allowed 45 minutes for switching and the making up of train No. 716 before returning to Pelican Lake. The train is shown here passing Elcho en route to its home base at Antigo during the summer of 1951. (Jim Scribbins)

Wooden combination car No. 402 served as coach service on various WP mixed trains, and later served as a caboose on way freights on the San Jose Branch. The photo was taken at San Jose in 1949. (Harold K. Vollrath)

The Soo Line and Wisconsin Central operated a fleet of local cabooses over their system lines. These cars, some fitted with coach seats, were operated on freight trains on various branches (such as Eau Claire, Wisconsin) and on certain main line segments, ie., Rhinelander to Sault Ste. Marie. This caboose was photographed at Trout Lake, Michigan in August, 1972. (Patrick C. Dorin)

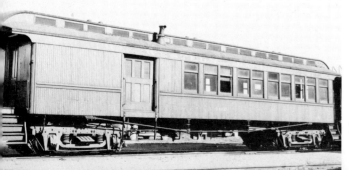

On a number of occasions the long distance local from Minneapolis to Chicago on the Omaha and Chicago & North Western Railroads would stall on the hill at St. Paul. Then the General Yardmaster at East St. Paul yard would dispatch an 0-8-0 to help No. 508 up the hill as you see here in this photo of August 9, 1955. Train No. 508, by the way, operated on a 14 hour, 20 minute schedule for the 409 mile run via Madison. 508 and its running mate, No. 501, rated a name, "The Viking," and carried a substantial amount of head-end traffic. (A. Robert Johnson)

The last Soo Line locals across North Dakota were trains 13 and 14. This particular train was photographed on June 29, 1963. The following year she had been discontinued and replaced by a mixed train service. In 1962, the train still carried an 8 section, 2 compartment, 1 drawing room sleeper. The year before that she was the famous Mountaineer running as long as 20 cars and 2 section operations were not infrequent. During that time the Soo operated still another local (trains 1 and 2) across the state of North Dakota. Soo Line 13 and 14 clearly show the rapid decline from limited status to local that took place all too often in the 1950's and 1960's. Train 13 is shown here at Minot in 92 degree heat. (A. Robert Johnson)

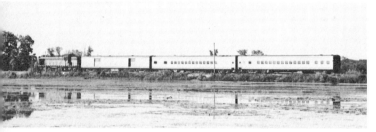

One of the more famous connecting train locals was the North Woods Hiawatha (or Hiawatha-North Woods Service if you prefer) between New Lisbon, Wausau and Woodruff, Wisconsin. Trains 202 and 203 connected with the Afternoon Hiawatha in both directions at New Lisbon for either the Twin Cities or Chicago. This photo by Jim Scribbins shows train 203 powered by an Alco RSC-2 (orange and black) with a 1934 Express car and two 1942 Hiawatha coaches (all yellow). The train is just north of the Necedah depot on July 25, 1959. (Jim Scribbins)

After the Afternoon Hiawatha was discontinued in early 1970, connecting local trains 202 and 203 were retimed and ran as passenger extras to connect with the last Hiawatha (trains 5 and 6) at New Lisbon. This photo shows the passenger extra connecting from No. 5 arriving at Wausau on September 1, 1970, with a consist of one FP-7 and one 1948 coach. (Jim Scribbins)

The southbound passenger extra en route from Wausau to New Lisbon to connect with Hiawatha train No. 6 passes Necedah (flag stop) with a single FP-7, one 1942 built coach and a 1948 coach on September 2, 1970. (Jim Scribbins)

A very rare local indeed was the Chicago Great Western's Minneapolis-Omaha trains. The trains regularly carried cement hoppers from Mason City to Dodge Center. The northbound is setting out at Dodge Center on May 15, 1965. (A. Robert Johnson)

The Milwaukee Road's Afternoon Hiawatha (on the right) passes the hybrid local/mail & express train No. 58 at New Lisbon, Wisconsin on July 25, 1966. (A. Robert Johnson)

CHAPTER 7

Commuter Trains

Of all the railroad passenger train services, commuter service has been almost 100% pure coach. To be sure, there have been some parlor car services such as on the Long Island's All-Parlor Car trains (still in service in 1974), and the Erie's Tuxedo. There has also been a number of private club commuter services where an individual pays an additional fee for special car traveling. Most of these types of operations could be found on the New Haven and the Chicago and North Western Railroads. Although some of these cars were former coaches, many were modified club lounge or parlor cars for the new private operation.

Basically, commuter service has been the operation of trains to and from the suburbs of large cities for people working in the downtown business sections. This means that a large part of the motive power and coach fleet and station facilities are run at capacity from about 6:30 AM to 8:30 AM and from 4:00 PM to 6:00 PM from Monday through Friday. This adds up to a grand total of 20 hours per week. Traffic is substantially lighter during all other time periods of the week. Because of this, the railroad companies have generally been in a tough situation with providing a large physical plant that is in full use only a small fraction of the entire week. This has produced substantial deficits.

Basically, commuter train trips are now quite comfortable in air conditioned streamlined coaches. It turns out that people commuting by train can save up to $200.00 or more per year in gasoline, parking, insurance fees and tires not to mention wear and tear on the car and one's nerves. Driving to work can be a real headache and more often than not, it is slower than by train. However such comfort and convenience has not always been the case. Only recently has such service been available.

Commuter train service has been in existence since before 1860 on a number of railroad lines in the eastern cities, Chicago, San Francisco and elsewhere. People in those early days had the same reason for catching the 7:15 AM as people do in 1975. It is a very convenient way of going to and from work, shopping or for pleasure in the big city. However, it was not always convenient or as nice as it is now.

Commuter coaches have historically been the hand me downs from main line service. In some cases, even former sleeping cars were stripped and equipped with flip over seats for commuter service. Prior to air conditioning, smoke and cinders often filled the cars on hot summer days. Open end coaches were in use even up to the 1950's. Aside from the historical significance of the equipment, they did nothing for the temperament and happiness of the people they were supposed to serve. The railroads had a monopoly up until 1920 or so, and the commuter trains were relatively profitable. After 1920 a number of events were going to take place that would change completely the commuter profit picture. Furthermore, the hand me down coaches would continue to remain in the picture of commuter train until a radical new design went into service in 1950.

The first event was the automobile and the new bus lines. These modes of transport were to cut into the railroad patronage almost immediately, particularly during the non-rush hour periods. This in turn brought a second event that is still plaguing the railroads. Most of the suburban passenger business is concentrated in two two-hour periods per day, the morning and evening rush hours. This means that nearly all of the equipment and facilities, as well as train crews, are idle nearly 20 hours every week day and even more so on weekends.

The result was that the profit picture slipped away, and a third event, the Depression, caused the problems to become even more pronounced. This in turn led to an attitude on the part of the railroad managements that the commuter operations were a hopeless situation, and they only ran by virtue of the State Regulatory Commissions. And even at that many services would die off completely by around the middle of the Twentieth Century. Los Angeles, St. Louis and New Orleans are but three examples.

World War II arrived and there was no way that any commuter operation problems could be solved during that time period. Besides, some of the problems dissipated during the war with gas rationing and no tires. After the war, people returned to some old habits, bought more and more automobiles, inflation sky-rocketed and most of the railroads tried in vain to raise fares to keep pace with rising costs. To further complicate matters, raising fares only served to drive more people to their autos; and motive power and rolling stock were in need of major repairs and/or replacement because of excessive war time use. The coaches were anything but comfortable, and the railroads and the commuters themselves were caught in a vicious circle. So they left the trains, took the car and a new vicious circle started as expressways, multi-story parking ramps and the simultaneous break down of both intra and inter urban trolley and bus systems sacrificed the cities and dissolved the tax base.

Meanwhile people that recognized that the train was the only way to go to work still rode in the old standard coaches. Aside from some light weight electric coaches built for the New Haven in 1938, and some re-building of cars by some lines; there was not to be a breakthrough in suburban coach design until 1950 when the Budd Company delivered 30 double deck streamlined coaches to the Burlington Route. These air conditioned beauties set a new standard in commuter coach comfort and style. Further, they reduced operating costs for the railroad because of the higher passenger capacity (in excess of 150) and lower rental costs in the Chicago Union Station. The seating was designed for the appropriate comfort index for suburban train travel. A major technological advancement had been made, and it set the stage for another Chicago railroad to show the world that commuters could mean a profitable operation.

Before we get into that particular operation, several railroads around the U.S.A. began re-building coaches and ordering new cars for commuter service in the early 1950's. In fact, the Chicago, South Shore and South Bend Railroad had rebuilt some of their cars right after World War II. The Rock Island purchased a fleet of 20 streamlined coaches in 1950. The New York Central, New Haven, Susquehanna, Reading, Long Island and the Canadian National all went to the car builders for new equipment around 1950. Although this equipment represented an improvement, the over all situation continued to deteriorate. In fact, this situation continued to exist for nearly all commuter lines right up until the early 1970's when relief from the States and the Federal Government began to pour in. And then this relief only began after people began to realize that the expressway craze could not go on, and still keep the city together. During this entire time, there was only one bright star on the horizon and that star was the Chicago and North Western Railway.

As we stated previously, the C&NW's commuter service was, and is, the brightest star in the commuter world. The railroad not only modernized its service with streamlined double deck Pullman Standard built coaches, but operated with a profit against overwhelming odds. Indeed, the city of Chicago and the state of Illinois is indebted to the C&NW for the service they have performed, and still are in 1975.

The C&NW has been operating a suburban service in the Chicago area since 1848. It was this service that provided the incentive for suburban population growth since the Civil War. During those early days, it was the C&NW service that made it possible for people to move out into the fresh country air as little as five miles from downtown Chicago. And it gave those early Chicago commuters a sense of punctuality.

Commuter or suburban trains have gone through a variety of styles since the 1850's, when such service began. This photo shows a Chicago & North Western suburban train at Williams Bay in 1896. Note the baggage cars and open end wooden coaches as well as the size of the 4-4-0 steamer. (Harold K. Vollrath)

Twenty five years later, equipment had changed only slightly. The steam power was heavier, but the C&NW was still using wood open-end equipment almost exclusively. This train was photographed at Wheaton, Illinois in July, 1921. (Harold K. Vollrath)

From those early times through 1955, the suburban service was provided largely with displaced steam power and down graded main line coaches. This condition existed on the C&NW, as well as other railroads, until 1961 when the modernization program was completed.

The service presently provided in the 1970's on the C&NW is generally recognized as one of the most modern in North America. Although not all of the problems have been solved, the service has gone through a major transformation since 1955 when the first streamliner coaches were purchased from St. Louis Car. Passengers ride in modern double deck coaches and the service is steadily attracting more and more riders. The significant point of all is that the service is operating on a profitable basis without a subsidy.

As most people know, the C&NW's service as recently as 1956 was in serious difficulty, financially and otherwise. Equipment was very old and obsolete. Locomotive power was a mixture of diesels and some 40 steam engines. Breakdowns were frequent and financial losses were exceeding $2 million annually. It was this situation that faced a completely new management, headed by Mr. Ben W. Heineman, when it took over the direction of the Company on April 1, 1956.

From that point on things began to look up. For example, 40 days later the commuter service was completely dieselized. At the same time, the company undertook a study to determine if there was a need for a soundly operated rail service to the suburbs on the three C&NW commuter lines. Despite competition from the new expressways that were under construction, it was found that indeed there was a need for a sound rail service. As a result of the research, the company assembled a modernization program and presented it to the Illinois Commerce Commission for its approval in late 1957. The Commission granted the railroad's requests almost in their entirety and the following was placed into effect in December, 1958:

1. The closing of 22 of its 88 commuter stations, almost all located within the city of Chicago. The railroad's studies showed that a substantial amount of service was being provided within Chicago, duplicating service already provided by the local city mass transit system.

2. A completed revision of fare structures, tickets and collection procedures was instituted for a three fold purpose of (a) establishing the entire suburban ticket structure and fares on the price of the

monthly commutation service as the basic type of transportation provided by the suburban service; (b) providing a ticketing system which had as its purpose an efficient collection of fares and the minimizing of cheating, and (c) establishing a price system resulting in commuters buying tickets related to need rather than haphazard price differentials which had developed through historical accidents. For example, 10 and 25 ride tickets were selling at substantially reduced rates at some stations, even though they were not in fact commutation tickets. The railroad replaced the old ticket system with a new one whereby it offered unlimited ride monthly, semi-monthly and weekly tickets which required no punching. In addition, it retained the one way and round trip tickets as well as a 25 ride convenience ticket booklet. The pricing policy followed was a complete reversal of historical practices in that the monthly unlimited ride ticket, rather than the one-way ticket, became the base, and all other tickets were priced to have a reasonable relationship to the basic monthly ticket, which on a per ride basis, carried the lowest rate.

3. Fares were increased 24 per cent.

While the C&NW was revamping its fare structure and the number of stations served,

the company was simultaneously taking steps to improve equipment. When the new management reviewed its suburban coaches, it found it had more than 400 cars, all conventional in design ranging from 30 to 40 years of age. Many were down graded long distance coaches with very low seating capacities.

The previous management had purchased 16 double deck coaches in 1955, and 32 more arrived on the property in 1956. The seating capacity of these cars ranged from 161 to 169 passengers. It was apparent that the double deck design was the direction the railroad should go with its equipment modernization program. However there was still one more problem concerning the trains and coaches that the North Western was determined to solve.

The C&NW's Chicago Terminal is a stub end station where every arriving train that came in had to be backed out or switched for out-bound movement with a consequent loss of time. The company was convinced it could achieve increased flexibility and efficiency if one of the chief advantages of rapid transit trains could be applied to the diesel powered trains. That is, a cab at each end of the train in order to eliminate switching and/or turning of power. The North Western's management believed that the same thing could be done with its diesel powered commuter trains whereby the locomotive would always be at the same end of the train regardless of its direction

The late 1920's saw the first steel equipment going into service, but that was the only real change that took place until diesels arrived in the 1950's. This photo shows a non-rush hour Chicago and North Western Railway suburban train at Kenosha, Wisconsin preparing to depart for Chicago in October, 1949. The first coach is a hand me down from the main line limiteds, the second and third cars were built by American Car and Foundry especially for suburban service. This photo could actually cover the time period from 1928 to 1955 when this consist could occur. (Harold K. Vollrath)

From 1955-1960 on however, dramatic changes took place in suburban service, not only on the C&NW but other lines as well. Double deck equipment went into service that was not only economical but pleasant to ride in. The latter is a quality that each car must have if passengers are going to desire to ride in the car again. This photo shows a C&NW rush hour train departing the Chicago Depot with an ex-Union Pacific "E" passenger unit leading a General Motors F-7 unit on the head-end of a long train. (Chicago & North Western Railway)

of movement. The company envisioned control cabs in its trailing coaches. In such cabs, the engineer would have the same controls as were available in the diesels at the opposite end of the train. Electric transmission lines would connect the controls in the coach cab with the diesel locomotive at the other end. The outcome of the careful thought was the famous "Push-Pull Trains" now in operation over the C&NW commuter lines.

The first push pull trains were ordered in 1959 when the company purchased 36 double deck coaches from Pullman Standard. These, incidentally, were the first to go into operation anywhere and this type has been adopted by other railroads. In January, 1960, the company ordered 116 more cars. These were all delivered by the Fall of 1961 when the transition from 417 conventional coaches to a new fleet of 200 double deck cars was completed. While the suburban fleet was completely modernized in 1961, the railroad has on several occasions purchased additional

coaches to meet increasing patronage. In 1971 the C&NW owned 280 double deck cars, 64 of which were equipped with cabs.

The C&NW commuter streamliners were built with the accent on comfort. The exteriors of the coaches, which are 15 feet, 10 inches high, are decorated in the sharp C&NW yellow and green. Inside the seats are cushioned in foam rubber and posture formed. Walls and ceilings are in light pastel colors that need never be painted. These colors are in vinyls of various textures permanently bonded to the steel interior linings. The vinyls are extremely durable and, unlike paint, do not peel, crack or discolor. In fact, there is no paint at all in the interiors. Exposed metal surfaces are either in stainless steel or aluminum. Continuous fluorescent lights run the full length of each car, both on the upper and lower levels. The result is that shadows are non-existent. Each coach is air conditioned and electrically heated. All electric power for the coaches originates in the locomotive. This makes

The C&NW has rebuilt a number of Union Pacific cabless passenger units for suburban train service. No one can say that the 504 looks like any other diesel anywhere. (Chicago & North Western Railway)

C&NW suburban trains are not just simply coach trains. Many carry a lounge or club car, and this photo shows the interior of the one of the original St. Louis Car double deckers rebuilt for lounge car service. The coach seats have been retained, but the windows have been modified with a false shade. (Chicago & North Western Railway)

unnecessary individual car motor generators for the air conditioning units. The cars have center vestibules, wide enough for three people to board or alight at the same time. The sliding doors on all coaches in a train are controlled by one trainman. The closing of all doors actuates a signal for the engineer, indicating that he may proceed.

As for motive power a number of modifications were made to a fleet of Electro Motive Division F-7's and E-8's, and also a number of "E" units purchased from the Union Pacific. These modifications permitted push pull operations, electric power for heating, lighting and air conditioning the coaches. The diesels were equipped with an auxiliary diesel generator installed in the compartment normally occupied by the steam generator. The auxiliary is completed divorced from the power plant used for propulsion. The only thing the two motors have in common is the fuel tank.

The attractive streamlined equipment with its increased efficiency, higher capacity and push pull flexibility made possible a number of service improvements. For example, in the past in an attempt to reduce costs, trains had been eliminated during the lightly patronized off peak hours. With the new equipment off peak schedules were revamped with increased service on

Former transcontinental club-lounge cars (once operated on the "Cities" and Flambeau 400) have also found their way into suburban service. What better way to travel to and from work. (Chicago & North Western Railway)

an hourly basis throughout the day until past midnight. This resulted in more suburban service than had ever been available before.

With the new equipment and operating techniques, the C&NW suburban service has been in the black ever since 1962. No other railroad in the world can boast such an accomplishment. The Chicago and North Western Railway Commuter Streamliner service can truly be called one of the great railroad success stories. A superb mode of travel to say the least.

With the various problems of expressway construction and increasing congestion, a number of states are now assisting the railroads with commuter train service. New Jersey, a state that literally taxed railroads into bankruptcy in the past, has made substantial improvements in its overall transportation situation. The Erie-Lackawanna now has a new fleet of Pullman-Standard push pull coaches and snack bar coaches. The older coaches are being phased out on all lines as the state acquires new or more up to date used equipment for each commuter railroad. The importance of this service for the general public cannot be underestimated. It is needed for all large city-suburban corridors because the expressways and highways, and the long term fuel situation cannot turn the wheels

of commerce efficiently. The commuter train is a very efficient way to travel to work, and with the exception of some parlor cars, the entire operation is by "COACH." Need we say more.

The push pull concept pioneered by the Chicago & North Western Railway has been adopted by other railroads, such as the Erie-Lackawanna who employs General Electric road-switchers instead of covered wagon units as found on the C&NW, Milwaukee Road and others. (Pullman-Standard)

123

Push pull coaches for the Erie-Lackawanna were also built by Pullman-Standard, who helped the C&NW pioneer the concept in 1960. The E-L's coaches, however, have been built with an eye toward future electrification and the cars can be equipped with pantographs and traction motors very easily. (Pullman-Standard)

Although Erie-Lackawanna did not go in for full lounge car service as did the C&NW, they did purchase a number of snack bar coaches for use on several trains. (Pullman-Standard)

The Chicago, South Shore & South Bend Railroad must still contend with street running in Michigan City, Indiana. This east bound train has just unloaded a load of TV sets from the Combine (a semi-streamlined car with picture windows) and is picking its way through the traffic en route to its next stop, the Shops. At that point, car No. 1 will be cut off and the lead car will continue to South Bend alone. The photo was taken during the summer of 1971. (Patrick C. Dorin)

The interiors of the E-L coaches feature over the seat lighting, baggage racks the entire length of the car and walk over (as opposed to flip over) contoured seats. The original seating arrangement was to have been a 3-2 set up, but opposition from E-L suburbanites brought about the more comfortable 2-2 seating. (Pullman-Standard)

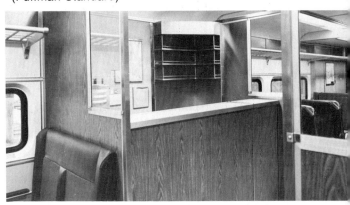

Snack bars on the E-L coaches were similar in many ways to snack bars found on main line coaches on the Penn Central and other lines. Food and beverage service included pastries and coffee, milk or tea in the morning, with light snacks, soft drinks, coffee, tea or your favorite beverage in the evening. Prices are reasonable, and the service gives many a commuter a real "pick-me-up" after a hard day's work. It makes traveling to and from work that much easier, and in fact, downright pleasurable. (Pullman-Standard)

Electric suburban has taken on a variety of styles over the years. The South Shore operated a high speed service between Chicago, Gary and South Bend with multiple-unit electric coaches equipped with non-reclining soft cushioned seats with foot rests. The exteriors were decorated in orange and maroon with silver roofs. Coach No. 20 will be the last car on a three car train that will soon depart for Chicago from Gary on one of the two stub tracks. (Patrick C. Dorin)

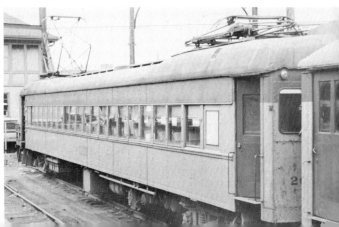

Not all electric coaches operated from overhead wire. All New York Central cars operated from a third rail. These streamlined electric coaches were built by Pullman-Standard in 1962. (Pullman-Standard)

On the other hand, still other electric coaches were designed to operate from either overhead wire or by third rail, such as these New Haven coaches constructed by Pullman-Standard in 1938 and 1953. This is train No. 368 near Sherwood Island, Conn. on the New Haven Region of the Penn Central Railroad on September 19, 1970. (J. W. Swanberg)

As we move into the 1970's, we still find main line hand me down coaches going into service in suburban territory. Here we see Pittsburgh and Lake Erie train No. 260 departing College (Beaver Falls), Pennsylvania en route to Pittsburgh with four ex-Louisville & Nashville coaches originally built for the Humming Bird and Georgian. The cars were purchased in November, 1970 and are painted Pullman green. It is unfortunate that Pittsburgh and Lake Erie is not spashed across the letter boards. This photo was taken in April, 1972. (Patrick C. Dorin)

Although there has been a vast transfusion of newer streamlined equipment in commuter service, we still find the old standard non-air conditioned coaches in service. These Rock Island coaches are sleeping out the weekend at Joliet in January, 1973. (Patrick C. Dorin)

The Metropolitan Transportation Authority has also purchased coaches from the L&N for suburban train service. Coach 2170 is ex-L&N 3100 and is part of the consist of train No. 914 at Brewster, New York on the old New York Central line. Note the word "Central" below the big "M". (J. W. Swanberg)

RDC's have gotten into the suburban train act too. Here we have ex-New York Central RDC-1 No. M-455 laying over at Jackson, Michigan on a weekend in July, 1972. The RDC was assigned to trains 357 and 374 on a daily except Saturday and Sunday basis. (Patrick C. Dorin)

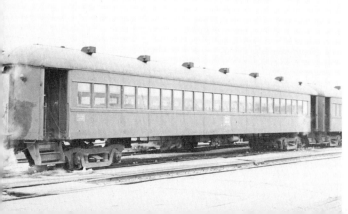

The Burlington Route purchased a small number of the Chicago & North Western "400" coaches, which eventually found their way into suburban service. There are three such cars in this photo, which was taken in June, 1971 at the BN's 14th Street yard in Chicago. (Patrick C. Dorin)

The Rock Island has very wisely co-ordinated their suburban train schedules with the Quad Cities Rocket. Here the east bound Rocket arrives at Joliet, and passengers destined to points between Joliet and Chicago can make a cross the platform change of trains to a streamlined double deck push pull train. The photo was taken in January, 1973. (Patrick C. Dorin)

Upon the departure of the Rocket, the suburban train begins its trip to Chicago as soon as the block signal turns yellow. Rock Island double deck coaches are painted in a fantastic red and yellow with white lettering. (Patrick C. Dorin)

Milwaukee Road Hiawatha coaches were also being converted for suburban service with the roads double deck push pull coaches. This is a mid-morning run from Chicago to Fox Lake, Illinois and she is rounding the curve just north of the Union Station: (Patrick C. Dorin)

CHAPTER 8
Milk, Mail and Express Trains

The milk and/or mail and express trains were assigned to a specific purpose of transporting milk, mail and express between terminals. The consist of the trains varied according to railroad and assignment but generally included baggage cars, box express cars, refrigerator express cars, sometimes milk tank cars, rail post office cars and a rider coach for the train crew and passengers. In some cases, mail trains also carried a sleeping car but the passenger carrying capacity of the train was small. Very rarely were any lounge or dining facilities operated on these trains.

Most of the coaches were again of the hand me down variety. Straight back coach seats of the walk over type and the car generally brought up the rear of the train. The Milwaukee Road, however, ran reclining seat coaches on their mail trains 55, 56 and 58 between Chicago and Minneapolis. Train No. 57 did not carry coaches at all.

In many cases the coach did not carry the markers for the train. In order to save time with switching set out and pick up mail and express cars at intermediate stations, the consist was such that a switch engine, or the road crew, would simply pick the car off the rear of the train for the set out operation. An example of this type of operation could be found with old Great Northern train No. 9, a run between St. Paul and Minot, North Dakota. In 1961 the train was made up of a baggage car, two mail and baggage cars (RPO's), a single coach, a piggyback with two trailers of mail and a baggage car. When No. 9 arrived at Willmar, Minnesota, the switch crew would uncouple the last two cars. The baggage car would remain at the depot, while the piggyback went to the ramp where two truck drivers were waiting to speed the mail to other destinations in Minnesota. The Willmar set out baggage car contained mail for Willmar itself, and mail for a Highway Post Office that went to Sioux Falls, South Dakota. The coach, in this case, was a reclining seat car. The Great Northern also ran reclining seat coaches on the Fast Mail (trains 27 and 28) during the last years of that famous train. The train also carried a News-Butcher for sandwiches

and refreshments and was one of few mail trains to offer such accommodations to passengers. Before the 1950's, the train did not carry reclining seat coaches and was more typical of most mail trains.

Some railroads identified mail and express trains in the time tables as being not recommended for travel by pointing out that the train was primarily for mail and express. The Santa Fe made such a notation specifically for trains 3 and 4 west of Kansas City in their time tables. Other railroads, such as the Union Pacific and the Pennsylvania simply noted that the train carried a rider coach only and there was no dining car or Pullman service.

Mail trains generally had an atmosphere about them that no other trains had. The Fast Mail meant speed and on time performance. When the train was late, the drama increased even more as the engine crew, train and mail car crews and station employees worked at a fever pitch running the train, loading and unloading at stations and in general yelling for everybody to hurry up. When a mail train was late, the dispatcher and everyone connected with the operation of trains was on the alert. Trainmasters and Division Superintendents were notified, and often requested to go to the office to supervise all attempts to make up time. An air of urgency existed until the train left the division or arrived at its final terminal.

As we move through the 1970's, the mail train no longer carries passengers. The baggage car and box express car is seen less and less in the consist of the trains, as piggybacks and containers replace such equipment in mail service. A caboose carries the markers instead of a rider coach, and very few Rail Post Office cars are in operation. The last of such equipment ran between New York City and Washington on the Penn Central. Flexi-van equipment is also part of the consist of mail trains on the Burlington Northern, Penn Central, Union Pacific and Southern Pacific. Although such trains continue to be important in the 1970's, passengers are unable to make use of them for travel and the air of urgency seems to be gone. The Fast Mail "ain't" what she used to be.

The fireman is watching railroad photographer-author Jim Scribbins as the 4007 wheels train No. 5, a mail and express train, thru Council Bluffs, Iowa. Although No. 5 was primarily a mail train, it did carry one or two coaches and a 10 section 3 double bedroom sleeper between Chicago and Omaha.

One of the eastern carriers that has disappeared from the Official Guide is the Rutland Railway. It too was famous for its milk trains, as is shown by this milk extra, with one tank and three refrigerator milk cars plus caboose at Middlebury, Vermont in August, 1951. (Harold K. Vollrath)

The New York, Ontario and Western Railway was famous for its milk trains. This milk train, with milk tank cars and an old, old coach, was photographed at Summitville, New York in 1947. The condition of the coach almost seems to say, "I am so Old & Weary." Note that even the marker lamp has lost its lenses. (Bob Lorenz)

Milk cars in the mid-west were typified by Chicago & North Western Railway 45 foot long wooden express refer. The wood cars were numbered 15262 to 15298 even numbers only. Cars were assigned to Wisconsin Milk Service and were operated on all trains except 400's, Streamliners and the North Western Limited. (Chicago & North Western Railway)

The New York Central operated a very large fleet of mail and express trains, and a few carried coaches for passengers. This fifteen car train is approaching the Marion, Ohio depot with two streamlined coaches on the rear end for passengers and crew. A good deal of NYC mail trains were powered by two tone gray geeps and looked very much at home on the head-end of such trains. (Bob Lorenz)

Four Union Pacific "E" units from General Motors head up a long mail and express train through Cheyenne, Wyoming. The train also carried a single coach and one 6 section, 6 roomette and 4 double bedroom sleeping car. (Bob Lorenz)

One of the more famous mail trains in the USA was the Milwaukee Road's Fast Mail between Chicago and Minneapolis. Train 57 did not carry passengers, but 56 did and provided one coach in the middle of the train. The Milwaukee Road held the mail contract between Chicago and St. Paul and operated as many as four RPO's on the train. The train was part of a transcontinental operation between Chicago and Seattle of which the Great Northern took over west of St. Paul. This photo shows No. 56 passing Wabasha, Minnesota in June, 1967. Normally the train did not pass here in daylight, but the long summer days of Minnesota permitted a brief time each year to see the train in daylight. (Bob Lorenz)

Three Southern Pacific "F" type units lead mail train No. 40 thru Tucson, Arizona on May 2, 1965. Trains 39 and 40 were the old Imperial and by the time this photo was taken had been reduced to a mail train only status with just one coach for the few passengers she carried. She operated to and from Chicago over the Rock Island Railroad. (Patrick C. Dorin Collection)

The Overland Route's mail train was 21 and 22 between Ogden and Oakland on the Southern Pacific. She connected with thru mail and express cars with Union Pacific trains 5, 6, 27 and 28 at Ogden, Utah. No. 21 is shown here at Reno, Nevada on May 28, 1967. (Patrick C. Dorin Collection)

Probably one of the strangest things about trains 21 and 22 was that very often 22 Roomette sleepers subbed for coaches that were in short supply during the summer time. It wasn't uncommon for two such cars to be running in coach service. This operation now goes down in history as being one of the more stranger types of coach service. (Pullman-Standard)

A number of mail trains carried the name "Fast Mail," but one of the more romantic names could be found on the Rio Grande where the Yampa Valley Mail, trains 9 and 10, operated between Denver and Craig, Colorado. This photo shows No. 9 at Tolland (just east of the Moffat Tunnel) behind an Alco PA with a three car consist. (Bob Lorenz)

Monon train No. 5, the Thoroughbred, literally transformed from a basic coach train to primarily a mail and express train over the years. This photo shows the ex-Army troop sleepers in head-end car service in the original red and gray color scheme as well two more head-end cars and single coach in the freight colors of black and gold. In fact, by October, 1962, most of the Monon's passenger equipment had been repainted to black and gold which had always been worn by the RS-2 powering No. 5. In the background is one of the three Fairbanks, Morse type H-12-44-TS units built only for the Santa Fe for passenger switching in Chicago. (Jim Scribbins)

Off comes the blue flag for the early evening southbound Santa Fe train No. 8 from Richmond, California. The photo was taken in the mid-1960's. The train was primarily a mail and express train and carried container cars, box express cars, baggage cars and streamlined coaches. For a short while No. 8 was a Golden Gate after No. 62 was discontinued and combined with No. 8, which was the mail and express train for that California route. (Richard Steinheimer)

Penn Central mail trains are a far cry from the mail trains of 20, or just 10, years ago as one can tell by this eastbound mail with GG-1 No. 4876 with four flexi-van cars and one caboose that is stenciled "For Passenger Service." The train is passing Frankford Junction, Pennsylvania on July 21, 1972. (J. W. Swanberg)

The Burlington Northern's "Pacific Zip" glides to a stop at Dayton's Bluff with 39 cars of mail bound for the Twin Cities, Fargo, Minot, Spokane, Seattle and Portland. All mail is carried in box express cars, piggybacks and flexi-vans. (Patrick C. Dorin)

BN's No. 3, the Pacific Zip, stops to change crews at North La Crosse, Wisconsin with its caboose adjacent to the home signal of Grand Crossing with the Milwaukee Road. Note the Great Northern box express car ahead of the caboose as well as the flexi-van cars. The consist of the train included 5 other box expresses as well as 17 piggybacks of mail on this June, 1972 day. (Patrick C. Dorin)

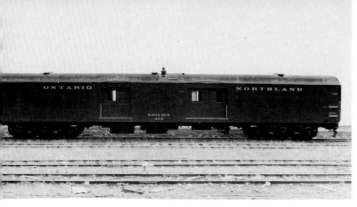

Ontario Northland Railway baggage car is typical of streamlined head-end cars operated for mail and express service. (National Steel Car Corporation Photo)

Spokane, Portland & Seattle Railway RPO-Baggage car No. 31 was a typical example of streamlined RPO cars with a 30 foot mail section. (St. Louis Car Company Photo)

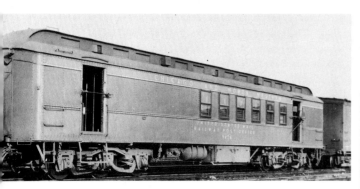

The workhorse of the standard era was these 60 foot Rail Post Office car. Different railroads had different styles, but by and large the full RPO was 60 feet long. This particular car was painted a two tone gray by the Chicago & North Western Railway to match Union Pacific two tone gray trains, such as the San Francisco Overland. (Chicago & North Western Railway)

The most modern RPO's were usually (but not always) 85 feet long and contained a 60 foot mail section with a 20 foot baggage section, sometimes used for mail storage. The Union Pacific operated this RPO car on the "Cities" streamliners. (John H. Kuehl)

The Milwaukee Road's long distance local train No. 58 from Minneapolis to Chicago was actually a relief mail and express train for the overnight speedster No. 56. Although 58 was a daylight run, its counterpart (No. 55) followed No. 57 out of Chicago and was actually a second mail and express train. Although 57 and 56 were the big guns of the mail trade, and carried the name "The Fast Mail," 55 and 58 were no small potatoes. The two trains consisted of from 10 to 20 cars depending upon the day of the week and time of year. This photo shows train No. 58 departing New Lisbon on July 25, 1966 and the eight car consist already reflects the mail traffic decline. (A. Robert Johnson)

One of the more famous mail trains in the world was the Great Northern's Fast Mail, trains 27 and 28. The Fast Mail was Great Northern's third transcontinental train, along with the Empire Builder and the Western Star until 1960. At that time, the Star and the Mail were combined with the name Western Star being retained, and the train numbers 27 and 28 adopted. The result was a very heavy train, such as Burlington Northern No. 27 shown here at Fargo on June 6, 1970. Powered by three diesel units, the consist included 20 cars. This view shows the forward portion of the train and the immense amount of mail being loaded and unloaded. The lead coach is an ex-Union Pacific leg rest chair car, while the second coach is an ex-Chicago & North Western ''400'' car. Although in BN service in 1970, one cannot help wondering if the two cars were ever coupled together in ''City'' streamliner service before 1956. (A. C. Phelps)

The complete consist of No. 27 on that June 6, 1970 day (before the tourist season really began for Glacier National Park), included three head-end cars, 5 coaches, 1 Ranch car, 1 sleeper and 10 head-end cars on the rear end. The consist of the train reflected the amount of mail business the farther west the train traveled. (A. C. Phelps)

A very interesting type of car was the Great Northern (and Milwaukee Road) baggage cars with rear end brakeman compartments. It solved very neatly the problem of how to have a flagman at the rear of the train, while the rest of the crew rode in the middle of the train in a coach. (A. C. Phelps)

One of the last runs of famous 27 and 28 is shown here with the west bound Western Star at Spokane, Washington on April 28, 1971. The Western Star was discontinued on May 1st, and the mail was replaced by ''Pacific Zip.'' trains 3 and 4. (A. C. Phelps)

CHAPTER 9

Amtrak

The opinions, hopes, wishes and desires for the National Railroad Passenger Corporation vary from extreme negativism to delightful positivism among the general public, railroad fans, management and labor. Talk to anybody about it, and one is liable to hear all kinds of comments concerning the present (1974) status of passenger service in the USA. It is sometimes difficult to get a realistic handle on the passenger situation, and to make matters worse, the same unfortunate thinking regarding passenger trains has now spilled over into the freight service. (The latter will be covered in a future volume by this writer.) However it is not the purpose of this chapter to rake the railroads over the coals for discontinuing passenger trains, or to accuse the public of abandoning the trains. The fact remains that a crisis situation was developing, and that a balanced transportation system is critical to the survival of society. Positive action had to be taken, and good or bad (depending upon who you talk to) Amtrak is here. Amtrak has taken on problems that nobody wanted to do anything about. And then to top it all off, too many people expected Amtrak to be a miracle worker and solve all of the problems at once. These were problems that have been plaguing the industry since the 1920's. Some can be traced directly to the United States Railroad Administration during World War I. Over 50 years of decline cannot be reversed in 50 or even 500 days. In view of the present energy crisis, it will probably be 5 to 10 years from now before the United States can have a truly balanced transportation system. A balanced transportation system is defined by this writer as a system that uses each mode of transportation for which it is best suited. Ironically the steel wheel on the steel rail is one of the most efficient transportation systems ever devised. Other fixed guide way systems simply cannot compare in terms of efficiency in power (air cushion vehicles) or technological feasibility (monorails have switching and other problems). The two rail system is economically sound and

the railroad industry has a strong future ahead of it.

Returning to the subject at hand, Amtrak was organized because of a crisis situation. If we go back for a moment to 1929, we find that the railroads operated over 20,000 daily passenger trains and carried 77% of the intercity passenger traffic by public mode in the United States. Buses carried 15.4% and the airlines carried an immeasurably small amount. Thirty one years later, more than 10,000 passenger trains had been discontinued and the rail share of the intercity public passenger traffic declined to 46.3%. The buses carried 37.7% while the airlines had jumped to 14.3%. By 1970 only 450 trains were still in operation and the rail share had dropped to 7.2%. The airlines and buses carried 73 and 16 per cent respectively. The reader should realize however that these percentages were split on what was left from the dominant mode of transportation — the automobile. In 1971, the private automobile carried 87% of the intercity traffic. The crisis that developed was the fact that it was increasingly evident that the US could not rely on further massive construction of highways and airports to meet transportation needs. The strangulation of our cities and environmental problems of air and noise pollution, excessive use of fuel and land, and the dislocation of people made unrestricted expansion of these facilities not only impractical but hazardous.

In view of the mammoth problem facing the United States, Congress finally began to take steps to positively face the problem. The Rail Passenger Service Act was signed on October 30, 1970 which authorized the National Railroad Passenger Corporation to manage the basic national rail network and be responsible for the operation of all intercity passenger trains — excluding commuter trains — under contracts with railroad companies. The spirit of the new law presented an image of the new corporation as a quasi-private, for profit organization although the scope and magnitude of the problems would

Amtrak is extensively rebuilding coaches of all types for use in trains Nationwide. In many cases, the interior decor is completely different from the original whereas in some cars, such as this former Great Northern dome coach, the original decor was retained during the refurbishing. In this instance, the cars have retained their "Northwest Indian" interiors. Bright and colorful, the wall murals lend a cheerful, relaxing and pleasant mood to these long distance cars. With the exception of the Santa Fe, the Great Northern was the only railroad to decorate their cars in such a manner. Amtrak is to be commended for retaining the decor. (Patrick C. Dorin)

Amtrak has completely redecorated the former Great Northern diner coaches, originally built for the Internationals between Seattle and Vancouver. The dining room tables of this coach have the most pleasant arrangement of dining room styles usually found on the railroads. The new decor includes a map of the Amtrak System, which is very much out of date with the route expansion program. (Patrick C. Dorin)

face Amtrak with several years of non-profit operation. The organization was specifically charged by Congress to do three things:

1. Provide modern, efficient intercity rail passenger service within the basic rail system of the USA.
2. Employ innovative operating and marketing concepts to develop fully the potential of modern rail service in meeting intercity transportation needs.
3. Operate on a "for profit" basis.

The job of rebuilding both the image and substance of the railroad passenger service cannot be viewed lightly nor with constant griping and bickering by railroad managements and labor, plus the unsympathetic attitude of many people. This incredible situation must be faced positively, and with constructive criticism from the public; and most important a co-operative effort must prevail among the Congress, Amtrak, the Railroads, the ICC and the Department of Transportation. They cannot pull against each other for if they do, the USA will never have a balanced transportation system.

As we said before, the size and complexity of Amtrak's task emphasizes that the rebuilding progress will be modest during the early months and years. The corporation's efforts are, therefore, aimed at a gradual revitalization of public confidence in rail service. (However when a railroad

employee fills a fuel tank with water in sub zero weather (Dec., 1973), public confidence can be a long time in rebuilding.) The first step in this task was for the corporation to increase regard for passenger needs through substantive service improvements. Although sleeping car services are being improved and expanded as time goes on, most of the service improvements have concentrated on the coach services. The above objective dovetails over the long term with Amtrak's overriding objective to attract the traveling public back to the rails. This is imperative if the corporation is going to be able to provide the financial means to offer new services, and ultimately position the corporation on a reasonably sound financial footing. This is not, in this writer's opinion, an impossible task; but it is going to take work, much patience and positive thinking.

In connection with the long term objectives of rebuilding public confidence, attracing more passengers and the development of a reasonably viable system from an economic standpoint, the corporation set some specific first year goals as follows:

1. Completing an efficient takeover of rail passenger service from the railroads in accordance with the congressional mandate.
2. Noticeably increasing the consideration with which Amtrak and railroad employees handle the public. These qualities of con-

sideration and courtesy must exist in fact and equally important, be perceived by the traveling public.

3. Improving the quality of service that can be noted readily by the riding public. These service improvements have been directed primarily toward on-time train performance, clean well-maintained equipment, and the provision of accurate information.

4. Building an effective, aggressive management team dedicated to the long term effort of making rail passenger service a successful operation. Further, and more specifically short term, is the task of developing positive programs to gain an increasing share of the travel market.

As we stated previously, the first few years must be viewed as a start-up and reconstruction period. It is totally unrealistic to believe the corporation can turn a profit and reverse the deplorable conditions that existed before May 1, 1971. However, things are continuously improving. Funding for example has expanded from $40 million initially in 1971 to $93 million in 1974. Authority to borrow has been increased from $100 million in 1971 to $500 million in 1974. Service has been expanded on many routes not originally included in the system. Some states, such as Vermont, have rail service again for the first time in several years. On other routes, the frequency of train service has been expanded. Each time table publication reflects improvements, and equipment is constantly being refurbished. It has been, and is, by no means a

Amtrak's rebuilding program has included the conversion of parlor cars to coaches. For example, the semi-streamlined New Haven parlor car, the Stamford, was rebuilt to a coach and carries Amtrak No. 7251. And so the process of converting First Class types of equipment to coach service continues during the Amtrak era. (J. W. Swanberg)

small job. Some trains have been pruned from the schedules, for example the Buffalo-Cleveland-Chicago trains have been discontinued because of a lack of patronage. On the other hand, the experimental Minneapolis-Bismarck-Spokane experimental run (The North Coast Hiawatha) has been expanded to a Chicago-Seattle run and began running on a daily basis in May, 1974. Metroliner service has been expanded to New Haven and additional trains placed in operation between New York and Washington. New suburban stops have been added, such as the Metropark station in New Jersey. Still other services are planned, and notwithstanding the critics, Amtrak is rolling and at a faster and faster rate of speed.

The most recent coach travel developments are the Metroliners and the Turboliners. (The Turbo Trains are included in these developments but were covered extensively in Chapter 22, *The Domeliners.* The Metroliners offer high speed service in the Eastern corridor, and as of this writing, non-electrified versions will soon be completed and Metroliner service will be offered in a wider geographical territory. They rank as among the finest coaches ever built, and for short distance operations, they are undoubtedly the best. This photo shows train No. 112 whipping past Frankford Junction, Pennsylvania en route to New York City. (J. W. Swanberg)

Amtrak Metroliner coaches are equipped with the latest model reclining seats and the decor includes carpeting on the walls. The latter is becoming quite common on many Amtrak coaches and provides a pleasant surrounding for coach travel. (Amtrak Photo)

Snack Bar Coaches are operated for meal service aboard Metroliner trains, which offer light meals, snacks and beverages. The interior also includes 60 reclining seats, and telephone service. (Amtrak)

AMTRAK COACH SERVICE

Amtrak operates five different types of coaches over its various routes. These can be classified as follows:

1. Streamliner Coaches (Both Day and Day-Night cars)
2. Turbo-Trains
3. Turboliners
4. Metroliners
5. Slumbercoaches

The streamliner equipment makes up the major proportion of Amtrak equipment. This equipment operates on virtually every train with the exception of the hi-level chair cars on the South West Limited, Turbo types and Metroliners. With the further exception of some electric coaches, the cars are equipped with reclining seats (for day coaches), and leg rest reclining seats for the day-night cars. Interiors are being decorated in cheerful colors and many include carpeting, not only on the floor but also on the walls. They range in seating capacities from 22 passengers (combination type cars) to 72 passengers with most equipment ranging from 44 to 60. Most leg rest seat cars contain 44 to 48 chairs, while the nonleg rest cars usually contain from 50 to 60 seats. All of this equipment is steam heated and many contain smoking lounge rooms at the ends of the cars.

Among the streamliner cars, Amtrak operates a number of varieties in the basic design. The hi-level coaches from the Santa Fe rank as among the most luxurious chair cars ever built. They have operated primarily on the Sunset Limited, Super Chief/South West Limited and Lone Star.

Another design twist is the 96 seat bi-level "400" coaches leased from the Chicago & North Western Railway. These 96 seat cars with spacious leg room and dome car level viewing have operated primarily on the Illinois Zephyr between Chicago and Quincy and on the Hiawatha service between Chicago and Milwaukee. These trains are powered by leased C&NW F-7 units which carry the special diesel generator for heating, air conditioning and lighting power for the train. To see these particular trains reminds one of the Flambeau and Peninsula 400's, and nostalga cannot help but creep into one's mind.

Dome coaches also operate on a number of trains, such as the North Coast Hiawatha, Empire Builder, Floridian, Lone Star, James Whitcomb Riley, San Francisco Zephyr and other trains. Domeliner service on Amtrak was covered in the book *The Domeliners*, and variations in such service has changed only a little during 1973 and 1974.

The Silverliner coaches operate on trains 600 to 630 almost exclusively between Harrisburg, and Philadelphia, Pennsylvania. These are the electrified coaches mentioned earlier in this section.

The day-night coaches are operated on long distance overnight trains, i.e., Chicago-New York City, Chicago-New Orleans, and so forth, while the day coaches are run on all other types of trains. The day coaches also run long distance service when required, and because of pooling equipment for maximum use, one will find leg rest cars on short runs.

As of the summer of 1974, Amtrak Turboliners have been serving exclusively in the Chicago-St. Louis run, and plans for 1975 include substantial expansion. Here the new French Turboliner rests overnight in Pittsburgh during its maiden voyage from Port Elizabeth, New Jersey to Chicago, Illinois. The reaction of many passengers to the trains is very positive, and it appears as of the moment that Amtrak made a wise decision in purchasing the trains. The low level profile reminds one of the Abraham Lincoln and Ann Rutledge which once operated over the same route. (Amtrak)

The telephone booth is located near the snack bar area in the center of the Metroliner coach. (Amtrak)

All streamliner coach passengers may use the Tavern Lounge or Club Lounge car facilities, the Recreation Car and Dining cars when operated. Most Amtrak trains, but not all, offer snack and beverage service on those trains that do not carry Tavern, Recreation or Dining car facilities. The coach passenger is permitted full use of dining and lounge car services.

As of early 1974, Amtrak operated three Turbo-Trains. Two of these special domeliners consist of five cars, while the third is a four car consist purchased from the Canadian National Railways. For the most part, these trains have been operated on the Boston-New York services. Depending upon the out come of certain operating tests and marketing studies, one might expect to find a Turbo-Train in operation elsewhere in the nation besides the east coast. All Turbo-Trains have been repainted in the Amtrak color scheme.

The Turboliners, which differ from the Turbo-Trains in both style and in national origin, have been placed in service on the Chicago-St. Louis runs. The two French trains have introduced a new concept in train travel to the United States. The trains operate on a double daily round trip basis on the former Gulf, Mobile and Ohio line of the Illinois Central Gulf Railroad. All four runs take 4 hours and 59 minutes for the trip. This compares favorably with the Wabash Blue Bird schedule of 5 hours, 15 minutes in 1955, and 5 hours, 10 minutes for the GM&O's Abe Lincoln in 1953. There is no doubt about it, these French trains out class the Jumbo Jets and it is good to see a touch of Europe and France on our rail-

road system. Thank you, Paris, for your contribution to the railroad transportation industry.

The Metroliners are in a class all by themselves. The electrified coaches operate only between New Haven, New York and Washington, D. C. Metroliner service has been expanded on the route and now 15 such trains operate in each direction every day from 6:00 AM to 8:00 PM. Running time is about 3 hours in each direction. The Metroliners are supplemented by additional trains from 5:00 AM to 10:30 PM northbound and from 4:15 AM to 9:45 PM southbound. Patronage on the Metroliners, which offer both coach and parlor car accommodations, continues to increase month after month. Further, Amtrak has ordered an additional 257 Metroliner type passenger cars for service between Boston and Washington. These new cars, capable of being pulled by either electric or diesel electric locomotives, will have interiors similar to the self-propelled Metroliner cars including food and beverage service, electrical heating and air conditioning systems with improved ride characteristics. The new coaches will be capable of operating up to 120 miles per hour. The Metroliners rank as being among the finest passenger cars ever constructed, and despite initial bugs, are turning out to be prime examples of American Know How.

In addition to the self-propelled Silverliners and Metroliners, Amtrak also operates self-propelled Rail Diesel Cars. Most of the RDC coaches are now equipped with reclining seats, and are pleasantly decorated in the interior and run on relatively short hops. Springfield and

The interiors of the Turboliner coaches are divided for the purpose of separating the smokers from the non-smokers. The interior includes baggage racks the entire length of the car and drapes on the windows. (Amtrak)

The train is one of the finest ways for a "Family" to travel. On a train everyone can talk with one another, play games, read and enjoy the scenery not to mention the lack of nervous tension common with highway travel. Many Amtrak trains carry a stewardess or a passenger service agent who provides onboard services for coach passengers. (Amtrak)

One of the niceties of traveling by train is the call for dinner. Dining room attendants signal meal times by the use of chimes walking the entire length of the train. This photo was taken in the dome lounge car of the San Francisco Zephyr. (Amtrak)

The center car of the five car Turboliner is a combination coach-bar and grill car. The dining room area includes 24 seats at tables where people may dine after they have picked up their food cafeteria style. The coach compartment of the car has 44 seats as compared to the full coaches with 80 and/or 76 seats depending upon the arrangement. Each power or Turbo-coach carries 48 seats. (Amtrak)

Coach passengers are greeted by either a uniformed trainman or coach porter who assists with luggage and other packages for the passenger. Many Amtrak trains carry coach porters, such as the Zephyrs, Broadway, Starlight and most of the transcontinentals. (Amtrak)

In May, 1971, most Amtrak passenger trains looked almost like their pre-Amtrak operation. However, changes were beginning to be made. For example, buffet car service was added to the Detroit-Chicago trains operated over the Penn Central. The Wolverine is shown here at Jackson, Michigan en route to Chicago with one baggage car, a New Haven lounge car and two coaches. There waslittle to indicate on the exterior that No. 361 was an Amtrak train. (Patrick C. Dorin)

Hartford to New Haven trains are typical of the type of operation Amtrak is using this type of car.

As we described in Chapter 1, the Slumbercoach is probably the most unusual coach ever placed in operation. Although more like a sleeping car, the car was and is called a coach and the B&O operated the car in the All-Coach Columbian. It did not run in the All-Pullman Capital Limited, even though the equipment was operated by the Pullman Company. A rare bird to say the least. Slumbercoaches have operated on the Broadway Limited, the Champion, the Vacationer, the Silver Star and a number of other trains and the service is being expanded. The Slumbercoach continues to be a hit and it ranks as being one of the more innovative creations in the railroad industry.

AMTRAK SERVICE IMPROVEMENTS

This book will cover only a small slice of the history of train service developments. There are two reasons for this. First, only one chapter is being devoted to Amtrak, and second, Amtrak is on-going and history will continue to roll on with new developments long after this book is written.

During 1973 to 1975, there were several new trains placed in operation. For example, new service was established between Chicago and Dubuque, Chicago and Urbana and Minneapolis and Duluth. On other routes, train frequency was expanded, such as the State House on the Chicago-St. Louis run; and there are many examples of improved train consists and on board services.

Improved service on the Chicago-St. Louis run began on October 1, 1973 with the French Turbine trains discussed earlier in this chapter and Chapter 1. The new State House went into service on the same route primarily for Springfield and Chicago service. Arriving in Chicago at 10:20 AM and departing that evening for southern Illinois at 6:15 PM, the new train gives businessmen and state employees a full day for work in Chicago. It is this type of planning and operation that brings people back to the rails. The State House carries reclining seat day coaches and a lounge car offering beverage, snack and light meal service.

Amtrak has had some spectacular successes with some of the new train services. The reader will probably recall that on September 29th, 1972, Amtrak placed in operation the international trains, the Montrealer and Washingtonian. This

One of the unfortunate side effects of the demise of the passenger train was the lack of clean equipment on many (but not all) railroads. Here an almost lost art is revived as a coach cleaner scrubs down the Twin Cities Hiawatha at Minneapolis in May, 1974. (Patrick C. Dorin)

Later the full buffet car service was replaced with rebuilt snack bar coaches. Actually this was a wise move since the buffet cars were combination sleeper lounge cars, and the sleeper space was pure non-revenue territory for the Chicago-Detroit daylight runs. If all Penn Central cars could have looked like this one, the PC would have been a sharp looking railroad. Snack Bar Coach No. 3215 was rebuilt from an ex-New York Central 64 seat coach built by Pullman-Standard in 1946. Amtrak has since re-numbered this car 3955. This photo was taken in June, 1973 as the east bound Wolverine paused in Jackson, Michigan. (Patrick C. Corin)

pair of trains has exceeded all expectations. The average number of passengers per day has exceeded 700 and during holiday seasons and the summer, the number reaches nearly 900. Most of these are coach passengers between New York and Washington, but a major percentage of the figure use the train north of New York City. The trains are equipped with Montreal-Washington sleepers plus a Montreal-Miami sleeper during the heavy winter travel time. A diner lounge car separates the sleeping cars and coaches and provides complete breakfast, lunch and dinner entrees. Cocktails, cordials and popular wines are also available with one's meal. Ahead of the diner lounge are at least two coaches in service between Montreal and Washington. The next car forward is the unique Pub Car. The Pub, equipped with a piano, is usually always located in the middle of the coach cars. The car serves snacks, cocktails and other beverages.

Former Illinois Central train, the "Shawnee," begins its trip to Carbondale, Illinois with two diesel units and five cars including one former Burlington dome coach. Trains 391 and 392 reflect the early changes made by Amtrak with cars literally roaming the entire Nation. In this case, former Louisville & Nashville coaches make up the rest of the consist of the train. For a great deal of time, each and every Amtrak train was a riot of colors. As we move into 1975, such color combinations are becoming less and less pronounced. (John H. Kuehl)

One of the more popular trains in the west is Amtrak's Coast Starlight. The consist shown here is typical. The Starlight operates over the Burlington Northern and Southern Pacific Railroads between Seattle and Los Angeles. (Tom Hoff)

In order to cater to the ski trade, Amtrak has added special ski racks in the baggage car. Skiers have taken advantage of the train which arrives in northern Vermont in the early morning on the rails of the Central Vermont Railway. The CV operated its last special ski train in the mid-1950's, and the new Amtrak service is reviving many memories. Trains 60 and 61 operate over the Penn Central (Pennsylvania and New Haven), Boston and Maine, Central Vermont and Canadian National Railways.

Through 1973 Amtrak made spectacular progress on many routes, and as things shape up 1974 and 1975 promise to be even better years. By late 1973, the Merchants Limited, Southern Crescent and Senator were upgraded for improved food and beverage service, parlor cars and coaches. These trains are designed to supplement the Metroliners, especially for businessmen unable to get reservations on the electric speedsters.

The popularity of the Broadway Limited has brought about a reversal of the unfortunate trend of combining local trains with limiteds. In late 1973, a new local train, the Valley Forge, was placed in service between New York City and Harrisburg, Pennsylvania to relieve the Broadway of local traffic requirements. The Valley departs Harrisburg after 6:00 AM and arrives in New York City before 10:00 AM for the 194 mile run. Westbound the train departs New York about 20 minutes behind the Broadway at 5:14 PM and arrives in Harrisburg at 8:27 PM (October 28, 1973 time table, p. 30). With the new train, the Broadway has discontinued carrying local traffic between New York City and Lancaster, Pennsylvania. The Valley Forge is equipped with coaches and a lounge car for beverage and snack service.

New York City-Philadelphia service has been rescheduled to provide departures each half hour all day long, and in many cases trains are as

145

Nearly all Amtrak trains are very heavy with coach class passengers as compared to sleeping car patronage. The same is true with even the transcontinental trains, such as the San Francisco Zephyr shown here at the 5,224 foot high Emigrant Gap in the Sierra Mountains between Reno and Sacramento (Amtrak Photo by Rich Tower)

close as 15 minutes apart. Trains depart New York City from 4:15 AM to 12:01 AM, while from Philadelphia schedules run from 5:45 AM to 12:55 AM. As of October, 1973, there were 38 southbound and northbound trains for a grand total of 76 passenger trains including 15 Metroliners each way daily. If one adds to this figure about 40 Philadelphia-Trenton Penn Central commuter trains, and 126 PC runs on the New York-New Brunswick/Trenton (and New York and Long Branch—see page 54, *Commuter Railroads*, Superior Publishing Company, Seattle, Washington, 1970), he can begin to get a handle on the amount of traffic on that section of the former Pennsylvania Railroad. Take into consideration freight and mail train traffic and the total number of trains is staggering. No other mode of transportation could handle the number of passengers and tonnage that flows over that New York-Philadelphia section of railroad with matching efficiency and safety.

The Florida trains have also gone through a substantial rebuilding, both in terms of service and in equipment. All Florida trains now feature the following:

1. An on board service director and/or passenger service representative, who acts as train host or hostess.
2. Hospitality hours and champagne punch.
3. Complimentary wake-up coffee and orange juice.
4. Special entertainment hours in the evening.
5. Complimentary morning and evening newspapers.

Amtrak added a winter season only train, the Vacationer (basically a replacement of the Florida Special), between New York City and Miami. In addition to the streamlined coaches and sleepers, the Vacationer carries a full dining car, bar-lounge diner and a club lounge car. Slumbercoaches are also featured on the Vacationer, as well as on the New York-St. Petersburg Champion and the Silver Star, which serves both Florida coasts. In addition, the Silver Meteor and Champion carry through cars to and from Boston and the Silver Star carries the Montreal cars.

The San Francisco Zephyr pauses at Laramie, Wyoming, which is now the only train serving the State of Wyoming. Somehow having a train with the name "Zephyr" on Union Pacific and Southern Pacific trackage doesn't seem to quite add up. It has been suggested that the train be re-named the San Francisco Challenger because it represents a challenge to the transportation problems of our age. (Amtrak)

The premiere Florida train is in the New York-Miami Silver Meteor. This train carries two 48 seat dining cars, a recreation car and a club lounge car. A passenger service representative on board acts as hostess for movies, bingo and other games, a fashion show and door and game prizes.

For the first time, the Chicago-Florida train, the Floridian, carries the full package of activities as the New York-Florida trains. In addition to the usual coach equipment, the Floridian carries two dome coaches plus full dining services, games, a children's hour and complimentary blankets for coach passengers. A complimentary continental breakfast is also served to all sleeping car passengers.

In March, 1974, two new rail routes went into service. The first was the Oakland and Bakersfield run through the San Joaquin Valley and the St. Louis-Laredo, Texas run.

The new San Joaquin Valley trains began running on March 6th and make direct connections at Oakland with the Coast Starlight. Bus service provided direct service between Oakland and San Francisco. The trains provide coach,

food and beverage service and operate on the Southern Pacific between Oakland and Port Chicago, and on the Santa Fe between Port Chicago and Bakersfield. The Santa Fe route was chosen because it serves Stockton directly and has a larger population than an all SP route.

The St. Louis-Laredo run began on March 13th and operates as a three times a week service. The new train combined the original Fort Worth-Laredo train, the Inter-American, with the new St. Louis-Dallas-Forth Worth service. The train offers coaches, sleepers, dining, lounge and baggage service. The train departs St. Louis on Sunday, Wednesday and Friday and Laredo on Sunday, Tuesday and Friday.

The Missouri Pacific handles the train from St. Louis to Texarkana. From there the Texas and Pacific takes the train to Forth Worth where the Santa Fe takes over to Milano. At Milano the MoPac gets it again for the last leg into Laredo. The train connects with the Natinal Limited for New York City at St. Louis, and also with the Turboliners for Chicago.

Coach travel under Amtrak is rapidly approaching the best it has ever been on the Ameri-

The Rail Diesel Car plays an important part in Amtrak coack service. Here train No. 146 with one RDC-1 and a lead car from the Roger Williams arrives Boston on August 19, 1973. Named the "Bay State" the train offers coach service with snacks and refreshments between New Haven and Boston via Hartford, which is known as the Inland Route. (J. W. Swanberg)

can Railroads. To be sure, the Santa Fe's El Capitan, the Pennsylvania Railroad's Metroliners and the Domeliners of the Burlington, Northern Pacific and the Great Northern as well as other lines were excellent, indeed, they were perfect in all respects. But coach service in general declined to a lowly state. Reduced budgets found cars running dirty. Roofs were leaking during rain storms, and cars would leak water and flood the interiors during the winter. Often the lights failed. Only a handful of railroads, such as the

Grand Trunk Western, Santa Fe, Seaboard Coast Line, and Union Pacific were making efforts to keep the cars in prime operating condition. Some lines were making token efforts, while some roads gave up altogether. Clearly something had to be done. Since Amtrak, business has increased again. From 1971 to 1972 the increase was about 12%. From 1972 to 1973, the jump was about 14%. New coaches and equipment are on order. This chapter on Amtrak cannot be considered complete as the history is on going. As this is being written, new coach and sleeper services are being planned for routes that in early 1974 have no train service. New chair car seats are being designed for maximum comfort, and training sessions are being held for on board crews. Progress is being made, and although it is difficult to predict the future, it certainly does appear that Amtrak is making inroads on a problem that has been plaguing America for 50 years.

Rail Diesel Cars are assigned to the Black Hawk between Chicago and Dubuque, Iowa on the Illinois Central Gulf Railroad. Train 371 departs Chicago passing a brace of Amtrak "E" units and an ex-Grand Trunk Western steam locomotive in the background. (John H. Kuehl)

The heaviest chair cars ever constructed are the hi-level cars built for the Santa Fe in the mid-1950's and again in the mid-1960's. Now operating for Amtrak, the cars grace the coach sections of the Southwest Limited and the Lone Star. (John H. Kuehl)

The former Chicago & North Western Bi-level 400 cars are now part of the Amtrak fleet, and operate on the Illinois Zephyr between Chicago and Quincy, Illinois among other trains. This photo shows train 347 departing Chicago en route to Quincy in August, 1974. (John H. Kuehl)

Train No. 3, the Southwest Limited, departs Chicago for Los Angeles with a substantial number of hi-level chair cars in the consist of the coach-sleeping car train. (John H. Kuehl)

The Bi-level coaches are now being repainted in the Amtrak color scheme. Soon the Iowa corn colors of green and yellow will no longer grace any long distance coach equipment. (John H. Kuehl)

The former Country Club lounge of the Peninsula 400 operated in Cafe Coach service on the Zephyr in 1974. When one thinks about it, it seems a little strange for "400" equipment to be operating in "Zephyr" service. Who would of thought in 1935 that forty years later we would see such a thing. After all what competition can one think of that was "hotter" than the Zephyr-400-Hiawatha runs between Chicago and the Twin Cities. (John H. Kuehl)

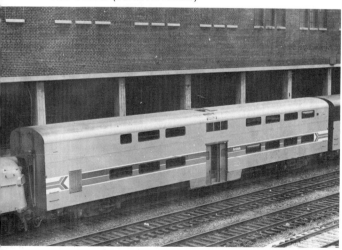

Train No. 15, the Lone Star, departs Chicago for the state with the same name in August, 1974. (William A. Raia)

On July 15, 1974, a full buffet lounge car substituted for the combination bi-level Coach-Country Club Lounge car. By mid-1974, not all of the Chicago & North Western bi-level coaches had been repainted by Amtrak. Also note the former Burlington "E" unit hastily put in service; and of all things the standard Penn Central coach in the Amtrak consist in the background. (W. A. Raia)

Amtrak train No. 326 arrives at Chicago from Milwaukee and is part of the Hiawatha Service fleet. Appropriately the train is made up of four Hiawatha coaches, which once operated not only on the Twin Cities Hiawathas, but the Pioneer Limited and the "Cities" streamliners. No. 326 is a Milwaukee Road operation as well as the other Chicago-Milwaukee services. (John H. Kuehl)

As Amtrak moves along, it has been offering more baggage and an expanded express service as well as carrying more U. S. Mail. Therefore it has purchased a number of cars from the U. S. Army that can be converted for head-end service, such as baggage car 1306 shown here. (John H. Kuehl)

The all-coach Turboliner arrives in Chicago from St. Louis after its fast run over the former Gulf, Mobile & Ohio rails of the Illinois Central Gulf Railroad. (William A. Raia)

151

Not all Hiawatha service trains have been assigned Milwaukee Road coaches. With the pooling of equipment, an all Amtrak consist sometimes shows up. This will of course be more frequent as time goes. All "Hiawatha Service" trains are "coaches only." (William A. Raia)

As time goes on, Amtrak is involved in more and more special movements. This Amtrak "E" unit No. 435 and coach No. 4472 await a wee hours in the morning assignment at Duluth, Minnesota. The Ice Capades are finishing up at the Duluth Arena, and after the last performance, the equipment will be loaded into baggage cars. The coach will serve as a rider car for the crew for this unusual special which will depart over the Milwaukee Road before sun rise. (Jergen Fuhr)

Amtrak's Black Hawk arrives at Chicago with two RDC-1's and one RDC-2 on April 3, 1974. The train also offers a buffet service, a feature not found on many RDC's. (William A. Raia)

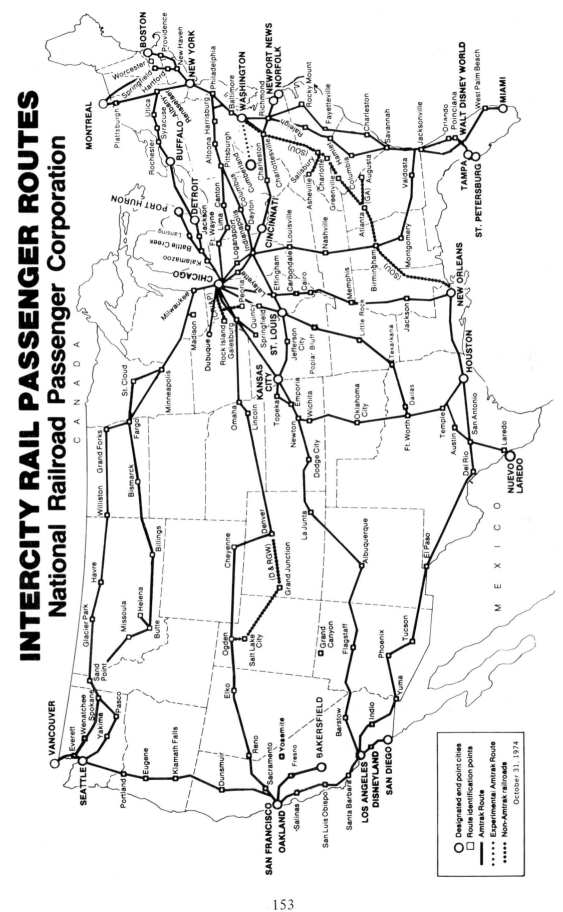

INTERCITY RAIL PASSENGER ROUTES
National Railroad Passenger Corporation

Legend:

○ Designated end point cities
□ Route identification points
— Amtrak Route
∙∙∙∙∙ Experimental Amtrak Route
∙∙∙∙∙ Non-Amtrak railroads

October 31, 1974

CHAPTER 10
Auto-Train

In this age of railroad problems, Auto-Train has to be the success story of all time. The passenger train has been a drain on resources of many railroad companies ever since the 1920's, depending of course on which railroad one was studying. But who would have thought in 1965 that a new concept in rail travel was going to be launched on December 5, 1971? Futhermore that concept was going to operate at a profit. This writer was often told that there was not a passenger train in the world that could operate at a profit. It was not in the cards some have said.

It was about 1965 that congress authorized a study for high speed ground transportation. The public study came to the attention of Mr. Eugene Kerik Garfield in 1969. He studied the report and decided that if done in the right way, a successful train could be placed into operation. He also decided that a need for auto-ferry service was critically needed between the northeast and Florida. With that decision made he went to work. He joined a small group of investors that provided the seed money for a two year developmental program, designed the Auto-Train, negotiated the necessary contracts with the Seaboard Coast Line and Richmond, Fredericksburg and Potomac Railroads, filed a corporate charter in Florida, obtained the necessary equipment, received all the regulatory approvals, staffed the operation and essentially did everything to begin a railroad company.

Railroad men and others were skeptical, and still are. They cannot see how Auto-Train can be making a profit, and some say it can only be done on the Florida run. However, Mr. Garfield's philosophy does not include the words "it can't be done." Many people tried to discourage him, but he never permitted that to sway him. His philosophy could be applied to many other aspects of life. At any rate the positive attitude of not only Mr. Garfield, but of the other staff members, placed in service on December 6, 1971 America's most innovative mode of travel.

As with most train operations in the U.S.A., a major percentage of Auto-Train's business is by coach. The corporation owns a fleet of both full length dome coaches and short or half dome coaches as reported by this writer in *The Domeliners*. These coaches are equipped with excellent leg rest reclining seats. The cars are fully carpeted and decorated in various colors that match the purple and red color scheme of the corporation. The colors are restful and give the passenger the feeling of being First Class. Indeed the First Class sections of jet liners, even the jumbo jets, cannot match the comfort provided by these Auto-Train coaches. They have been totally rebuilt by Pullman-Standard and other companies. The ride is smooth and quiet, and in addition, blankets and pillows are provided to all coach passengers for their sleeping comfort during the all night journey. As of 1974, it is doubtful that any transportation company can match the luxury and economy of coach class travel on Auto-Train.

Auto-Train luxury coaches were once part of such trains as the El Capitan, California Zephyr and the Union Pacific "Domeliner" fleet. In addition, the Santa Fe and Union Pacific supplied the sleeping cars of the double bedroom variety. The auto-carriers were purchased from the Canadian National, who also operates a smaller scale service between Toronto, Ontario and Edmonton, Alberta. The train includes two buffet dining cars purchased from the Seaboard Coast Line Railroad. These two cars are separted by a kitchen-dormitory car which is used for storage and quarters for the crew. A dome Night Club Lounge car completes the beverage and recreation areas on board the train.

As I stated above, there are two buffet dining cars on each train. One is decorated as the Lemon Tree car while the other is known as the Purple Plum. In either car passengers are served a complimentary buffet supper including a variety of three entrees, salad, desert and choice of bever-

Train No. 2, the northbound Auto-Train, arrives at Lorton, Virginia with 28 cars in May, 1972. The Louisville-Sanford train looks very muck like the original Lorton-Sanford service. (H. H. Harwood, Jr.)

age. Live entertainment is provided in the Starlight Lounge (the dome night club lounge car), the only car of its kind in the Western Hemisphere. Passengers participate in sing-alongs while they enjoy their favorite beverage and snacks. Feature length movies are shown twice in each buffet car. The first showing is after the final dinner setting, and the second immediately follows the first. Complementary evening and morning newspapers are provided and a newsstand/boutique, selling magazines and commemorative souveniers is open in the evening.

Potato chips, candy bars and playing cards are available for sale in the Night Club Lounge which is open past the midnight hour. All night coffee bars are open for the passenger's convenience in the lounge areas on the lower level of some of the coaches. Hot water for tea, Sanka, Postum or hot chocolate is available in the buffet diners. A complementary late evening snack is also served.

Each train crew consists of a Service Director, Senior Hostess, 3 Passenger Service Assistants and 11 Hostesses. This crew is very positively orientated and is most happy to assist the passengers with any questions and problems that they may have. The Hostesses patrol the coaches while the Passenger Service Assistants are available in the sleeping cars throughout the trip.

The total train consist includes two General Electric U36B's for motive power, up to twenty auto carriers, one steam generator car (for supplying steam for the train heating and steam tables in the buffet and kitchen cars), up to seven coaches, one night club lounge car, two buffet

dining cars, one kitchen dormitory car (coupled between the buffet cars) and finally three or four sleeping cars for a total train length of up to 38 cars. Auto-Train now ranks as being one of the largest, if not the largest, passenger train in the United States. The only other 30 car passenger train regularly operated that this writer knows of was the Great Northern's Western Star during the summer seasons in the early 1960's.

The train travels at a cruising speed of 79 miles per hour with an average speed of just under 60 miles per hour for the entire run. The distance of the Washington-Florida run is 856 miles and the train incurs five scheduled stops for servicing and railroad operating crew changes. The crews are provided by the RF&P and the SCL (including the L&N on the new midwest route) and consist of an engineer, fireman, conductor, brakeman (on the SCL) and flagman. These five stops are at Richmond, Virginia; Rocky Mount, North Carolina; Florence, South Carolina; Savannah, Georgia; and Jacksonville, Florida. The stop at Florence permits the refueling and watering of the locomotive and train, and also includes time for passengers to walk their dogs.

Auto-Train is a success story. Although the company lost $2,479,863 during the first fiscal year from December, 1971 to April 30, 1972, most of this was the preoperating costs consisting of salaries, management services and promotional costs incurred from date of incorporation (April 11, 1969) to commencement of operation on December 6, 1971. Included in these costs are the equipment acquisitions plus land, terminal construction and other rentals and contracting

Auto-Train operates bi-level enclosed auto carriers which insures the complete safety of the passenger's automobile. Auto-Train is also experimenting with tri-level enclosed cars. This particular car was originally owned by the Canadian National and was rebuilt by Pullman-Standard for Auto-Train. (Pullman-Standard)

Autos are easily loaded and unloaded by Auto-Train crews at all three terminals (Auto-Train)

that had to be undertaken to get the train on the track. Many people thought that the loss figure meant that Auto-Train was not going to make it. But the pessimists did not get to have their day. The new company was operating in the black within 90 days from the commencement of service. The net income from May 1, 1972 to April 30, 1973 was $804,872. During that year the company carried 61,740 automobiles and 186,201 passengers. From May 1, 1973 to April 30, 1974, the company earned a net income of $1,568,890 and carried 95,302 automobiles and 261,067 passengers. As one can see, this is a substantial increase over the previous year.

There is no doubt about it, Auto-Train is a progressive company, and progress has been made

on several fronts. The company can now operate anywhere in the USA subject to the ICC approval. This development was brought about by the passage of the Rail Passenger Service Amendments Act of 1973. Because of this, the Louisville, Kentucky and Sanford, Florida operation went into operation on May 24, 1974.

The new route extends over the Louisville and Nashville Railroad and Seaboard Coast Line. As of early 1975, there is one train per week each way. The consist of the new train service is similar to the train operated on the Washington-Florida run, and the company expects the potential on the midwest route to be even greater than the original route. The scheduled running time for trains 5 and 6 is 22 hours for the 988 miles.

With the fuel situation being what it is, Auto-Train services could be a boon to the American

Steam generator cars are operated at the end of the train and supply steam for train heating and the steam tables in the buffet cars. Not all steam generator cars were rebuilt from baggage cars, such as this car purchased from the Santa Fe. Auto-Train operates a number of ex-Great Northern steam generator cars. (Patrick C. Dorin)

Dome coach No. 510 is an ex-Santa Fe dome lounge dormitory car. Auto-Train has retained the dormitories in cars 510 to 515. Note the steam generator car ahead of coach 510. (Auto-Train)

Dome coach No. 523 is an ex-Santa Fe dome lounge with a lounge section beneath the dome. Again Auto-Train has elected to retain those facilities. 523 is one of five such cars. Cars 541 and 542 look very similar but are operated as Night Club Lounge cars and coach seating was not installed. (Patrick C. Dorin)

Coach seating in Auto-Train cars is made up exclusively of leg rest chairs with arm rests in the middle. Chairs are very colorful with reds, oranges, purples and other complementary and restful colors. Coach service includes pillows and blankets. (Auto-Train)

Full domes are not the only dome coaches in service on Auto-Train. This photo shows ex-Western Pacific coach No. 817 (known as a "mini-dome") after rebuilding as Auto-Train No. 472. (Photo by C. K. Marsh, Jr. Collection of H. H. Harwood, Jr.)

traveling public. For example, if the Auto-Trains between Washington, D. C. and Florida are fully utilized, the train service saves 11 million gallons of fuel annually. For one family to drive from Florida to Washington, D. C., they would burn about 90 gallons of gasoline. In contrast, the Auto-Train burns about 25 gallons per family. Moreover General Electric locomotives incorporate design advances that provide for maximum operations with a minimum of fuel, which at the same time reduces smoke emissions (which are low on railroads anyway) to help keep the environment clean and fresh. In other words, not only is Auto-Train providing a fine service by bringing together automobile and railroad in complete harmony, but they are doing a public service in the saving of precious fuel. Therefore it appears that the potential for Auto-Train is literally unlimited. Services of this type are desperately needed to many places, such as the Pacific southwest and northwest, the Lake Superior, Colorado and South Dakota vacation lands and many other places to and from all of the populated areas of the USA. Only time will tell what expansion will take place with America's most innovative train operation since the Pullman sleeper was invited. Thank you Mr. Garfield and all of your nearly 700 employees for doing such a fine job for the American traveler, the railroad industry and the United States of America.

Auto-Train dome coach No. 708 (known as a "maxi-dome") is ex-Union Pacific dome coach No. 7012. Seating on the main level of the car is identical to that shown previously in the full dome interior photo. (Photo by C. K. Marsh, Jr., Collection of H. H. Harwood, Jr.)

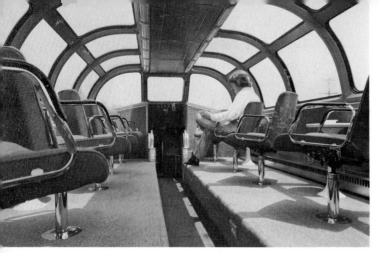

Interiors of some of the mini-domes are equipped with single seating for lounging and viewing the passing scenery. (Auto-Train)

Exterior of one of the buffet dining cars operated on the Lorton-Sanford route. (Pullman-Standard)

Interior of the buffet dining cars is built cafeteria style. This photo was taken before the addition of chairs at the tables, which is designed for both couples and seating for four. these food service cars are among the most attractive ever operated. (Pullman-Standard)

Dormitory-Kitchen cars are operated between the buffet cars. Auto-Train owns five of these cars, which were purchased from Seaboard Coast Line. The kitchen serves both buffet cars. (Patrick C. Dorin — David J. Overhouse)

Coach passengers disembark from Auto-Train after their overnight trip on the Washington-Florida run. (Auto-Train)

CHAPTER 11
The Algoma Central Railway To Agawa Canyon

The Lake Superior Region of North America is one of the most scenic areas of North America. At the eastern end of that Great Lake, we find the Algoma Central Railway winding its way northward through the pines, around lakes and mountains, over gorges and river valleys to the fantastic Agawa Canyon. This scenery has drawn people from all over the United States and Canada for a trip over the Algoma Central Railway.

Prior to the 1960's, the AC ran passenger trains 1 and 2 between Sault Ste. Marie and Hearst, Ontario in what might be termed a conventional manner. Eventually the trains operated on a less than daily schedule, sometimes during the off season as few as four trips per week were made. The railroad serves an area surprisingly void of roads. Fishermen, hunters and lumberjacks were the primary customers. As more and more sportsmen noticed the area to the east of Lake Superior, more of them began making use of the ACR for transportation. Word also spread among wives and families of the beauty to be seen in the Algoma country, and there was only one way to get there—by Algoma Central passenger train.

People began to ride the ACR to Canyon and return on vacation days and weekends. It was a convenient place to get off and return on the southbound train. The railroad then set up tours and park facilities were expanded and improved at the Canyon station. The tours allowed people to make a one day trip to the Agawa Canyon. Business mushroomed throughout the 1960's and into the 1970's. It is not unusual for trains 1 and 2 to operated in two sections between Sault Ste. Marie and Canyon. Trains are operated with up to 20 cars including 2 dining cars.

At the present time (1974), the train departs the Soo with up to four GP-9's, a heater car, one or two baggage cars, a long string of coaches and dining cars. The run to Canyon takes about 4 hours for the 114 mile run and arrives just after 12:00 Noon. The entire train except for one GP-9, 1 baggage, 1 heater car and one coach is set out at Canyon. The passengers detrain and have approximately two hours to rest, relax, hike and just look at God's handiwork in the Agawa Canyon.

The Algoma Central offers three types of tours. The most famous is the One Day Wilderness Tour mentioned above. This tour operates from mid-May to mid-October. The Snow train is a one day Winter Wonderland Tour that runs from January to March. The third type of tour is the "Tour of the Line." The railroad advertises "Visit the Frontier North" and such tours are available the year round. This last tour actually runs for two days. The passenger rides the through coach which operates to Hearst. Hearst is a connection with the Canadian National Railway and is 296 miles north of Sault Ste. Marie. The round trip is handled with a single coach and no dining car service is provided. There are also hunting and fishing lodges, camp sites, canoe trails and other recreation areas along the ACR's route. Many of these sites are accessible only by Algoma Central Railway.

At the present time (1974), the ACR operates a fleet of ex-Canadian Pacific smooth side coaches. The interiors still contain reclining seats, while the exteriors are painted maroon with a light grey roof and gold lettering. The cars advertise the Agawa Canyon Tours below the windows in the center of the car. The 15 to 20 car passenger trains, unheard of on the ACR 20 years ago, make a splendid picture as they move through the Lake Superior Wilderness of Ontario—God's Country.

Trains 1 and 2 originally operated between Sault Ste. Marie and Michipicoten, which is located on Lake Superior. Michipicoten is located at the end of a branch line that leaves the main line at Hawk Junction. Trains 3 and 4 operated from Hawk Junction to Hearst. When the Michipicoten service was discontinued, trains 1 and 2 were re-routed to the Sault Ste. Marie-Hearst circuit. Train No. 1 is shown here arriving Michipicoten with two cars, a typical local, in October, 1948. (Dale Wilson)

Tour traffic had not yet caught on in the mid-1950's when this photo was taken showing train No. 2 arriving at Sault Ste. Marie during the winter season. None of the Algoma Central geeps are equipped with steam generators. Therefore all passenger trains must be assigned one steam generator, such as shown here coupled to the 162. Ex-U.S. Army Pullman troop sleepers are also operated as baggage cars. The Algoma Central left the exterior of these ex-troop sleepers virtually unchanged in their conversion to either baggage car or steam generator service. (Algoma Central Railway)

Southbound train No. 2 has arrived at the Agawa Canyon depot and will soon pick up the tour coaches. This photo shows the park and some of its facilities that passengers may enjoy during their layover in the canyon. This area is very beautiful, and words cannot really describe the scenery. It must be seen to be fully appreciated. The tour to Agawa conyon is especially suited for family travel. (Algoma Central Railway)

Train No. 2 rounds a bend and through a rock cut on the homeward journey with a tremendous train. The consist included four geeps, one steam generator car, one ex-Army troop sleeper baggage car, one standard baggage car, two dining cars and well over a dozen coaches most of which are ex-Canadian Pacific cars. (Algoma Central Railway)

A good deal of the AC coach fleet are ex-Canadian Pacific Railway coaches, such as the 423 shown here at Sault Ste. Marie. Most are painted Tuscan Red with a light grey roof and gold lettering. "Agawa-Canyon-Tour" is splashed across the side. A number of the cars still carry their old CP colors of silver with Tuscan Red striping, but are re-lettered for the Algoma Central. (Patrick C. Dorin)

Dining cars on the Algoma Central could be classified as "shorties" and contain vestibules at each end, as they are rebuilt coaches. Again the cars are lettered "Agawa-Canyon-Tour." (Patrick C. Dorin)

The **Algoma Central** has continually added to their coach fleet, and sometimes so fast that the former Canadian Pacific color scheme has remained with only the words Algoma Central replacing the former road name. The year 1974 was no exception for the addition of equipment. As this is being written, the road is rebuilding 14 articulated coaches with electro-mechanical air conditioning from the Southern Pacific, two coaches from the Gulf, Mobile and Ohio and four from the Central of Georgia. This equipment will be in service by the 1975 tour season. (Patrick C. Dorin)

Train No. 2 arrives at Sault Ste. Marie with three units and 18 cars on July 7, 1973. (Patrick C. Dorin)

Tours continue in the winter time and here we see the snow train (No. 2) southbound from Agawa Canyon with one geep, one steam generator car (this one has been modified extensively), one baggage car, two coaches with a diner sandwiched in between. The winter tour is equally beautiful, and one should remember the Ontario winters are much more pleasant than weather in the Detroit-Chicago areas. (Algoma Central Railway)

It's June 17, 1952, and Algoma Central train No. 4 pauses at Hawk Junction, Ontario to wait for No. 2 from Michipicoten. Upon arrival from the Lake Superior port, the two trains will be combined for the final leg of the run to Sault Ste. Marie. During the early 1950's, the AC offered buffet service between Sault Ste. Marie and Hearst, Ontario. (Elmer Treloar)

Upon arrival the three Geeps and one steam generator return to the roundhouse as passengers continue to unload from the train. (Patrick C. Dorin)

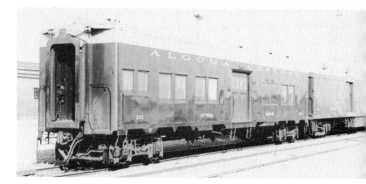

The Algoma Central operates three basic types of head-end cars on trains 1 and 2. The former Army troop sleepers have served nicely in this service not only on the ACR but many US roads as well. (Patrick C. Dorin)

The second type of head-end car is the full express baggage car, such as the 207 shown here. (Patrick C. Dorin)

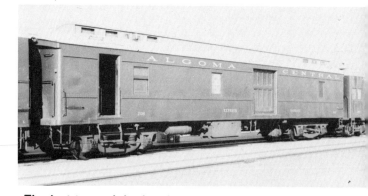

The last type of the head-end car is the former Rail Post Office Baggage cars such as the 208. All head-end cars are equipped to handle canoes and other outdoor type of equipment for campers, hunters, fishermen and other passengers whose livelihood takes them into the woods. (Patrick C. Dorin)

164

CHAPTER 12
The Ontario Northland's Polar Bear

The Polar Bear can lay claim to being the only train in North America that is both a mixed train and a tour train. In fact, it is actually two trains, a tri-weekly local and a summer season passenger train operating daily except Friday. The Polar Bear operates between Cochrane and Moosonee, Ontario, otherwise known as the Island Falls Subdivision. The subdivision cuts through the muskeg of the James Bay lowlands where swamp spruce and jackpine struggle with their growth in the subarctic climate. It is Ontario's fabled Northland, and it is one of few truly romantic train rides in the world.

The land north of Cochrane has been tamed little beyond the Ontarion Northland Railway right of way. The scattered inhabitants are pioneers in every sense of the word. The railroad clings closely to river banks as it moves north through the muskeg and the land is thickly forested.

The last road disappears dead end into the muskeg just a few short miles north of Cochrane. From there on, the mixed train becomes the milkman, breadman, mailman, neighborhood bus, ambulance, newsboy, delivery service and the center of attractions. Train 421 runs north on Monday, Wednesday and Friday, while 622 rumbles south on Tuesday, Thursday and Saturday. The trains run as third class trains in the operating time table and take 6 hours for northbound run. Southbound, 622 is scheduled to make the run in 5 hours, 35 minutes. The trains leave Cochrane and Moosonee at 8:25 AM and 8:40 AM respectively. However the time table is only a rule of thumb and is not a word of law. Although the mixed has four scheduled stops and five flag stops, the train will stop anywhere, anytime, for anyone who flags it down. How is that for service?

The mixed train runs with a single FP-7 diesel locomotive, any number of freight cars and a small string of varnish, including a snack lounge car. Passenger accommodations are, however, all-coach. 421 and 622 connect with the Northland at Cochrane in both directions.

Trains 423 and 624 are a different story. This train too is an all-coach train with restaurant car service. As stated before it runs daily except Friday and stops only at Fraserdale and Otter Rapids. It is a tour train that provides passengers with a five hour stay in Moosonee. Passengers can elect however to stay overnight at Moosonee and catch the mixed train south the next morning if they wish. 423 departs Cochrane at 8:30 and arrives at its destination at 1:00 PM. No. 624 departs at 6:00 PM and arrives Cochrane at 10:15 PM. It does make connections with the southbound Northland from Kapuskasing en route to Toronto. The train carries about a dozen cars including a former mail and baggage car in use as a recreation and snack car. It is powered by two FP-7's, features streamlined coaches and sing-a-longs in addition to the spectacular scenery that rolls by outside. The cars are painted with Polar Bears on the sides facing the center of the car. The train name, "Polar Bear Express" is between the two bears, all of which is below the window line. The railroad name is in the letter board where it can be seen by all. It is interesting to note that the equipment goes into commuter service at Toronto during the fall, winter and spring months. One might compare this to the old operation of Pullman cars that went west and north in the summer, and south in the winter. Commuter business is heavier during the non-vacation months of the year and the cars are put to good use. Vacation periods reduce commuter patronage, and the cars go north for the vacationers to ride them. A very interesting passenger car pool to say the least.

Freight business of the mixed train is not addressed by town or village, but by mile post. The engineer blows the whistle and the forestland resident knows that a package is waiting for him by the track.

Hunters, fishermen and trappers are let off anywhere they desire, while their canoes, tents and supplies are unloaded from the baggage car. Whenever they appear, the Polar Bear will be back to pick them up, hopefully with a moose, deer, bear, furs or freezer load of fish.

One of the significant things about coach train travel is that people become friends very easily. This is especially true on the Polar Bear. Scien-

The Polar Bear of 1974 is a far cry from the Polar Bear of just 10 years ago. Now, not only a mixed train on a year around basis, but also a special tour train similar to the Algoma Central's run to Agawa Canyon. Here we see two immaculate FP-7's heading for James Bay with 11 cars including one ex-RPO-baggage car running as a Recreation Car. There is no doubt about it, the train is one of the greatest ways to view the far north. (Ontario Northland Railway)

tists and miltary men heading for Hudson Bay pay close attention to the grizzled trappers and loggers that ride the train regularly. It is often said that there are no strangers in the northland, and no strangers aboard the Polar Bear.

The train follows a route north from Cochrane that French Military Officer Chevalier de Troyes followed in 1686 to capture the British fur trading post at the mouth of the Moose River.

The excursion trains 423 and 624 stop at mile post 93 at the immense Ontario Hydro Otter Rapids dam and powerhouse in the valley. This stop is soley for the benefit of the passengers so that they may photograph the facility and in general look at the scenery.

Mile post 142 is an engineering triumph to the men who built the Ontario Northland Railway. At this point, the railroad crosses the Moose River, which is a half mile wide. The river is one of changing moods from the solid ice and calm quiet of winter to the raging ice flow torrents of spring and the warm murky sluggishness of summer. Originally, the river fought the ONR time and time again to keep itself from being bridged and conquered. Finally, the construction crews dumped eight trainloads of ballast off a temporary trestle until the flow of water was stopped. Then working through the winter, with temperatures as low as 50 degrees below zero, the crews spanned the rest of the river with concrete piers and steel bridge decking. The cost

was more than $1,000,000 in depression era money. The next 44 miles to mile poast 186, Moosonee, is all downhill.

Summer or winter, train time is important to the residents of Moosonee. The station platform is always packed with people waiting for friends or freight, or just simply to watch the Polar Bear come in. The winter passenger will find few, if any, cars or trucks but plenty of snowmobiles and dog teams. It is as far north as one can go by train, from here on it is either by airplane or a 22 foot Rupert's House freighter canoe. It is a true wilderness country where one can gaze at the stars and Northern Lights through a smogless sky, and the charging tempo of the twentieth century disappears as silently as a winter morning or the tide in James Bay.

Except for the summer months, 421 and 622 are the only trains on the Island Falls Subdivision. One never can tell what the future will bring to this area of the Polar Bear trains, whose very engines carry the Polar Bear insignia. A lignite coal deposit has been discoverd at Onakawana, mile post 127, and who knows but perhaps coal trains will share the line with the Polar Bear mixed trains and summer excursion trains. However, if there is one thing that people can be sure of, it is the fact that the coaches and chair cars of the *Polar Bear* are the best way to travel through and to see, feel, and smell the goodness of the far reaches of the Ontario Northland.

CHAPTER 13

Ski Trains

Sometimes the train is a special way of getting some place, and it can accomplish much more than just simply taking passengers from one place to another. A good deal of these types of operations had to do with various special events or seasonal operations including ski trains. A short lived operation in the New York Central and the Long Island were hiking trains. These trains departed New York City early in the morning on Saturdays and Sundays and took passengers to various parks for hiking. Another example is businessmen renting a train, or riding a train with a private coach or lounge for the purpose of conducting meetings—and be away from phone calls and other interruptions. However the most spectacular of all such trains were probably the ski trains.

A number of railroads operated ski trains both in the west and in the east. Such trains died out fast in the late 1940's and there was only a sprinkling of snow trains in the 1960's. It was not until Amtrak established service between Washington and Montreal that any revival of ski train service was even thought of. With the possible exception of the Rio Grande service out of Denver, most of the western trains carried Pullman sleepers. In the east however, most of the trains were all-coach specials with additional equipment for recreation, dining and outfitting. The peak of popularity was probably during the latter part of the Depression. Record crowds patronized these trains from Christmas through Easter of those years. Let's turn back the pages of history now and take a look at the "Snow Train" which was—more or less—originated by the Boston and Maine in 1931.

The B&M originated the ski train in the USA on January 11, 1931. On that day it transported nearly 200 winter sports enthusiasts on a special train from Boston to Warner, New Hampshire. By the winter of 1935-1936, the B&M was running 25 or more snow trains during a season. This did not include those trains that orignated on the New Haven or other railroads and terminated on the B&M. Furthermore, some of these

trains operated in up to four sections. During the winter of 1935 and 1936, the B&M reported carrying well over 25,000 winter sports passengers to the hill country of Vermont and New Hampshire. Most of these went to the White Mountains.

The B&M operation included both one day and weekend excursions with the 1935 level fares varying from $1.75 to $3 round trip for the one day trips and about $4 for the weekend runs. The trains consisted of as many coaches as required plus a dining car and a sports equipment car. If more than one section were operated the sports equipment car ran in the first section. It offered for sale or rent skis, ski clothing, toboggans, ski wax, books on skiing and even red flannels. All sections carried a small supply of incidentals, and the equipment car was available to all passengers before departure and at the destination.

Hotels and local chambers of commerce at the ski areas met the trains and people not having reservations were accommodated. The B&M itself even made reservations at the ski areas for passengers requesting it. Passengers were taken from the trains to the ski areas by truck, buses or automobiles for rates of 25 to 50 cents depending upon the distance. The B&M advertised its snow trains extensively, and during the 1930's was quite pleased with the snow train profits.

The Maine Central also operated several snow trains for ski enthusiasts of the Portland area. These trains ran to the Fryeburg, Rumford, and the Dover-Foxcroft areas. Maine Central trains were not as heavy as Boston and Maine services, but nevertheless operated some trains in two sections. The all-coach consists carried from 400 to over 700 passengers per individual train section. The Main Central also participated in some joint through operations with the B&M and New Haven from time to time.

The New Haven snow train operations attained major proportions during the 1930's as it served skiers from the populous New York City and New Haven, Conn. areas. The company operated one day trains to Pittsfield, Mass.,

Each ski trip arrived and departed at a large city depot, and may have made a few stops at some suburbs. The result, either going or coming, was piles of skis, equipment, luggage and other hand baggage. It was a congested process in either direction as passengers arrived by car, bus and taxi or en route home from a fabulous week-end. This photo shows the Union Station in Los Angeles after the arrival of a Union Pacific ski tour. Union Pacific tours were of the long distance variety running from both Los Angeles and Chicago to points in California, Idaho, Colorado and to points on the Southern Pacific. (Union Pacific Railroad)

The UP extensively advertised their ski tours, and this photo was part of such advertising. Ski passengers traveled to the slopes by UPchair cars, while their baggage and skis rode up front in the baggage cars. Passengers were also given pillows as well as a copy of Skiing Magazine. Most UP ski trips were overnight on such trains as the City of Denver. However the transcontinental trains such as the City of Portland, San Francisco Overland and City of Los Angeles were part of the act. The City of Portland and Portland Rose carried substantial numbers of passengers to the Union Pacific's most important ski center, Sun Valley, Idaho. (Union Pacific Railroad)

South Lee and Norfolk, Conn., and weekend trains to Waterbury, Vermont. Passengers were able to board the trains at several locations, which originated at both New York City and New Haven.

Many of the weekend trains were operated on an all-expense basis while for others the New Haven only made hotel reservations upon request. Special facilities were provided on all trains including dining cars, club and lounge cars and the sports equipment car. The latter functioned the same on the New Haven as on the Boston and Maine. It is interesting to note that the New Haven made careful surveys of winter sports areas in order to assure passengers of ample skiing trails and slopes. This was done before train schedules were set up, and it shows that at least some marketing research was already with us in the mid-1930's.

Advertising the trains was done with New York department and sporting goods stores who were interested in promoting skiing and their winter sports equipment. It was an unusual advertising arrangement that benefited the public, railroad and stores in one swoop. The snow country communities were also anxious to cooperate with the New Haven. Most of these areas were pri-

marily summer resort orientated and they welcomed the opportunity of adding a winter time business.

The New York Central System, as one might guess, carried a substantial amount of passengers to the ski slopes in special ski trains. The NYC operated both one day and weekend trips from New York City to Phoenicia and Woodstock in the Catksills; from New York to Lake Placid; from Syracuse and Utica to Old Forge; from New York City to Bear Mountain and over the Delaware and Hudson to Gore Mountain, North Creek, New York; and on the Boston and Albany from Boston to Hinsdale, North Adams and Middlefield. And if we travel west abit, we find that the Michigan Central operated ski trains from Detroit to Grayling, Michigan. The New York Central System would carry in excess of 30,000 passengers during a winter season, and charged from $1.00 to $3.00 for a round trip ticket depending upon the distance and if it was a weekend or a one day trip. Generally, the weekend rates were higher and were further away from New York City or Boston.

Advertising the trains was also conducted in cooperation with department stores and also ski clubs. Also the railroad maintained an indicator to report snow conditions at various points in the Grand Central Terminal.

As usual the trains carried coaches and dining cars, sometimes two diners with their kitchen ends coupled together. An unusual twist though was that the sports equipment cars were operated by a New York department store.

The Delaware and Hudson, in addition to the joint New York Central trains to North Creek, operated ski trains out of Schenectady and Albany. These were one day affairs with round trip charges of $1.50. D&H ski trains generally handled from 400 to 600 passengers per train and consisted of coaches, dining car and a baggage car for skis and equipment. All ski trains ran to North Creek where they were parked for occupancy all day. The diners remained open during the day and offered combination breakfasts at 65¢ to $1.00 while dinners were about a dollar. The D&H advertised the trains in newspapers and placed colored window cards in department and sporting goods stores.

The Delaware, Lackawanna & Western Railroad operated one day ski trains from New York City to Pocono Summit, Pennsylvania in the Pocono Mountains. There were also additional ski train services from Scranton, Pennsylvania to the same destination. Patronage on the Lackawanna was not as heavy as on other lines with the average passenger load being only about 200 per train. Round trip fares from New York were $2.50 and just 75¢ on the trains out of Scranton. Department stores in Newark, New Jersey co-operated with the Lackawanna in much the same manner as stores did with the New York Central and New Haven in New York.

Each train carried a recreation car and a diner where special priced meals were served. The trains were parked at Pocono Summit from which buses carried passengers to the slopes of Pocono Manor Inn. The Inn had available for rental skis, bobsleds and other equipment.

On February 12, 1936 the DL&W operated a very special ski train. On that day a train, sponsored by a group of New York society people, ran to the Pocono Mountains for the benefit of a nursery. The fare was $7.50 and the amount above the railroad fare went to the charity. Very few trains have been operated for such beneficial reasons.

The Baltimore and Ohio also operated a small number of ski trains. Basically these ran out of Buffalo, New York and Pittsburg, Pennsylvania plus a number of others, known as Sunday Coach Excursions, from the Baltimore-Washington, D. C. areas.

Trains out of Buffalo ran as one day trips to Salamanca, New York, a distance of about 60 miles for a round trip fare of $1.25. These trains

Most Depression era Ski trains looked very much like this New York Central ski passenger extra at Phoenicia, New York. Typical day coaches were operated, and just as often as not, even commuter or suburban cars got into the show. Such trains always included a baggage car and many carried a cafe lounge or dining car. On the one day tours, the steam engine remained coupled to the train for heating at the ski location. On weekend runs, the train would often go to some intermediate terminal so that the engine could be serviced and the cars cleaned before the Sunday afternoon trip back. The advantage of taking the train to the slopes was that it often arrived right next to the ski area. All one had to do was get off the train and start skiing. (Ed Nowak — Penn Central)

consisted of coaches, cafe car and a baggage car for sports equipment and carried an average of about 425 passengers per train. The slopes available were those of the Allegheny State Park which was seven miles from Salamanca. Bus service was provided for 75¢ for the round trip and the administration building at the park was available for rest and eating lunch and snacks.

The trains from Pittsburgh operated to Kane, Pennsylvania, a distance of 195 miles at a round trip fare of $4.00. These trains departed Pittsburgh about midnight Saturday with Pullman sleepers, coaches, dining car and a baggage car for checking skis and other equipment, and for carrying the rental equipment. These trains usually carried about 250 to 275 passengers on the average. At Kane, the trains were parked with steam permitting the passengers to maintain headquarters at the train. The Kane Chamber of Commerce provided free transportation by horse drawn bobsleds, trucks and automobiles from the station to farms where ski trails and other winter facilities were available.

The B&O also participated in joint advertising with the sport shops and radio-newspaper medias at both the origins and destinations of the ski trains. Although B&O operations were not as elaborate as the New York Central and other lines, the trains provided a service to areas that otherwise would not have had such service.

Many railroads such as the Milwaukee Road, Union Pacific, Great Northern and others, operated their own ski areas. This photo shows the Milwaukee Road Ski Bowl located at the summit of Snoqualmie Pass in the heart of the Cascade Mountains 60 miles east of Seattle. (The Milwaukee Road)

With such arrangements, it was easy for the railroad company involved to make complete trips or tours on one neat ticket package for the skier. Here a group of skiers and spectators are detraining from a Milwaukee Road passenger extra ski train at the Ski Bowl in March, 1947. The fare for these tours in 1946 and 1947 was $1.77 from Seattle and $2.09 from Tacoma round trip. Most Milwaukee Road ski trains were one day affairs, but the company ran special Night Snow Trains and passengers could ride the Olympian or Columbian for weekday trips. (The Milwaukee Road)

The Milwaukee Road's Copper Country Limited also handled a substantial number of skiers on its daily winter runs to and from the snowy Upper Peninsula of Michigan. Both Iron Mountain and Houghton feature ski areas. The train operated between Chicago and Calumet in a joint arrangement with the Milwaukee Road and Soo Line (the former Duluth, South Shore & Atlantic Railway). This photo shows the Copper Country Limited prior to its departure as South Shore No. 10 from Calumet during the summer months. (Jim Scribbins)

The Burlington Route's Denver and California Zephyrs carried many skiers to the Rocky Mountain and Sierra Nevada Mountain ski resorts. Often the two trains departed Chicago in several sections and Friday nights the crowds were so thick it was difficult for commuters to find their trains. Although some of these Colorado skiers were going only for the weekend, most of the passengers were traveling west for a week or more on the slopes. This photo shows CB&Q No. 17, the California Zephyr, heading west from Chicago on December 6, 1964. The Ski season had already begun in the Western Mountains. (Louis A. Marre & Gordon B. Mott)

The Reading Railroad too, got into the snow train act in the mid-1930's. Some of their trains ran from Philadelphia to Bear Mountain, New York, with the operation over the West Shore from New York City. The round trip fare for this operation was $3.25 and some of the excursions ran in two sections. The number of passengers carried for a single trip ranged from about 175 to nearly 800. The trains consisted of coaches, dining cars and baggage cars for checking skis and other sports equipment. The dining cars featured special "snow train" menus with breakfasts at 50 to 75¢ and dinners at about $1.00. In contrast to other lines, the Reading made no special arrangements for the passengers at Bear Mountain. The company felt that the many, many events scheduled annually by the Bear Mountain Park provided sufficient inducement. The Philadelphia department and sporting goods stores also cooperated with the Reading in advertising the trains on the radio and newspapers. Although the Reading's ski train operations were small, they were by no means the smallest in the east.

The Pennsylvania, not one to be left out in the cold, also ran one day snow trains from Philly to Bear Mountain via its own line to Jersey City and the West Shore beyond. The trains consisted of coaches, dining car and a refreshment car. The PRR was among the few lines that operated refreshment cars in their ski trains. Patronage on the PRR was relatively small, and the company carried most of its ski business in regular trains from Philadelphia to the Pocono Mountains. The company offered one day trip tickets and special four day round trippers for winter sportsmen. These special excursion tickets were advertised in flyers and booklets, and in the Broad Street Suburban Depot (Philadelphia), there was a large animated window sign with a skiing scene and a series of thermometers which showed temperatures and snow conditions daily at about a dozen winter sports centers.

Of the eastern railroads, the Erie brought up the rear with ski excursions. Very few trains did they run, and none were operated on a regular basis. They did, however, run some special coach trains for certain ski clubs of the New York area. Salisbury Mills, New York was one such destination for these ski club trains, which did not carry the general public nor were they advertised in any way.

Ski trains in the west operated some very long distances compared to the trains in the east. The Burlington Route and Rio Grande ran trains from Chicago to Colorado ski slopes. Often these ran

Another convenient train for winter skiers and summer time tourists was the North Western's Arrowhead Limited, which operated as a section of the North Western Limited between Chicago and Eau Claire. En route to Duluth with 14 cars, we see Omaha Road "Pacifics" numbers 384 and 510 double heading the heavy train near Eau Claire, Wisconsin on August 10, 1948. The train was particularly popular with skiers and tourists because of the late departure from Chicago and early morning arrival at the popular centers in Northwestern Wisconsin. The train departed Duluth early in the evening for an equally early arrival in Chicago, which made the schedule a convenient one in both directions. (A. Robert Johnson)

as extra sections of the Denver or California Zephyrs. It was not uncommon in the winter time for the DZ to run three sections from Chicago right up through the mid-1960's. Ski trains in the east had been long forgotten by this time. The Rio Grande Railroad ran ski trains from Denver to Rocky Mountain ski slopes right through the winter of 1974—the time of this writing.

The Union Pacific provided ski vacations in some of the western parks, especially Sun Valley, Idaho. The Great Northern, Northern Pacific, and the Milwaukee Road also promoted ski trips by train to points in the Rocky and Cascade Mountain Ranges.

The midwest too had its ski trains on the Milwaukee Road, Chicago and North Western and Soo Line Railroads. The Milwaukee Road ran special ski trains to Iron Mountain, Michigan from Chicago. These trains went north on Friday nights and returned on Sunday afternoon. Other skiers were accommodated on the Copper Country Limited to the northern part of the Upper Peninsula. Skiers rode the Peninsula 400 and the Iron and Copper Country Express to Northern Michigan on the Chicago and North Western. The C&NW also served northern Wisconson and Ironwood, Michigan with the Ashland Limited and Flambeau 400, two other favorite trains for skiers. The Soo Line provided service to northwestern Wisconsin slopes with their Laker, and the C&NW did the same with the famous Duluth-Superior Limited.

Ski trains seem to have a special personality. It was an atmosphere of good, clean, wholesome fun and a comradship that can only be found on a train. Even the trains that accommodated skiers with the regularly scheduled operations seemed to have had that atmosphere. The trains left the cities behind and went out to the country with fresh air, clean snow and a chance to relax with vigorous exercise on the slopes. The entire trip did something for one's soul. Fortunately the ski train has not yet been totally lost.

Amtrak is now running special package tours for ski trips, not only to the west, but also to Vermont. The Montrealer, running over the Central Vermont Railway, has been an instant success. This coach and sleeper car train has far exceeded forecasted patronage, and now the quiet of the Vermont winter is again drawing skiers to the slopes by that superb mode of travel— The TRAIN.

As with the Copper Country Limited, this writer was not able to secure winter time photos of the Laker and the Arrowhead Limited during the time those trains carried skiers. The Soo Line's Laker is shown here at the Duluth station in early June, 1953. The consist does not yet reflect the summer tourist trade to the Indianhead Country, which will soon swell the consist to double and triple its five cars shown here. The same happened on weekends during the ski season. (A. Robert Johnson)

CHAPTER 14

Rail Fan Trips and Special Events

Railroads have operated special trains for particular reasons or special events ever since they have been in operation. There have been numerous reasons for such runs including picnics, marriages, the Kentucky Derby, political campaign trips, the Indianapolis 500, European royalty visiting the USA and Canada, state governors' conventions, weekend excursions to the Wisconsin Dells and other parks and rail fan trips. And this list is by no means conclusive. One might say there are as many reasons for operating special passenger trains as there are grains of sand on the beaches of Lake Michigan. Furthermore, these types of trains have often been made up of the strangest combinations of passenger car equipment. Often business cars, club and lounge cars, dining cars, sleepers, parlor cars, gondola and flat cars fitted with seats and cabooses are operated as coaches in coach service. In other words, First Class tickets were not required to ride the sleepers and parlor cars that were pressed into such extra special service.

For the most part these passenger extras have looked just like any other passenger train with the possible exception of sleeprs and business cars being used as coaches; and the use of a so-called baggage recreation car in the middle of the train. This type of a car is a baggage car fitted with a bar and grill for the use of passengers. Not only does the car provide the food and drinks, but is also used for dancing or whatever else the passengers had in mind. Sometimes lounge cars were used in this type of service. On one occasion the Milwaukee Road removed all of the furniture from a lounge car for a square dancers' special train from Chicago to Minneapolis. The square dancers danced the entire 421 miles from Chicago to the City of Lakes and Wheat. That will be one train ride that those people will never forget.

Rail fan trips have held center stage on many railroads for decades. Most of these trips have often combined not only a steam locomotive

excursion, but also a trip to a car or locomotive shop with a special tour of the facilities. These trains are also equipped with special baggage cars coupled behind the locomotive. Such equipment is fitted for tape recorders and other sound recording equipment to pick the steam engine sounds for people to enjoy for many years to come. Nearly all rail fan trips are equipped with coaches, but such is not always the case. A recent trip over the Duluth & Northeastern Railway for the author and his family has to rank as one of the most unusual consists for a rail fan trip.

As we arrived at Cloquet on a beautiful August, 1973 morning, we were greeted not by a string of coaches but by a consist of Burlington Northern extended vision cupola cabooses, a Northern Pacific wood caboose, Duluth, Missabe & Iron Range Railway wood cabooses and a DM&IR combination baggage-business car. The latter is probably either the only or one of a very few such cars in the USA or Canada. In addition, the train was equipped with a flat car fitted with sides and seats. The entire excursion was carried in the D&NE's regular freight operating between Cloquet and Saginaw. One could say it was one of a rare number of excursions that actually could be classed as a mixed train. Many railroads such as the Union Pacific, Southern, Reading, and Canadian National have operated steam powered fan trips that are famous the world over—and that is no exaggeration.

Other organizations have run steam trips, such as Iron Horse and the Green Bay, Wisconsin Railroad Museum. Other organizations, such as the Lake Superior Transportation Club, are planning trips in the future.

One could literally write a book about special passenger trains. Because of space, this chapter is being kept rather short but before closing, this author would like to point out that some of the special trains have been substantial sized trains. Many have carried in excess of 1000 passengers, such as the Race Track Specials on the Illinois

One of the more famous of the regularly operated steam specials is the immortal 8444 of the Union Pacific. The all-coach specials include a baggage recreation car on the head-end for the sound boys and a cafe car. A dome coach has also been retained by the Union Pacific for special runs. (Jim Morin)

Central, Chicago and North Western and other lines. However, the special that tops all specials was one operated by the Burlington Route on May 23, 1964 commemorating one hundred years of suburban passenger service. On that day, passenger extra No. 5632 West (dual service Northern type 4-8-4, steam type 0-5B class) ran from the Chicago Union Station to Aurora, Illinois with 3,300 passengers. The train equipped with about 20 double deck coaches holds the record for the largest number of passengers ever hauled on a single train. This is a feat that can only be exceeded by another passenger train. Perhaps the next celebration will find a train of 30 double deck coaches with 4500 passengers. It could be done, and only a train can do it.

Special trains are usually alot of fun to ride because everybody on board has a common purpose. Trains are always a place where people make friends easily, but this seems especially true on specials. Song fests, special meals and other activities seem to hasten the breaking down of psychological barriers to friendships, and it is a known fact that many life long friends have met on such trains. What more can one ask for and when it happens on a train—the memories seem to be just that more pleasant.

An ex-Canadian Pacific Ten Wheeler No. 1057, now the Credit Valley (an Ontario Rail Fan organization), wheels a seven car rail fan trip over the CPR about two miles south of the Forks of the Credit River. The Credit Valley operates over a section of railroad which was once called the Credit Valley until taken over by the CPR. (Elmer Treloar)

Many different types of equipment have been operated for rail fan trips. This Western Pacific trip, headed by Ten-Wheeler No. 94, consisted of four mill type gondolas, one coach and a wood combine. The special was run in October, 1954. (Harold K. Vollrath)

One of the more unusual consists was the Duluth & Northeastern Railway trip of August, 1973. Seven cars were attached to the regular local freight and consisted of a flat car with benches and railings, one baggage sleeper lounge car (DM&IR) and five cabooses. Northern Pacific caboose No. 1311 is now on display in the Lake Superior Transportation Club museum at Duluth, Minnesota. 100 passengers were on board this trip, nearly all in family groups. (Patrick C. Dorin)

Duluth, Missabe & Iron Range Railway side door caboose C-9 was part of the D&NE consist. Many, but not all, side door cabooses carried coach seats and were operated in mixed train service on railroads all over the USA. Such cars often provided the last remnants of rail passenger service over a given line. (Patrick C. Dorin)

Burlington Northern extended vision cabooses were also part of the consist. It was probably the first time that these modern cabooses were pressed into coach service. (Patrick C. Dorin)

176

There are a number of steam operated museum services throughout the USA. Some are run on a circle of track such as at the railroad museum at Green Bay, Wisconsin. Here a Lake Superior and Ishpeming Railroad 2-8-0, long accustomed to switching ore on the Marquette Iron Range, pulls a single Chicago & North Western wood combine at Green Bay. (William A. Raia)

With the demise of railroad operated passenger service, many organizations have had to acquire their own coach equipment. A former Richmond, Fredericksburg & Potomac coach, No. 524, is now part of Steam Tours and is shown here on a railroad excursion at Gettysburg, Pennsylvania on the Western Maryland Railway. (J. W. Swanberg)

Of the three Milwaukee Road Skytop Lounge parlor cars that survive in 1974, the No. 187, Coon Rapids, has been utilized in coach service on rail fan excursions. In May, 1974 rail-photographers detrain along the Escanaba & Lake Superior Railroad for a run-past on a superb trip. The roof of this deluxe car has since been refinished. (Jim Scribbins)

Former Milwaukee Road 10 roomette, 6 double bedroom sleeper, Lake Oconomowoc, was also operated in the May, 1974 rail fan trip over the E&LS. This is but one of many examples of sleeping cars being operated in coach service. This photo was taken in February, 1973 at the E&LS yards in Wells, Michigan. (Patrick C. Dorin)

A former Burlington "Black Hawk" coach was also part of the excursion on the E&LS. This car was photographed at Wells in February, 1973. (Patrick C. Dorin)

On September 12, 1954, the Railroad Club of Chicago operated a special coach train over the C&NW utilizing Class D Atlantic No. 395. The special occasion was the last run of the 395. The train is shown here arriving at Chase Yard in Milwaukee. The Class Es Pacific No. 647 was coupled ahead of the 395 in order to operate the Automatic Train Stop. The train consisted of four "400" coaches and two standard lounge cars and carried 250 passengers. (Jim Scribbins)

C&NW Pacific Class E-2b No. 2901 departs Milwaukee with an all-coach passenger extra packed with fans from the Railroad Club of Chicago. In addition to the coaches, the train carried a dining car and a refer express car which separated the coaches from the engine. The train was en route to Fond du Lac, Wisconsin with the June, 1948 excursion run. (Jim Scribbins)

Special events or parties often reserve an entire car for coach service, and many times the reserved car is not a coach. In this case, a party for a hockey game at the Duluth Arena has reserved an ex-Empire Builder dining car, No. 1032 — the Minnesota, on the rear of the Great Northern's Badger at Superior, Wisconsin in February, 1967. The train was en route from St. Paul to Duluth. (Patrick C. Dorin)

One of the last standard trains to operate over the Western Pacific was this passenger extra en route from Oakland to Stockton on April 17, 1966. The train, powered by two F-7 diesel units, consisted of eight leased Southern Pacific coaches, a single standard Pullman car painted in the streamlined two tone grey scheme and the WP's unique observation lounge. The lounge ran backwards behind the engine on this east bound run which is shown here passing San Leandro, 14.8 miles from San Francisco. (Patrick C. Dorin Collection)

Although this is not a photo of the highest quality, it is being used here for several reasons. First of all, the Veterans' Special (Northern Pacific employees) was the last Northern Pacific Railway passenger train to arrive and depart the Duluth Union Depot. The consist of this June, 1969 passenger extra included one head-end car, three Slumbercoaches, one California Zephyr sleeper, one NP coach and the Yakima River. Furthermore, on very rare occasions, business cars would be operated in coach service. Aside from the CZ sleeper, the train would have been an all coach train capped off with a streamlined open end car. The purpose of the train was the Duluth convention of Northern Pacific Veteran employees. (Patrick C. Dorin)

Duluth, Missabe & Iron Range Railway equipment has often been used in coach service, such as this Duluth Rotary Club special departing the Duluth Union Depot in 1957. With white flags flying, Pacific No. 400 leads coach No. 33, combination car No. W24 and the Northland. (Wayne C. Olsen)

The most extensive of all Class I railroad steam excursions are those of the Southern Railway. Mikado No. 4501 was built for the Southern by Baldwin in 1911. Since 1964, she has been the property of Paul Merriman, President of the Tennessee Valley Railroad Museum, Chattanooga, Tennessee. She has powered many passenger extras over the past years with consists of mixed standard and streamlined cars, and always with a baggage recreation car on the head-end for the tape recorder boys. (Southern Railway)

179

Southern steam locomotive No. 722 was obtained by the Company in 1967. It was one of two steam engines acquired from the East Tennessee and Western North Caroline Railroad Company in exchange for two Southern Railway Alco diesels. (The other was the 630.) Originally the two engines were owned by the Southern but were sold to the ET&WNC in 1953. However the Southern wanted them back for both display and excursion purposes. After extensive work required to bring the engine up to Southern "steam" standards, the 722 made its debut on September 4, 1970 for a National Railway Historical Society special from Augusta, Georgia to Charleston, S. C. (Southern Railway)

One of the more unusual engines in steam excursion service on the Southern is Savannah & Atlanta steam locomotive No. 750. (The S&A is part of the Southern Railway System.) This 4-6-2 was built in 1910 by American Locomotive Company and was originally owned by the Florida East Coast. It was sold to the S&A in 1935. In 1962 the Savannah & Atlanta Railway donated the 750 to the Atlanta Chapter of the National Railway Historical Society for exhibition and excursion operations. The 750 is often double headed with other power as shown here with the 630, and with the 722 in a previous picture in this section. As of 1974, the Southern System has more steam power for operation than any other line in the USA. (Southern Railway)

The twin of the 722 is the 630 purchased from the ET&WNC at the same time. The 630 is shown here with a rail fan special out of Charleston, S. C. with six cars including a baggage car behind the engine, one coach, a baggage recreation car and three more coaches. (Southern Railway)

Many passenger specials carry a baggage recreation car, and the Arrowhead Civic Club train was no exception. BN baggage car 7025 was pressed into such use for this train. (Patrick C. Dorin)

Next to the baggage recreation car was Great Northern coach No. 1003. The coach is a former Union Pacific chair car and is one of a very few cars that never carried GN's classic Omaha Orange and Pullman Green, the Empire Builder color scheme. A color scheme that is sadly missed by many throughout the former Great Northern territory. (Patrick C. Dorin)

The Burlington Northern has retained a fleet of passenger equipment, and among that equipment are two former Great Northern coaches Numbers 1115 and 1116. The two cars seat 60 passengers and are operated in special trains. Both cars operated in the Arrowhead Civic Club train. (Patrick C. Dorin)

Passenger Extra 6331 West arrives at West Duluth where the passengers will get off after a full and exciting day. Some of the children were so happy upon boarding the train in the morning that they were literally "crying." Many of the children were seriously ill, and so the entire trip was a rare opportunity for them all. Bringing up the markers end was the combination sleeper buffet lounge St. Croix River complete with a drum head sign identifying the "Arrowhead Civic Club Picnic Special." (Patrick C. Dorin)

Passenger Extra 6331 West was a most unusual train. The date is July 17, 1974 and Amtrak and Burlington Northern have teamed up for a special passenger train for disadvantaged and disabled children. Many of these children could not walk and had to be carried on and off the train. The train was sponsored by the Arrowhead Civic Club of Duluth, Minnesota and the train operated from that point to Moose Lake and return. The children were treated to a picnic while at Moose Lake. The ten car special was donated by the Burlington Northern and Amtrak, and the crews donated their time. It demonstrates that large companies and organizations can be sensitive to the *unusual* needs of our children. Extra 6331 West is shown here waiting at Moose Lake for the Children to return, and the way freight has tied up on the "freight house" track waiting for the passenger to depart. (Patrick C. Dorin)

A very bright and cheery Sunday morning, September 15, 1974, found Duluth, Missabe & Iron Range Passenger Extra 130 North carrying 348 passengers from Duluth to Two Harbors and return for a tour of the Autumn leaves, the Knife River Marina on Lake Superior and the ore docks and museum at Two Harbors. The train is shown here departing Knife River for Two Harbors. (Patrick C. Dorin)

A lack of coaches found two Burlington Northern sleepers (non-Amtrak equipment) pressed into service as coaches. Former Empire Builder sleepers Big Horn Pass and Jefferson Pass made up part of the consist. (Patrick C. Dorin)

The BN dining car Lake Michigan was also operated as a coach and did not provide food and beverage service. (Patrick C. Dorin)

The complete consist included the St. Croix River, BN coaches 1115 and 1116, Lake Michigan, Big Horn Pass, Jefferson Pass and Duluth, Missabe & Iron Range Railway W-24, a combination sleeper baggage. The train is shown here at Knife River during the tour of the marina. (Patrick C. Dorin)

On September 14, 1974, the American Institute of Mining Engineers rode an eight car special train from Duluth to Two Harbors and return. The consist of the train included six cars from the Burlington Northern as well as the DM&IR's W-24 and the Northland. It is not unusual for the mining engineers to ride such trains at least once a year. The photo was taken in East Duluth in the rain. (Patrick C. Dorin)

CHAPTER 15

Just a Note on Parlor Cars

Parlor cars came into being as the result of passenger demand for *First Class* day train service. In many respects, the parlor car was and is identical to the exterior of the coach, but it's whats inside that counts. Parlor cars have usually been equipped with carpeting, single soft cushion revolving seats, drawing rooms, large spacious restroom lounges and porter service. In this case, one porter was assigned to each car and in many cases parlor car service was Pullman operated. Indeed, it was not uncommon for 12 section, 1 drawing room sleeping cars to be operated in parlor car service.

Parlor cars were constructed as full parlor cars, parlor lounge observation, dome parlor cars, parlor dining cars, parlor lounge cars and even combination parlor coaches. Parlor accommodations also came with the Chicago & North Western's bi-level cars with a single 60 seat parlor car and a combination parlor coach.

Many parlor cars had a definite Pullman look to them. While others on the other hand, looked identical to coaches operated by the owning railroad. Many parlor cars were rebuilt coach cars and the outside window configuration was not changed.

Parlor cars were generally separated from the rest of the train by lounge and dining cars, however this was not always true. Again it depended upon switching requirements en route.

Travel by parlor car added a luxurious note for many day trains. Prior to the 1920's, there were a fair number of *All-Parlor* car trains in the east. However they all but disappeared by the 1930's, and only the Long Island continued to operate them through the 1960's and 1970's. However, as we move through the 1970's, parlor cars are an important part of the consist of many Amtrak trains. The parlor car is still very much a part of American Rail Travel.

With the exception of the heavy weight Pullman parlor cars, most parlor cars were identical or nearly identical to the exteriors of coaches. Painted for ''Eagle'' service MoPac parlor car No. 752 is an ex-Chesapeake and Ohio parlor car. (Missouri Pacific Railroad)

It was the interiors that made the difference. Nearly all parlor cars were equipped with single reclining rotating seats that were larger than the average coach seat. Carpeting on the floor and a closet for hanging coats plus a private drawing room were the essential differences. Other items such as luggage racks, overhead reading lights, wall murals and window curtains were all things that one could find in a luxury coach. (Missouri Pacific Railroad)

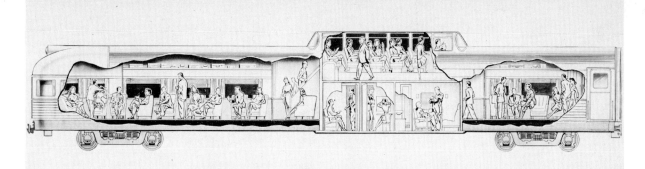

Parlor Cars were built in many different styles and should be the subject of a book all their own. The Burlington was famous for dome observation parlor cars. This cut away view shows the interior of the Twin Cities Zephyr dome parlor car equipped with movable soft cushion chairs, a drawing room beneath the forward end of the dome, two wash rooms beneath the rear of the dome, two parlor rooms fore and aft of the dome plus a small observation room. The car was so popular that the CB&Q purchased an additional parlor for each train and that too was equipped with movable chairs. (Burlington Northern)

What must be classed as the most spectacular, or at least the most unusual are the Milwaukee Road Skytop Lounge Parlor cars. Cedar Rapids was one of four such cars constructed in 1948 for Twin Cities Hiawatha service. Washrooms and drawing rooms were located at the forward end. The main section contained 24 revolving, reclining seats plus 12 sofa type lounge seats in the lounge area. The car is shown on train No. 5 en route to Minnesota in July, 1966. (Jim Scribbins)

The Milwaukee Road parlor car "Red River Valley" was built for Hiawatha service in 1948. She contains 30 reclining rotating seats, drawing room and men's washroom at the vestibule or forward end, and the ladies' washroom at the opposite end. The car is shown on train No. 5, the Morning Twin Cities Hiawatha, at the old depot in Milwaukee in July, 1965. (Jim Scribbins)

Just as there have been cases of parlor cars being rebuilt for coach service, there have also been coaches rebuilt for First Class passengers. The "Linoma" is an ex-C&O, an ex-Rio Grande dome coach that has been rebuilt by Auto-Liner Corporation. The car has run in parlor car service for Amtrak but not exclusively for that type of operation. This dome car probably has the widest travel experience of any dome car built. (Auto-Liner Corporation)

Interior of the observation room of the Auto-Liner dome car "Linoma." (Auto-Liner Corporation)

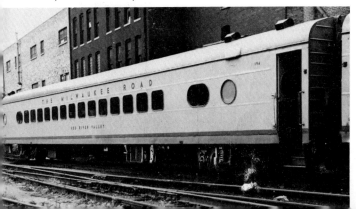

Parlor cars generally operated on the end of passenger trains, such as the "Twin Cities" shown here bringing up the marker's end of train No. 20, the Great Northern's Gopher departing St. Paul for Duluth. The three coaches are ex-Empire Builder coaches of 1937 and the first car has been modified for a "News-Butch" and his cart for selling sandwiches, soft drinks, coffee and those Wenatchee apples, for which the Great Northern was World famous. (Collection of Wayne C. Olsen)

The Great Northern also operated heavy weight parlor cars on the rear of certain trains, such as the Puget Sounder, train No. 359, shown here departing Vancouver, British Columbia in May, 1949. This train carried a combination observation cafe parlor car. (Harold K. Vollrath)

The Puget Sounders were replaced by the streamlined Internationals, and parlor car service was expanded and improved upon with parlor observation cars. Here the "Port of Vancouver" brings up the rear of the Morning International train No. 357 en route to Seattle, Washington from Vancouver. The train was photographed at Bow, Washington by J. W. Swanberg.

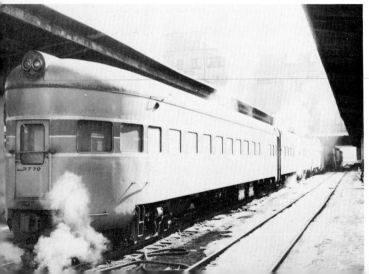

After Amtrak, the ex-Great Northern parlor observation cars were taken out of service and the Pacific Northwest and were, for awhile, assigned to Hiawatha service between Chicago and Minneapolis. Here the Twin Cities Hiawatha shines in the Sun on a cold winter day in February, 1974 with the "Port of Seattle" carrying the markers for train No. 10. The photo was taken at the old Great Northern depot in Minneapolis. (Patrick C. Dorin)

The interior of the "Port of Seattle" is very attractive, but the old Great Northern atmosphere is missed. The car is still very pleasant to ride in and passengers may make use of the rear observation room to watch the passing scenery through windows of the "picture window" variety. (Patrick C. Dorin)

The newest style parlor cars to hit the rails are the "Metro clubs" of the Amtrak Metroliners in the Washington-New York City corridor. The new parlors feature the most modern type seating as well as all of the comforts normally associated with parlor car service including both stewardess and porter services. (Amtrak)

Metroliner parlor car passengers may have their meals served at their seats with small tables for each individual seat. The comfort index of this equipment is exceptionally high. (Amtrak)

To this writer's knowledge, the last parlor car to be outshopped in 1974 by a non-Amtrak firm was Burlington Northern's Deschutes River. To be operated in special train service, the car contains 26 parlor seats, table seating for 10 at triangular tables and a buffet kitchen. (Patrick C. Dorin)

As a large number of parlor cars are actually observation cars. they must be turned after each run. The combined North Coast and Twin Cities Hiawatha leaves a parlor at Minneapolis on its way to the West Coast. Upon departure of No. 9, a Burlington Northern switcher turns the parlor car on the wye just outside the old Great Northern depot. On the day this photo was taken, the dome observation parlor "Silver Tower" had graced the marker's end of the Hiawatha. Although a very fine car, it is a far cry from the Milwaukee Road Sky Top Parlor Cars. (Patrick C. Dorin)

Epilogue

As we begin the year 1975, the transportation situation in the USA continues to follow the patterns of the past few years. Virtually no progress has been made toward a balanced transportation system since this writer wrote the Epilogue for *The Domeliners* in 1972. At the moment we are continuing with an energy crunch and it is obvious that the USA cannot continue the transportation patterns of the heavy emphasis on highway and air travel. The misuse of our available petroleum fuels on an unbalanced transportation system can only lead to an eventual break down in our total overall transportation organization.

Yet we have a solution for this problem. It has been with us for the past 80 years, but because it is not a fancy, far out, venture the USA has chosen to ignore it. That solution is our rail system.

There are four basic areas that rail transportation can be of high potential use for Americans. The first, and probably the least important, is the transcontinental or cruise type of train. However it is an excellent way to view the country with an excellent period of time for relaxation. The second is the intermediate distance trains for service in the 400 to 1000 mile categories. In this case fast train service can be provided for both daylight and overnight runs, the latter of which is now very badly neglected in the USA. The third classification is the short distance train serving the 50 to 400 mile districts. The final or fourth classification is the commuter services.

All of these services are vital to America's future if for no other reason than the fuel conservation need. According to the *Report to the Congress on the Rail Passenger Service Act* (submitted by the Secretary of Transportation in July, 1974), the inter-city passenger train leads all others in energy effectiveness based on seat capacity. This means that no other mode of transportation can match the passenger train in terms of fuel efficiency. A nine car passenger train with 720 seats and powered by a 3,000 horsepower type SDP40F diesel locomotive gets 360 seat miles per gallon. A six car train with 480 seats powered by an older E-8 or E-9 diesel locomotive gets 300 seat miles per gallon.

Intercity buses with 47 seats on the other hand come up with 282 seat miles per gallon, while the maximum seat miles per gallon for a 4 jet engine aircraft with 200 seats is 51 seat miles per gallon and a jumbo jet's maximum is 60 seat miles per gallon.

Fuel conservation is not the only reason for a balanced transportation system. Higher usage of public transportation will decrease automobile traffic on the highways, which in turn will decrease traffic accidents and lower the construction and maintenance costs of our streets and highways. Canada has, in many ways, already proven this concept. Canadian National Railways has demonstrated that the public will travel by rail if the trains are attractive, run on time and scheduled appropriately. The Government of Ontario with the CN has further shown that commuter rail service co-ordinated with bus service can attract passengers from their automobiles, and in turn reduce or eliminate the need for additional expressways.

Ontario was faced with the problem of additional expressway construction in the Toronto area. Yet they knew that as soon as the roadways were completed, they would be filled to capacity with traffic. This in turn would require additional expressways, which in turn would mean additional parking ramps, etc. in downtown Toronto. This would sacrifice the city and destroy the tax base.

With this condition prevailing, the Government sought out other alternatives for moving people to and from downtown Toronto. The train was, and is, the most effective means for doing this. The decision was made to work with Canadian National to set up a rail commuter service covering about 60 miles of main line with Toronto situated almost in the middle of this territory. The route selected already had a high density of traffic and is part of the Montreal-Windsor population corridor. Yet because rail lines have a high train frequency capacity with appropriate signaling and Centralized Traffic Control, the GO Transit system began operating trains co-ordinated with bus transportation on hourly schedules during most of the day with 20 minute headways during rush hours. The system has saved the Province of Ontario millions of dollars even though the system itself operates at a loss. This alternative is far superior to expanding the highway system.

The next question that comes to mind is just what can the United States do to handle the present problem? To just simply say we must add passenger trains on every route would be ignorant. The author would like to recommend that each state set up an advisory council of citizens, railroad, air and highway people to investigate the state's transportation needs, and to determine how those needs can best be met. The people assigned to such a council should be of the highest caliber so that selfish and/or political interests will not interfere with the decisions, recommendations and overall study. The Federal Department of Transportation should have the responsibility to co-ordinate the findings of the various state advisory councils. The first task of the councils should be the study of passenger service.

As far as Amtrak is concerned, it has been four years since that May 1, 1971 start up. They have made substantial progress with a problem that has been a serious illness for over 50 years. More work must be done, however, and one thing is certain and that is that rail passenger service must become an integral part of the Nation's public transportation system. There is no other choice when we think of fuel conservation, not to mention the other benefits of faster and safer service and the fact that rail service is the only all weather transportation system.

INDEX